EAT THE RICH

❖

P. J. O'ROURKE

EAT THE RICH

ATLANTIC MONTHLY PRESS
NEW YORK

Published simultaneously in Canada
Printed in the United States of America

Library of Congress Cataloging-in-Publication Data

O'Rourke, P. J.
Eat the rich / P. J. O'Rourke.
p.   cm.
ISBN 0–87113–719–4
1. Economics—Humor.   2. Money—Humor.   I. Title.
PN6231.E295076 1998
330' .02'07—dc21
98–27100
CIP

Design by Laura Hammond Hough

Atlantic Monthly Press
841 Broadway
New York, NY 10003

98 99 00 01   10 9 8 7 6

FOR TINA AND ELIZABETH

CONTENTS

❖

1   LOVE, DEATH, AND MONEY   1

2   GOOD CAPITALISM: *Wall Street*   11

3   BAD CAPITALISM: *Albania*   36

4   GOOD SOCIALISM: *Sweden*   56

5   BAD SOCIALISM: *Cuba*   77

6   FROM BEATNIK TO BUSINESS MAJOR:
Taking Econ 101 for Kicks   104

7   HOW (OR HOW NOT) TO REFORM (MAYBE) AN ECONOMY
(IF THERE IS ONE): *Russia*   124

8   HOW TO MAKE NOTHING FROM EVERYTHING: *Tanzania*   160

9   HOW TO MAKE EVERYTHING FROM NOTHING: *Hong Kong*   199

10   HOW TO HAVE THE WORST OF BOTH WORLDS: *Shanghai*   216

11   EAT THE RICH   231

ACKNOWLEDGMENTS

❖

I stole the title. But I don't know from whom I stole it. I may have lifted it from the 1993 Aerosmith CD *Get a Grip,* which has a song by the same name. But Colorado journalist Dan Dunn informs me that Aerosmith might have nicked it, too. Dunn says there's a tune with that moniker on Motorhead's 1988 album, *Rock'n'Roll.* And Motorhead may have filched the thing themselves, because I first saw the phrase on T-shirts worn by the Shi'ite Amal militia in Lebanon in 1984 or 1985. I don't know where the Amal got the phrase, but I assure you that they stole the T-shirts. Perhaps "Eat the Rich" is a part of the world's folk-music heritage, the original version to be unearthed, by some archivist, from a forgotten Folkways recording, *Songs of the Economic Advisers*:

> *Kill the poor,*
> *Eat the rich,*
> *Screw every other son-of-a-bitch.*

The rest of the book is my own work, for good or for ill, although I had a tremendous amount of help putting it together. As has been the case for the past thirteen years, *Rolling Stone* paid for the travel. All the foreign adventures and my trip to Wall Street first appeared, in modified form, in that magazine, and part of Chapter II appeared in *Rolling Stone*'s brother publication *Men's Journal*. I owe a huge debt of gratitude (and unfinished assignments) to *Rolling Stone*'s founder and editor in chief, Jann S. Wenner. Besides being a good friend, he has been a remarkably tolerant boss. *Rolling Stone* already had someone writing about political-economy issues, my ideological pal-in-opposition, National Affairs editor William Greider. When I went to Jann in 1995 and told him I wanted to write about economics, he was momentarily taken aback. But he didn't fire me. He just sighed and said, "You mean I now have two lunatic economists on the staff of a rock and roll magazine?"

Part of Chapter X also appeared in the *London Sunday Telegraph*. Editor Dominic Lawson thereby allowed me to get my anti-British feelings about the Hong Kong handover off my chest in a way that would offend the largest number of British people. Sorry. I'm over it. I now realize that if I'd owned Hong Kong, I would have given it back to the Chinese, too. Although not until they bought me some drinks. But I'm Irish.

This book could not have been finished—or, at least, published—if I hadn't gotten fabulous and fabulously necessary editorial help from Andrew Ferguson, senior editor at *The Weekly Standard,* and gotten good advice and hand-holding from Denise Ferguson. Whatever shape and structure the book has is due to Andy. The flabby and pointless parts are (as in my person, so in my work) mine. The manuscript was then vetted by Nicholas Eberstadt, visiting scholar at the American Enterprise Institute and visiting fellow at Harvard's Center for Population Studies, and by Mary Eberstadt, writer for *The Weekly Standard* and other fine journals. Nick did his best to make the logic of my economic arguments actually logical and tried to show me how to use statistics in an unstupid manner. Mary helped put flesh and (more's the pity) blood into the descriptions of the damage that totalitarianism does to people, and she tactfully pointed out a number of not-unstupid solecisms.

The magazine pieces that formed the raw material of this book were assigned and, in many cases, conceived by *Rolling Stone* managing editor Robert Love. His editorial craftsmanship was great, and his patience was extreme. Bob has a knowledge of journalistic storytelling, something that has always eluded me. Specifically he knows what part of a story is the beginning, what part is the middle, and what part is the end—no small matter to the reader. Also a blessing was the help I received on Chapter II from an old friend, *Men's Journal* editor Terry McDonell, the person who hired me at *Rolling Stone* in the first place. Terry and *Men's Journal* senior editor David Willey helped me to explain high finance without exposing myself as the person who, in 1997, bought precious metals, held on to Japanese yen, and sold Pfizer short.

An enormous amount of unsung research-and-development grunt work was done by Tobias Perse. And more of the same was accomplished by Mike Guy and Rodd McLeod. Exhaustive—and exhausting—fact checking was done by Mary Christ, Sarah Pratt, Kim Ahearn, Erika Fortgang, and Gina Zucker. Any remaining errors of fact are the result of my own pigheaded persistence in error. Heroic copy-editing tasks (I cannot spell well enough to find the SPELL CHECK icon) were undertaken by Eric Page, Marian Berelowitz, Corey Sabourin, and Thomas Walsh. And Eric Page returned to do a copy edit on the book text and ruin his Memorial Day weekend with a case of Dictionary Eyes because the author didn't get the manuscript to him until the last possible minute.

The cover photo was taken by the brilliant David Burnett, who always makes me look more or less human. (His secret is that he uses someone else for the model.) Tommy Jacomo, magnificent manager of the Palm in Washington, D.C., threw all the semi-inebriated Capital big suits out of his establishment so that David could take the picture. The Washington Palm is the best restaurant in the world and the only place where you can see James Carville eat something other than Ken Starr's lunch. The little rich guy running away from me was drawn with skill and flair by Daniel Adel. And the whole cover composition was pulled together by Grove/Atlantic art director Charles Rue Woods, assisted by Whitney Cookman. They are geniuses. (One of the best things about writing "Acknowledgments" is that it gives a journalist a break from saying bad things about people. Also, sometimes he gets a free lunch.)

There are scores of other people about whom I have good things to say. When I started writing this, I was so ignorant of my subject that I thought "economics" were plural. A number of friends in the financial industry helped walk me through the basics, particularly Hugh Eaton, Richard Morris, and John Ricciardi, partners in the Cursitor-Eaton Asset Management Company, which is now a part of Alliance Capital; and Briget Polichene, former general counsel for the House Banking Committee. I was also assisted by the faculty and students of the Owen School of Management at Vanderbilt University. Dewey Daane, the Frank K. Houston Professor of Finance, emeritus, and a former governor of the Federal Reserve Board, explained money to me—very slowly and using words even I could understand. Luke Froeb, associate professor of management, gave me a pep talk and a reading list, but, most importantly, donated an item of his own classroom material titled "A Traditional Economics Class in Only One Lecture." It was while reading this that economics began to make sense to me, specifically with the first two sentences of Froeb's text: "The chief virtue of a capitalist mode of production is its ability to create wealth. Wealth is created when assets are moved from lower- to higher-valued uses."

My best and most-extensive source of economic understanding, however, was the Cato Institute, the libertarian think tank run by President Ed Crane and Executive Vice President David Boaz where I hold the unpaid (and I earn it) position of Mencken Research Fellow. The Cato Institute loves freedom, embraces responsibility, and displays a grumpy nonpartisanship in politics. Plus, donations are tax deductible, so give it a bunch of money. Cato has provided me with research and analysis for all my books for the last ten years. (Except *Give War a Chance*—folks at Cato believe that killings should be made in the marketplace.) I'd like to thank Ed and David, and Cato scholars Doug Bandow, Ted Carpenter, James Dorn, Stephen Moore, Tom Palmer, Roger Pilon, José Piñera, Jerry Taylor, and the late Julian Simon, and I'd like to thank Nicole Gray for years of getting Cato events together and getting me to those together events.

Another organization that has been a great help and to which I hope I've been a little help in return is the National Forum Foundation, founded in 1984 to promote democracy and human rights in places that didn't have those things. Forum Foundation provided me with contacts in Russia and Cuba. President Jim Denton got me into the various political headquarters during the 1996 Moscow elections, and chief financial officer Therese Lyons showed me around St. Petersburg. The National Forum Foundation has since merged with Freedom House, which has been fighting the same excellent battles since it was started in 1941 by political odd couple Eleanor Roosevelt and Wendell Wilkie. Jim and Therese now serve, respectively, as the executive director and the vice president for finance and administration in the new organization. You should give it a bunch of money, too.

The chapter on Good Capitalism would not have been possible if some of the best capitalists in America hadn't been willing to waste hours answering Kiddie Investment Klub–type questions from me. That time could have been turned into money, but instead it's become prose. Therefore it is both heart- and wallet-felt thanks that I give to Michael Meehan, Sean McCarthy, Merrill Lichtenfeld, Tom Leander, Al Ehrbar, Alan Braunshweiger, Jeffrey Leeds, Jay Duryea, Kevin O'Brien, Myron Scholes, and Robert Merton. And thanks to Kim Kirkpatrick for the Scotch-and-Water Park joke.

In Albania, Eton Tocaj and Dave Brauchli were a tremendous amount of help with important things, such as keeping me from getting killed.

In Sweden, Peter Stein played a splendid Virgil to my poor imitation of Dante as we toured the environs of socialistic Heck. The people I met there were forthcoming, welcoming, and kind even though they knew I was going to make fun of their country. (Thanks, by the way, to Peter Berlin, author of *The Xenophobe's Guide to the Swedes,* for the phrase *orgy-borgy.*) In Stockholm I was treated to innumerable dinners, lunches, and intelligent conversations, and maybe there's something to that Social-Democrat nonsense after all—as long as I keep my legal residence in New Hampshire for tax purposes. My thanks to Odd and Ingrid Eiken, Thomas Gür, Anders Isaksson, Jean Louis Gave, Nils-Eric and Kerstin Sandberg, Carl and Jeanne Rudbeck, Johann Kugelberg, Rolf Albert, Eva Norlin, Åke Ortmark, Thomas Atmer, Elizabeth Langby, the Swedish free-market think tank Timbro, and to American ambassador Thomas Siebert and his wife, Deborah.

Sweden, however, does have an evil twin—Cuba. The darker side of socialism was made less dark by David Beard, Chris Isham, Jennifer Maguire, Pascal Fletcher, Douglas W. Payne from Freedom House, and Frank Calzòn, executive director of the Center for a Free Cuba.

Jonas Bernstein did everything possible in the way of finding all the pieces with a straight edge in that gigantic jigsaw puzzle that is Russia. I'd like to thank him and Richard Conn, David Nunley, Michael Caputo, Dmitry Volkov, Claudia Rosett, the Honorable Chris Cox, Garry Kasparov (who introduced me to the Boris Yeltsin campaign staff—let's see Big Blue do that), Intourist guides Ana and Paul, the International Republican Institute, and the Jamestown Foundation.

My travel through Tanzania would have been pointless without the intelligence, information, and friendship of J. J., who did all the hard work. The trip was arranged by the commendable firm of Abercrombie & Kent. I thank Edward Hudgins of the Cato Institute, and Rahim Azad and Kephas Mavipya for the insights they provided, and Zanzibar's Mbweni Ruins Hotel and Mnemba Club for welcome respites from journalism.

The handover of Hong Kong to China was a grim occasion and also a great party. It was homecoming week at the Foreign Correspondents Club. Thanks for all the tips (and tipples) I got there from past president and old (and, John, I do mean "old") friend John Giannini, present president Keith Richburg (whose book *Out of America* was also a big help in writing about Tanzania), Dave and Celia Garcia, Hugh and Annie Van Es, Jimmy Lai, and Bill and Julie McGurn. (And special thanks to Bill for his articles and essays on Sir John Cowperthwaite.) The handover ceremonies were also turned into fun by the totally amusing company of Lauren Hutton, John Cleese, Alyce Faye Eichelberger, David Tang, Dominic Lawson, and Rosa Monckton. I look forward to seeing all of you again at the next triumph of bad governance—maybe in Belfast.

And my visit to Shanghai would have been much less comprehensible without Yeung Wai Hong and Kate Xiao Zhou, and much less pleasurable without Jim Whitaker and my fellow members of the cobra-blood-drinking fraternity: Jerry Taylor, Gary Dempsey, and Aaron Lukas.

I want to thank my publisher and friend Morgan Entrekin and everyone at Grove/Atlantic for printing this book (probably against their better judgment) and paying me for it (definitely against their better judgment). I want to thank Grove/Atlantic's Associate Publisher Eric Price, Director of Publicity and Marketing Judy Hottensen, Managing Editor Michael Hornburg, Assistant Editor Amy Hundley, Subsidiary

Rights Manager Lauren Wein, and all the other people whom authors do not customarily thank and without whom authors would have nothing but wiggles on a computer screen to show for their efforts.

My gratitude to Scott Manning for arranging the book tour and putting up with my ingratitude while I'm out touring and am temporarily under the impression that fifty-year-old writers should act like twenty-year-old rock-band drummers.

More gratitude to my longtime and long-suffering agent, Bob Dattila, who barely winced when I proposed a book on economics ("Oh, Hollywood is going to leap on that"). And more gratitude yet to Jacqui Graham, who keeps publishing me in Britain despite my continued outbursts of provincial Anglophobia, and to Don Epstein and everyone at Greater Talent Network, who keep finding people who will pay me for lecturing so that I don't have to get a real job or write books that can be made into movies.

With all these thanks said, I now come to one of the great conundrums of literature. How does one give full and sufficient credit to one's wife without sounding like a mealymouthed pig or giving the readers mental images of the tambourine-playing spouse in *This Is Spinal Tap*? I'm going to go for mealymouthed pig. Tina O'Rourke has a business degree and understands the stuff in this book, which is more than its author does. She accompanied me on several of the foreign trips, or, I should say, I accompanied her. She helped with the travel arrangements and tour research. To her I owe the slogan "America—it doesn't suck." And Tina, supplied with *Rolling Stone* journalist credentials for the Cuba trip, was forced at one point to actually ask a pop-music star, "What's your favorite color?" Then, as this book was being written, Tina edited, fact-checked, proofread, entered the whole manuscript into the word processor that remains a Delphic mystery to her husband, managed the household, changed diapers, and gave our infant daughter her 1 A.M., 3 A.M., 3:30 A.M., 3:45 A.M., 4 A.M., and 5 A.M. feedings while I . . . stared out my office window and picked adverbs. Thank you for not killing me, dear.

A NOTE ABOUT THE BIBLIOGRAPHY

There isn't one. I'm too lazy. And who ever heard of humor with footnotes? But there are certain books which I found crucial to a neophyte student of economics, especially if (and I mean no insult to the texts by this) that student is uninformed, innumerate, light-minded, and a big goof-off. In other words, these are the books to read if you want to know something about economics but have never gotten further into the subject than figuring out a trifecta at Belmont:

Free to Choose and Capitalism and Freedom by Milton
     and Rose Friedman
New Ideas from Dead Economists by Todd G. Buchholz
The Road to Serfdom by Friedrich A. Hayeck
Economics in One Lesson by Henry Hazlitt
The Tyranny of Numbers by Nicholas Eberstadt
How the West Grew Rich by Nathan Rosenberg and L. E.
     Birdzell Jr.
The Armchair Economist by Steven E. Landsburg
The History of Money by Jack Weatherford
Money, A History edited by Jonathan Williams

There are also certain books you should avoid, such as anything with the words Investment and Success in the title and everything ever written by John Kenneth Galbraith.

A NOTE ABOUT THE NUMBERS IN THIS BOOK

How accurate are the statistics in the following pages? How long is a piece of string? All statistics are fraught with error. And I, personally, cannot add a 15 percent tip to a ten-dollar bar tab and get the same number twice. Not that I've ever had a bar tab as small as ten dollars. And that may be part of the problem. But, even sober, I'm no mathematician. And neither, apparently, are the other people who publish statistics. For example, I refer the reader to the debates about Cuban gross domestic product in Chapter V and Tanzanian per-capita GDP in Chapter VIII. The numbers seem as random and inadequate as the change I ended up leaving that surly bartender.

Statistics, however, can have some value for comparative purposes, and this is the way I've tried to use them. Unless otherwise noted, the population, GDP, vital stats, and other principal figures in Eat the Rich come from the 1997 edition of the CIA's World Factbook and the 1997 edition of the U.S. Department of Commerce's Statistical Abstract of the

United States. Yes, I know, the CIA is the espionage agency that had to read about India's nuclear tests in *The Washington Post.* And now Pakistan is making mushroom clouds, too. Pretty soon every cabdriver and 7-Eleven manager in the world will have the bomb. And I also know that the Department of Commerce is no Plato's Academy in Athens. But the baloney in the *Factbook* and the *Statistical Abstract* is presumably all cooked from the same ground-up scraps and innards, and comes packaged in easily compared slices.

Although even our government doesn't always agree with itself about these things. The *FB* says the estimated mid-1997 population of the United States is 267,954,764, while the *SA* says 267,645,000—a discrepancy of almost 310,000 people. That's as if all the residents of Wichita, Kansas, had disappeared. Check the tornado reports. Call Dorothy. Anyway, when forced to chose between numbers, I've picked the CIA's for the simple reason that nobody's ever been terminated with extreme prejudice by the Department of Commerce.

There is another problem with the statistics in this book. They're outdated. All statistics are outdated. They are the record of a certain arbitrary moment, and by the time that record is processed and printed, it is, in effect, your senior-class picture in the high-school yearbook and you're very embarrassed by last fall's hairstyle. My statistics are even more outdated than usual, having been collected over a period of two and a half years. It would have been nice if I could have visited eight countries in one week, written about them over the weekend, published my work on Monday, and had an au courant book. But the thing could not be done. I went to Sweden, Cuba, and Russia in 1996. I went to Tanzania, Shanghai, Hong Kong, and Wall Street in 1997. And my manuscript went to press in the spring of 1998. Things have changed in all those places. Economic conditions are somewhat better in Sweden, Albania, and Tanzania; worse in Russia and Shanghai. The pope has breezed through Cuba, to what effect I do not know. Hong Kong has suffered less at the hands of the mainland Chinese than I feared it would—so far. And what's going to happen to the stock market remains the riddle it's been since 1792, when twenty-four brokers gathered under a buttonwood tree on Wall Street and agreed to a set of rules by which they would sharp and cozen each other.

I ask readers to take the numbers herein with the single grain of salt that the Romans believed to be an antidote to poison. The purpose of this book is to make some broad points about economics, freedom, and responsibility. If the reader examines my work too carefully, he may discover that I'm only a journalist. This means that when it comes to knowing what I'm talking about, I'm no different than the next person; I just get paid for the talking.

"In this state of imbecility, I had, for amusement, turned my attention to political economy."
—Thomas De Quincey
Confessions of an English Opium Eater

1

LOVE, DEATH,
AND MONEY

❖

I had one fundamental question about economics: Why do some places prosper and thrive while others just suck? It's not a matter of brains. No part of the earth (with the possible exception of Brentwood) is dumber than Beverly Hills, and the residents are wading in gravy. In Russia, meanwhile, where chess is a spectator sport, they're boiling stones for soup. Nor can education be the reason. Fourth graders in the American school system know what a condom is but aren't sure about 9 × 7. Natural resources aren't the answer. Africa has diamonds, gold, uranium, you name it. Scandinavia has little and is frozen besides. Maybe culture is the key, but wealthy regions such as the local mall are famous for lacking it.

Perhaps the good life's secret lies in civilization. The Chinese had an ancient and sophisticated civilization when my relatives were hunkering naked in trees. (Admittedly that was last week, but they'd been drinking.) In 1000 B.C., when Europeans were barely using metal to hit each other over the head, the Zhou dynasty Chinese were casting ornate wine vessels big enough to take a bath in—something else no contemporary European had done. Yet, today, China stinks.

Government does not cause affluence. Citizens of totalitarian countries have plenty of government and nothing of anything else. And absence of government doesn't work, either. For a million years mankind had no government at all, and *everyone's* relatives were naked in trees. Plain hard work is not the source of plenty. The poorer people are, the plainer and harder is the work that they do. The better-off play golf. And technology provides no guarantee of creature comforts. The most wretched locales in the world are well-supplied with complex and up-to-date technology—in the form of weapons.

Why are some places wealthy and other places poor? It occurred to me, at last, that this might have something to do with money.

But I didn't know anything about money. I didn't know anything about money as a practical matter—did I have enough to pay the mortgage? And I didn't know anything about money in a broad or abstract sense. I certainly didn't know anything about economic theory. And I wasn't alone in this.

I couldn't answer the central question of this book because I was an economic idiot. I got to be an economic idiot by the simple and natural method of being human. Humans have trouble with economics, as you may have noticed, and not just because economic circumstances sometimes cause them to starve. Humans seem to have an innate inability to pay attention to economic principles.

Love, death, and money—these are the three main human concerns. We're all keen students of love. We are fascinated by every aspect of the matter, in theory and in practice—from precise biological observations of thrusting this and gaping that to ethereal sentimentalities marketed in miles of aisles at Hallmark stores. No variety of love is too trivial for exegesis. No aspect of love is so ridiculous that it hasn't been exhaustively reviewed by the great thinkers, the great artists, and the great hosts of daytime talk shows.

As for death, such is the public appetite for investigation of the subject that the highest-rated television program in America is about an emergency room. The most hardheaded and unspeculative of persons has his notions of eschatology. The dullest mind can reason extensively about what causes kicking the bucket. Dying sparks our intellectual curiosity.

But money does not. All we care about is the thing itself, preferably in large amounts. We care a very great deal about that. But here our brain work stops. We don't seem to mind where our money comes from. And, in an affluent society, we don't even seem to mind where our money goes. As for larger questions about money, we shrug our shoulders and say, "I wish I had more."

Why is it that we are earnest scholars of amorosity and necrosis but turn as vague and fidgety as a study hall in June when the topic is economics? I have several hypotheses, none of them very good.

Love and death are limited and personal. Even when free love was in vogue, only a certain number of people would allow us to practice that freedom upon them. A pious man in the throes of Christian agape may love every creature in the world, but he's unlikely to meet them all. And death is as finite as it gets. It has closure. Plus the death ratio is low, only 1:1 in occurrences per person.

Economics happens a lot more often and involves multitudes of people and uncountable goods and services. Economics is just too complicated. It makes our heads ache. So when anything economic goes awry, we respond in a limited and personal way by searching our suit-coat pockets to see if there are any wadded up fives inside. Then we either pray or vote for Democrats, depending on our personal convictions of faith.

Or maybe economics is so ever present, so pervasive in every aspect of our lives that we don't really perceive it. We fail to identify economics as a distinct entity. We can watch a man slip and fall and almost never hear him say, "God-damned gravity!" And we can watch a man fall ten times and not see him become interested in how gravity works. Almost never does he arise from the eleventh tumble saying, "I went down at a rate of 32ft./sec.^{2}—the force being directly proportional to the product of the earth's mass times my weight and inversely proportional to the square of the distance between that patch of ice on the front steps and my butt." And so it is with economics. No amount of losing our jobs or our nest eggs sends us to the library for a copy of John Maynard Keynes's *The General Theory of Employment, Interest, and Money*.

The very pervasiveness of economics keeps us from getting intellectual distance on the subject. We can view death from afar for an average of 72.7 years if we're a male American, and 79.5 years if we're a female. Although love is notorious for fuddling the brain, there is matrimony to cool the passions or, failing that, sexual climax will work in the short term. But there is no such thing as a dollargasm. Money is always with us. What am I going to do to take my mind off money? Go shopping? Drink and drugs will cost me. I suppose I can play with the kids. They need new shoes.

Constant money worries have a bad effect on human psychology. I'd argue that there is more unbalanced thinking about finance than about anything else. Death and sex may be the mainstays of psychoanalysis, but note that few shrinks ask to be paid in murders or marriages. People will do some odd things for political or religious reasons, but that's nothing compared to what people will do for a buck. And if you consider how people spend their dough, *insane* hardly covers it.

Our reactions to cash are nutty even when the cash is half a world away and belongs to perfect strangers. We don't ridicule people for dying. Or, in our hearts, despise them for fooling around. But let a man get rich—especially if it happens quickly and we don't understand how he did it—and we can work ourselves into a fit of psychotic rage. We aren't rational and intelligent about economics because thinking about money has driven us crazy.

I'm as much of a mooncalf as anyone. I certainly had no interest in economics as a kid, as kids don't. Children—lucky children at least—live in that ideal state postulated by Marx, where the rule is, "From each according to his abilities, to each according to his needs." Getting grounded equals being sent to a gulag. Dad in high dudgeon is confused with Joseph Stalin. Then we wonder why so many young people are leftists.

I had no interest in economics at college, either. I belonged to that great tradition of academic bohemia which stretches from the fifteenth-century riots of François Villon's to the Phish tours of the present day.

For university hipsters, there is (no doubt Villon mentions this in his *Petit Testament*) nothing more pathetic than taking business courses.

My friends and I were above that. In our classes we studied literature, anthropology, and how to make ceramics. We were seeking, questing, growing. Specifically, we were growing sideburns and leg hair, according to gender. It did not occur to us that the frat-pack dolts and Tri-Delt tweeties, hurrying to get to Econ 101 on time (in their square fashion), were the real intellectuals. We never realized that grappling with the concept of aggregate supply and demand was more challenging than writing a paper about "The Effects of Cool Jazz on the Poetry of Edgar Allan Poe." What the L-7's were being quizzed on was not only harder to understand than Margaret Mead's theories about necking in Samoa, it was also more important. The engine of existence is fueled by just a few things. Unglazed pottery is not among them.

If the Rah-Rah Bobs and Pin-Me Sallys had been taking Love or Death courses, we would have been right there with them. But money was a different matter. We weren't interested in money. Actually—what we weren't interested in was work. Maybe we guessed that it would be a lot of work to b.s. our way out of memorizing such formulae as:

$$\text{Price Elasticity} = \frac{\text{\% Change in Supply}}{\text{\% Change in Price}}$$

Not that we weren't up to the task: "Like, price—that equals wasting natural resources and the pollution thing, if you're into the whole capitalist, monopoly rip-off, man."

And, of course, we *were* interested in money. I remember we'd get excited whenever we had any. It's just that we were determined not to earn it. We would never go in search of money. Money was something that would come looking for us after we'd choreographed our world-shattering modern-dance recital or mounted our famous empty-gallery show of preconceptual post-objectivist paintings or when our folk-rock group, Exiles of Dayton, learned to play "Kum Ba Ya." And we weren't going to "sell out" no matter how much money was lavished upon us.

Business majors intended to (it was a loaded phrase in those days) "make money," and they were going to do this even if it involved some activity that wasn't a bit artistic, such as running IBM. We artsy types would have been shocked if anyone had told us (and no one had the nerve) that making money was creative. And we would have been truly shocked to learn that a fundamental principle of economics—"Wealth is created when assets are moved from lower- to higher-valued uses"— is the root of all creativity, be it artsy, IBMsy, or whatever.

"Putting money first" was crass. It was as if you'd gone to a party with dozens of wild, swinging chicks and, instead of drinking Mateus and making small talk about Jean-Paul Sartre, you just whipped out your unit. Except we would have thought that was a blast. But go into business? Never.

If you don't count selling drugs. Which we were all doing. We knew everything about price elasticity when it came to pot, not to mention aggregate supply and demand. In point of fact, we hirsute weirdos probably had more real business experience than any business major on campus. And one more thing—we all fancied ourselves to be marxists. As a philosophic recipe, marxism is a cannelloni of the economical, stuffed with economics, and cooked in economic sauce.

Still, we were not interested in economic ideas. And, to be fair, the business majors weren't, either. Econ was not something they took because they were fascinated by the elegant complexities of economic relationships or because mankind cannot survive without economic activity. They took Econ and forgot everything in the text so they could get a job from somebody else who took Econ and forgot everything in the text.

I turned into a square myself, of course, as everyone who lives long enough does. I got a job as a journalist—but without ever considering that journalism was a business. (Although I would have been unpleasantly surprised to get a hug instead of a paycheck at the end of the week.) And I continued to ignore economic issues even though I had a press pass to the most spectacular extravaganza of economics in this century.

It was the 1970s, and the economy was changing almost as often as bed partners. The Great Depression may have been more dramatic, but it was a one-trick pony. In the '70s, globalization suddenly included the other three-quarters of the globe. The places that used to make our windup toys were making our automobiles. Everything was being imported—except oil, which had hitherto been given away free with a windshield wash and a set of highball glasses at most brand-name gas stations. Then, one day, you couldn't buy oil for money. Not that there wasn't plenty of money around in the '70s. It just didn't happen to be worth anything. We had a previously unimaginable combination of fever inflation and hypothermia business slump. You could make more money buying Treasury bills than you could make breaking into the Treasury. The gold standard disappeared from the scene. Maybe it joined a cult. International currency-exchange rates were determined with mood rings. The most powerful nations in the world had, at their helms, an amazing collection of economic nincompoops—Nixon, Carter, Mao, Harold Wilson, Georges Pompidou, Leonid Brezhnev. And the electronic-media revolution was under way so that bad ideas about economics were spreading around the world at neural speed.

I dozed through it. And I was covering politics, too. Even I realized that money was to politicians what the eucalyptus tree is to koala bears: food, water, shelter, and something to crap on. I made a few of the normal journalistic squeaks about greed and self-interest, and let the thing slide.

It wasn't until the 1990s, when I'd been a foreign correspondent for ten years, that I finally noticed economics. I noticed that in a lot of places I went, there wasn't anything you'd call an economy. And I didn't know why. Many of these countries seemed to have everything—except food, water, shelter, and something to crap on.

I decided to go back to the Econ texts I'd finessed in college and figure things out. And my beatnik loathing returned full-blown. Except this time it wasn't the business majors I despised; it was the authors of the books they'd had to study. It turns out that the Econ professors were economic idiots, too.

Looking into a college textbook as an adult is a shock (and a vivid reminder of why we were so glad to get out of school). The prose style

is at once puerile and impenetrable, *Goodnight Moon* rewritten by Henry
James. The tone varies from condescension worthy of a presidential
press conference to sly chumminess worthy of the current president.
The professorial wit is duller than the professorial dicta, and these are
dulled to unbearable numbness by the need to exhibit professorial self-
importance. No idea, however simple—"When there's more of something, it costs less"—can be expressed without rendering it onto a madras
sport coat of a graph and translating it into a rebus puzzle full of peculiar signs and notations. Otherwise the science of economics wouldn't
seem as profound to outsiders as organic chemistry does. And then,
speaking of matters economical, there's the price of these things—$49.95
for a copy of *Economics,* fifteenth edition, by Paul A. Samuelson and
William D. Nordhaus.

Economics has been, as its edition number indicates, in use as an
Econ text forever—that is, since 1948, which counts as forever to the
baby-boom generation. The book is considered a fossil by many economists, but it has been translated into forty-six languages, and more than
4 million copies have been sold. *Economics* was what the current leaders of international business and industry were afflicted with in school.
And here was another shock. Professor Samuelson, who wrote the early
editions by himself, turns out to be almost as much of a goof as my friends
and I were in the 1960s. "Marx was the most influential and perceptive
critic of the market economy ever," he says on page seven. Influential,
yes. Marx nearly caused World War III. But perceptive? Samuelson
continues: "Marx was wrong about many things . . . but that does not
diminish his stature as an important economist." Well, what would? If
Marx was wrong about many things *and* screwed the baby-sitter?

Samuelson's foreword to the fifteenth edition says, "In the reactionary days of Senator Joseph McCarthy . . . my book got its share of
condemnation." I should think so. *Economics* is full of passages indicating that Samuelson (if not William-come-lately Nordhaus) disagrees with
that reactionary idea, the free market. The chapter titled "Applications
of Supply and Demand" states, ". . . crop restrictions not only raise the
price of corn and other crops but also tend to raise farmers' total revenues and earnings." Increase your corn profit by not growing corn?

Here's a wonderful kind of business where everybody can get rich if they'll just do nothing.

In the chapter "Supply and Allocation in Competitive Markets," the book seems to be confused about the very nature of buying and selling. "Is society satisfied with outcomes where the maximal amount of bread is produced," it asks, "or will modern democracies take loaves from the wealthy and pass them out to the poor?" Are the rich people just going to keep those loaves to grow mold? Why would they produce "the maximal amount of bread" to do that? Or are we talking about charity here? If so, let us note that Jesus did not perform the miracle of the loaves and taxes. We all know how "modern democracies take loaves from the wealthy." It's the slipups in the "pass them out to the poor" department that inspire a study of Econ.

It was not reassuring to learn that the men who run the companies where our 401(k)s are invested have minds filled with junk from the attic of Paul A. Samuelson's *Economics*.

There were newer texts than *Economics* for me to look at, and what they said wasn't so obviously wrong. But then again, what they said wasn't so obvious, period. Here are the first three sentences of *Macroeconomics* by David C. Colander (donated by Eric Owens, who lives next door to me and is taking Econ at the University of New Hampshire): "When an artist looks at the world, he sees color. When a musician looks at the world, she hears music. When an economist looks at the world, she sees a symphony of costs and benefits." Somebody change the CD, please.

The textbooks weren't good. This sent me to the original source material, the classics of economic thought. But here I had to admit, as I was tacitly admitting thirty years ago, that I don't have the brains to be a Tri-Delt. *The Wealth of Nations, Das Kapital, The General Theory of Whatchmacallit* were impressive works and looked swell on my bookshelf, but they put me to sleep faster than the economic news of the '70s had.

There were, of course, popular books on economics, but the really popular books were about extraordinary people doing extraordinary things and getting fabulously wealthy or going to jail—preferably both. I was interested in ordinary people doing ordinary things and getting by. And the less popular but more worthwhile books on economics all seemed to presume that I'd made it through something like *Economics* without blowing a fuse.

So I gave up trying to be smart about economics. I decided that if I wanted to know why some places were rich and other places were poor, I should go to those places. I would visit different economic systems: free market, socialist, and systems nobody could figure out. I'd look at economically successful societies: the U.S., Sweden, Hong Kong. I'd look at economically unsuccessful societies: Albania, Cuba, Tanzania. And I'd look at societies that hadn't decided whether to be successful or not: Russia and mainland China. I'd wander around, gape at things, and simply ask people, "Why are you so broke?" Or "How come you're shitting in high cotton?"

2

GOOD CAPITALISM

❖

WALL STREET

An investigation of money might as well begin where lots of money is being made—for the moment, anyway—on the New York Stock Exchange. Maybe the magic of Wall Street can work for everyone in the world. Perhaps the peasants of China can all "go public" and form a billion corporations with assets of "1 water buffalo, 2 conical hats, wok." Each peasant will then make an initial public offering, sell his stock, get rich, and put a lap pool in the rice paddy.

This is actually happening, or will be soon, say economic and political experts. They claim there's a triumph of free-market capitalism occurring around the globe. If that is true, then the New York Stock Exchange really does merit inspection. The NYSE is the world's largest single trading center for investments. Investments are the "capital" part of capitalism. The NYSE's market is free in the sense that no government, religion, or discernible law of physics controls its prices. And the prices have been rising triumphantly. Hence: "Triumph of free-market capitalism."

Of course, how long this free-market triumph will last is another question. Can men who have guns restrain themselves from interfering in the affairs of men who have nothing but checkbooks? And is the free market really that triumphant? Recent events in Asia show how corruption and the collusion of governments and businesses can cause the rules of capitalism to be violated—as you noticed if you lost all your capital by investing it in Asia.

But international politicians are crowing about the free-market victories they've achieved. Never mind that politicians are cheerleaders who have themselves confused with the people who carried the ball. (And never mind that many politicians are cheerleaders for the other side.) Laissez-faire—as the theory of the hour—seems to have displaced central planning, nationalization, democratic socialism, and the thoughts of Senator Edward Kennedy. The free market—triumphing or not—has been recognized as a potent and ultimately unavoidable force in human events, and as something that's going to get in our hair for the rest of our lives.

And here is another reason to look at the New York Stock Exchange. It's personal. That's our own money in the stock market, jumping up and down like a maniac on the price trampoline. Either we've made somersaulting investments of our own or pension funds and insurance companies have done it for us. We're worried our money is going to break its neck. Even if we don't have a cent in stocks, we're concerned about the economy in general—what will happen to Bill Clinton's sex life if the Dow Jones goes down?

So the stock market is important. We should pay attention to it. However, we're already paying attention to it—too much attention. And almost all of that attention is the wrong kind.

The New York Stock Exchange has achieved celebrity status. It appears on the network news every night and in *The New York Times* headlines every day, is kidded during Jay Leno monologues, and attracts 700,000 tourists a year to live performances. Expect the secondary effects of fame to kick in soon. Nike merger-and-acquisition shoes. Tommy Hilfiger margin-call sweat suits.

This is an era of strange renown, but the New York Stock Exchange is an odd star even by current standards. It's just a room, or actually three rooms: the Main Room (it's the main room), the Blue Room (the walls are blue), and the Garage (it used to be one). These are big, dumpy, overlit spaces festooned with coaxial cables and mobbed by gesticulating clerks and hollering middle-aged men all wearing ridiculous jackets and scurrying around with complete absence of dignity. Thousands of telephones ring. The floor is covered with trash. Large boards full of little lightbulbs blink astronomy-class strings of digits. Hundreds of video screens display runic symbols and funny numbers. And girdling it all, at cricked-neck height above the frenzy, is the ever-changing stock ticker, a crawling electronic ribbon of gibberish.

Behold the hero of the late '90s. We thrill with its victories, shudder at its defeats, admire its resilience, sympathize with its shortcomings. And now there are the effects of the "Asia crisis" to add tabloid interest.

We identify. Generation X has given up playing in garage bands and trying to make indie films, and has gone back to grad school en masse to get that MBA. An older, even loopier generation is spending the money in its IRAs and Keoghs and 401(k)s on stocks, betting the ranch (or the ranch house it expects to inherit from its folks) on no-load mutuals, index funds, and 100 shares of Intel bought at . . . bought at the peak of the market, probably, but we're in this for the long haul, right? We're fans of the American economy. Rock and roll will be as a passing fad compared with the baby boom's loyalty to growth-oriented investment planning.

This is a big change. Something has happened to the huffy indignation that right-thinking people felt about getting rich during the "greedy Reagan years." Finance has been famous before, and not long ago, but it played the heavy. There was the movie *Wall Street* with its Gordon Gekko, the hubris-oozing Masters of the Universe in Tom Wolfe's *Bonfire of the Vanities,* and preppie hysteric Michael Lewis at Salomon Brothers taking notes for *Liar's Poker* and tut-tutting about "big, swinging dicks."

In the modern-celebrity tradition, money making has re-created itself. It has acquired a new, burnished, lovable image—the way Rich-

ard Nixon did with years of post-Watergate statesmanship poses and
Princess Di did with a car wreck.

But we never really know these luminaries, do we? And nobody knows
the stock market. The unpredictable rise and fall of stock prices prove it.

Watching the market all the time doesn't really help. When we see
the moil and tumult on the exchange floor, we're looking at something
we aren't seeing and seeing something that isn't there. The something
we aren't seeing is, essentially, nothing. We think of stocks as being
constantly bought and sold—1,201,347,000 shares traded on October
28, 1997, the NYSE's busiest day to date. But there are 207 billion shares
registered on the New York Stock Exchange. In an absolute buying and
selling frenzy, less than 0.6 percent of those shares changed hands. Investment usually stays invested.

What we're seeing that isn't there is "a rush to get into the stock
market" or "a panic to get out," depending on the day. In a bull market we have an idea that stock is only being bought. Street people are
cashing in their pop cans for a share of Microsoft. Dogs bring their
bones to the stock exchange. In a crash we think stock is only being
sold. The wealth of the nation has been converted into T-bills or Franklin
Mint commemorative plates. But every share of stock that sells has a
buyer. There are no stocks sitting empty with OPEN HOUSE ON SUNDAY
signs out front. At the end of the worst possible day for stocks, the
market contains the same number of shares it started with. The market is not a different size, we just like it less. And this isn't some fuzzy
hormonal mood we're in. Our feelings can be measured precisely, in
dollars.

In fact, when we own any "financial instrument" (as people in the
money business call anything worth money), what we basically own is
an opinion. When the British pound loses value, the number of pence
in a pound doesn't change. We just don't feel the same way about pounds
anymore; we're nuts about Euros now. It always takes the same number
of pigs to make 1,000 pork-belly futures, but next year's bacon suddenly smells bad to us. One share of common stock continues to repre-

sent the same percentage of a corporation's assets, and the corporation is probably not growing or shrinking very fast, but our love for that corporation can swell or pop overnight.

We have an opinion. That opinion is a price. And since prices are constantly changing, our opinion is always about to be wrong. Think of the stock market as an endless Gallup poll with 207 billion things that people can't make up their minds about.

So in order to understand the stock market, we have to realize that, like anything enormous and inert, it's fundamentally stable, and like anything emotion-driven, it's volatile as hell. Got that? Me neither. Now what about all those people running around on the stock-market floor in a state of utter chaos?

There isn't any. The New York Stock Exchange is enmeshed in rules. There are rules about everything. To sell even one share of stock in the U.S., a corporation has to file a "full-disclosure statement," complying with the Securities Act of 1933. The law itself is eighty pages long with four hundred additional pages of Securities and Exchange Commission regulations. Then, to get a stock "listed" on the NYSE, the corporation has to meet further requirements about the size, value, and soundness of the offering. Once a stock is listed, there are myriad rules about how it can be bought and sold. And no running around is involved; there's a rule against it. (Formidable power walking is allowed.) The NYSE is one of the most organized places on earth. But the organization is so complex that I stood, stupid, on the trading floor for two days before I noticed that there was one.

During my first hour in the Main Room, I didn't notice anything at all. I was too fascinated by the littering. You don't see good littering in America anymore. In the 1950s, people used to chuck their newspapers in the gutter, heave sandwich bags from cars. Your mom would tell you to do it: "Now put the candy wrapper out the window, honey." Stockbrokers are the last nonpsychotic people in the U.S. throwing garbage over their shoulders. Four thousand pounds of canceled buy and sell orders, scribbled stock quotes, and phone messages from the ex-wife about taking the kids this weekend are removed from the stock-exchange floor each day.

I talked to one stockbroker who said he knew the market was getting intense when he caught himself tossing empty milk cartons on the kitchen linoleum at home.

It's the littering as much as anything that gives the stock market its free-for-all atmosphere. But it's not free, and it's not for all. In order to trade stocks on the NYSE, you need a "seat" on the exchange. The 1,366 seats are traded the way the stocks are and currently sell for more than $1 million apiece.

Possessors of these seats do no sitting. A stockbroker may conduct millions of dollars of business in a day, but instead of a corner office with a Statue of Liberty view, he has an eighteen-inch space filled with phones, computer screens, and the infinite pieces of paper that attach themselves to anything involving money. And he can't even get near this because a couple of clerks are in it taking orders to buy and sell.

There are various kinds of brokers on the stock exchange. The floor broker works for a brokerage house. When you get a tip from your acupuncturist that Disney is going to buy Seagram and open a Scotch-and-Water Park in Boca Raton, the floor broker is the person who buys you your shares. He is your actual stockbroker. (And he will be a he. Only 169 seats on the Exchange are held by women.) The person you call your stockbroker is a salesman who doesn't even sell stock, or buy it, either. He just sells you on buying and selling. The brokerage house makes money on the commissions, no matter which you do.

Besides floor brokers, there are competitive traders who are independent businessmen buying and selling for their own accounts, specialist brokers who deal only in certain stocks, and two-dollar brokers who handle excess business for floor traders and can buy and sell for any brokerage.

Two-dollar brokers are so-called because they used to get a two-dollar commission for every 100 shares of stock they traded. The commissions are now negotiated, but "what-the-fuck-is-this-costing-me brokers" takes too long to say. And that is how it would be said. One of the old-fashioned charms of the NYSE, besides the littering, is the constant use of *fuck* as a noun, verb, adverb, and adjective with every possible meaning except "sexual intercourse."

Around the walls of the NYSE trading rooms are the tiny workstations grandiosely called "telephone booths"—more than 1,200 of them. In the middle of the rooms are the horseshoe-shaped counters with banks of video screens overhead, the "trading posts." Here the hollering middle-aged men gather, looking like they're doing something foolish. This is what we see on television.

The middle-aged men are there because of the specialist brokers. Each specialist has a location at a trading post, and every stock that's listed on the NYSE is assigned to one specialist. If a floor broker wants to buy or sell a certain stock, he has to go to the specialist's post.

The broker who goes to a post is called the "trading crowd" even if he's the only person in it. Although usually he isn't, because the cattle-herd instinct is as strong on Wall Street as it is, for example, in a cattle herd. The specialist's job is to give a "quotation" on the stock—to tell the trading crowd the highest price that anybody is currently willing to pay for a share and the lowest price at which anybody is willing to dump it. The video screens above the trader's head show the last price at which a stock was traded and whether that price was an "uptick," a "downtick," or no tick at all. The stock "ticker" running around the room is a compilation of the trading prices from all the specialists' posts.

What's going on in the trading crowd is a double-jointed, Hydra-hatted auction—as though Sotheby's had a dozen guys with gavels, each with the same Rembrandt, and not only could the bidders raise their prices but the auctioneers could lower theirs.

It sounds complicated because you and I don't buy a lot of Rembrandts at Sotheby's. But shopping for a car this way would be a pleasure. You want a Lexus. You know exactly how much the last Lexus sold for—with the same option package you intend to get. All the Lexus dealers in the world are in one place. You can hear their lowest prices. You don't have to read their fibbing newspaper ads or spend all day traveling to their dealerships in the outer 'burbs and getting soft-soaped. All the Lexus buyers are in one place, too. You can listen to each of them bargaining. Now you know—to the fraction of a dollar—how much you should pay for a Lexus.

To an outsider, however, especially an outsider being assed and elbowed aside and trod upon by people walking at thirty-five mph, it is confusion. And the language doesn't help. The hollering is done in a form precisely dictated by the stock exchange. The number of shares is expressed in units of a hundred. *At* means you're selling. *For* means you're buying. All bids are made "price for size." All offers are made "size at price." Price increments come in arithmetically boggling one-sixteenths of a dollar—6.25 cents. This is called a "teenie" on the floor.

"Twenty-five and three teenies for twenty."

"Ten at twenty-five and five teenies."

The teenies inject an odd note of juvenility into the baritone roars. One expects "itsy-bitsies" and "itty-bitties" to pop out next.

Meanwhile, the specialist is "maintaining a fair and orderly market," which basically means keeping middle-aged men from hitting each other. And the specialist is also acting as a "market maker," which is a role analogous to what Dad plays when the kids are running a lemonade stand on the front sidewalk. If there are too many sellers of a specialist's stock and not enough buyers, the specialist is expected to "make a market" by buying some of the stock for his own account. If there are too many buyers and not enough sellers, he is expected to sell some of the stock he holds in inventory—the NYSE equivalent of going inside to squeeze more lemons. (Somehow, specialist brokers make out better on this than Dad does.)

What about the floor trader who went to the specialist's post several paragraphs ago? He's gone. Half a dozen trades can be made in the time it takes to read about one.

"Take it."

"Sold."

A large chunk of money has just changed hands without lawyers, contracts, notary publics, or even handshakes. The two traders put their heads together for a moment, jotting on order forms.

"I am . . ." One names his brokerage and gives his NYSE badge number.

"I am . . ." The other does the same.

And we are . . . able to buy the beach house. Or we should start to look for a second job.

† † †

I was interviewing one of the floor brokers, whom I'll call David, or, rather, I was trying to interview him. Besides hollering in teenie language, brokers are consulting their beepers, using the banks of telephones on the trading floor, and shouting into cell phones. A good broker—and David is one—can do all four things at once. At any given moment, he's supposed to be buying or selling several different stocks, each trade requiring him to be at a different specialist's post. Also, the buy or sell demands come with complicating instructions—"Limit orders," "Stop orders," "Fill or kill"—with meanings like "Don't buy for more than such-and-such," "Sell if it gets to so-and-so," "Buy this much or nothing."

"I have to ask my clerks," says David, "'Do I have time to pee?'"

David moves from post to post. I can barely keep up with where he's going, let alone with what he's doing. More than 3,000 corporations are listed on the NYSE. Their stock is worth more than $9 trillion. The New York Stock Exchange is the Super Bowl of money. Being allowed on the trading floor is like being allowed on the football field during the game and getting to follow the players around. Under the circumstances, Q&A is necessarily truncated.

Finally, around noon, there was a pause. I had the chance to pose a question. There was so much I needed to know. There were thousands of puzzling aspects to the stock market. Possible queries flooded my mind.

"What's with the ugly jackets?" I asked.

David's was a polyester-cotton blend, with a lawn-and-leaf-bag shape in the prescribed, and horrible, color of his brokerage house. It was rumpled and creased and slightly sweat stained. The sides bulged with notepads, order books, and memoranda. Twenty pens and pencils were shoved into the breast pocket.

"You wreck your clothes," said David.

The traders wear dress shirts, expensive neckties, and well-tailored trousers, but most of them leave their suit coats in the members' lounge, and their wing tips, too. They put on the gaudy sack blazers and the least-fashionable kind of lumpy sneakers. As a result, the average trader is dressed like a combination bank president, produce manager, and ghetto kid who lets his mom pick out his shoes. Nike and Tommy Hilfiger doing a NYSE line of clothes is not really a bad idea.

† † †

We in the general public have an idea that there's something WASPy or, anyway, stuffy about the stock market. But the accents belie this.

There are WASPs on the floor, saying "fuck" with the best of them. But the traders are predominately Jewish, Italian, and, most predominately of all, Irish. The NYSE is the Brooklyn of fifty years ago. (And one reason *fuck* may be used so often is that immigrants didn't understand why the slang for making love was dirtier than the slang for going to the bathroom.)

I asked a specialist broker, who's Irish himself, why so many stock-exchange members are micks. We're not known for our business acumen.

"They were cheap labor," he said.

The Irish were hired as clerks and runners and boys who chalked up prices before video screens were invented. They figured out how the whole thing worked, and they stayed.

"How come there are so few black and Hispanic traders?" I asked the specialist.

"They're next," he said.

And, indeed, many of the nonbroker employees on the floor are black, Puerto Rican, Dominican, and so forth. And more than a quarter of them are women. In twenty years the traders will be saying "mo'fo," "caramba," and "oh, fudge."

A lot of brokers never went to college. And the rest don't care if they did. I asked David what kind of economic theories people who trade stocks believe in. Do they belong to the "classical school," which says the forces of supply and demand are uncontravenable and self-correcting? Are they Keynesians, who think that government programs can create prosperity and full employment? Are they monetarists, who postulate that economic cycles are tied to Federal Reserve policy?

"I don't think they give two shits," said David.

They're tough guys. David, for instance. He's a wiry man in his fifties, a former college wrestler. He took up running at forty and ran in half a dozen marathons with times well under five hours. When he left for the Boston Marathon, the last things to go in his suitcase were four packs of Marlboros.

"I look forward to this job every day," says David. He takes the subway to work from the Upper East Side and stands the whole way: "It never occurs to me to look for a seat."

"I had some marital trouble years ago," he says. Lots of people would blame such difficulties on their work. "This job got me through some rough personal times," says David.

And then he is off into the trading crowd again, six strides ahead of me and holding more numbers in his head than I can count to.

Upstairs from the trading floor is the New York Stock Exchange Luncheon Club, looking the way that something to do with the stock market should look. The ceilings are lofty, the windows are Palladian, and the help is obsequious. The leather armchairs are wide and deep. The china is monogrammed. The stalls in the men's room are made of marble. And all day long the New York Stock Exchange Luncheon Club is empty. David hasn't eaten there in seven years.

The traders gobble take-out food, standing up, and not just because they have too much work. They're in the groove. They're wholly absorbed in what they're doing. They're lost in total concentration on the market or on one segment of that market. In the middle of the afternoon, I mentioned to David that the Dow Jones average was down a hundred points. He'd had no idea. He hadn't bothered to look.

The traders spend their day in that eerie, perfect state the rest of us achieve only sometimes when we're playing sports, having sex, gambling, or driving fast. Think of traders as doing all those things at once, minus perhaps the sex.

The great surprise of the stock market is that it's a happy place—not only happy in a bull season, when everybody's making money, but also happy, in its way, when everything is falling apart. All free markets are mysterious in their behavior, but the New York Stock Exchange contains a mystery I never expected—transcendent bliss.

The New York Stock Exchange does $23 billion in business on an average day. Five times a week it buys and sells an amount of stuff equal to the annual gross domestic product of Tanzania. The NYSE is the world's largest clearinghouse for corporate shares, but there are plenty of other big stock markets. The American Stock Exchange, a block away, trades 6 billion shares a year. The stock of newer, smaller, or less-illustrious corporations—more than 5,500 of them—is bought and sold in the Over-the-Counter market. Here the hollering and wearing of ugly clothes take place across a network of computer terminals and phone lines—the National Association of Securities Dealers Automated Quotation system, or NASDAQ.

There are regional stock exchanges in Boston, Philadelphia, Chicago, and San Francisco. Most capitalist countries (and some communist nations such as China) have stock exchanges. More than $19.4 trillion worth of stocks was traded worldwide in 1997.

And stocks are only one way to bliss out with money. The bond market is also huge. Americans have more than $2 trillion invested in corporate and foreign bonds, another trillion-plus in state and municipal bonds, plus the Treasury bonds and T-bills we (and the Japanese) have bought to cover our $5.5 trillion national debt. Then there are commodities, derivatives, money-market instruments, and just plain money itself. More than $1 trillion of international currency changes hands every day. All of these things are traded with the same frenzy of incomprehensible glee as stocks.

The trading floor was starting to spin again. A feeling of desperation began to rise, and so did the take-out food that was gobbled standing up. For us civilians, savvying financial markets is like taking calculus when the last course we had in the field was high-school practical math. Not only that, but—because we didn't pay any attention to stocks, bonds, interest rates, or the business section of the newspaper until it all got famous about a year ago—we have, in effect, hooked the first dozen calculus lectures. What are we going to do?

And this is not just a matter of idle journalistic curiosity as far as I'm concerned. I mean, I may want to know why some places are as rich as Wall Street and other places are as poor as a visit to Wall Street makes me feel, but I'm also planning to retire. It seems everybody is planning to nowadays. Although I can remember a time when we all intended to die before we were thirty. We're saving our butts off, putting $3,000 a year into our savings accounts. By 2028, we'll be able to . . . live comfortably for thirty-six months. Of course we get dividends from those savings accounts. We consult the compound-interest tables in *Money Management for Fools*. At 3 percent, the $3,000 we put in the bank today will be worth $7,281.79 in thirty years. But Democrats are going to get back into Congress sooner or later. Inflation will return. We tell our kid to find the consumer-price-index Web site. It turns out today's dollar is worth only about a quarter of what a dollar was worth thirty years ago. That means our $3,000 that will become our $7,281.79 may equal $1820.45 when the golden years begin. Of course, there's always Social Security. I understand Meow Mix is one of the more palatable cat-food brands.

We need to invest. But investing presupposes a certain basic knowledge about investment and not just knowledge about whether corporate bonds will go up or down but knowledge more basic than that. Like: What the hell *is* a corporate bond?

There are two main kinds of investments: debt and equity. Debt is just lending money. A General Motors corporate bond is a "debt instrument." You lend GM money, and GM promises to pay you back, plus interest. Your savings account is also a debt instrument. You lend the bank money, and the bank promises to let you withdraw it, never mind that the interest is less than you'd get from keeping a sock full of buffalo nickels under your bed. And your checking account is a debt instrument, too. You lend the bank money and they . . . charge you for it? Plus ATM fees? This is probably why so many pistol-waving people rob banks and why so few pistol-waving people rob General Motors.

Various companies, such as Standard & Poor's, provide bond ratings from AAA to D to help you estimate how safe your debt instrument is. A D-rated bond is like money lent to a younger brother. An AAA-rated bond is like money lent to a younger brother by the Gambino family. U.S. government bonds are considered "riskless"—unless Vince Foster is still alive *and* Iraq has the bomb.

Bonds rated BB and lower are called "junk bonds." Junk bonds are just loans that are risky and therefore pay higher interest rates. The credit-card debt that you've run up is essentially a junk bond held by Visa. There's no collateral except the Benetton sweater that the dog chewed.

And Visa knows what your Standard & Poor's rating would be if you had one. Visa knows more about you than your parents and psychotherapist. There's a good reason you get soaked on your credit-card balances.

Debt means that you're renting your money to someone. Equity means you're buying something from him. If you buy a share of a corporation's common stock rather than buying its corporate bond, you own part of the corporation. You don't get a mere loan payment, you get the profits. Specifically, you get the profits that are left after the corporation settles its tax bill, pays off its bond debts and other prior obligations, gives enormous bonuses to its top executives, uses part of its earnings to buy other corporations and Indonesian real estate, and retains another part of its earnings in case it needs to buy more Indonesian real estate later. You get those profits, or, rather—since there are, say, a couple million shares of common stock outstanding—you get $\frac{1}{2,000,000}$ of those profits.

This is your stock dividend. Oh, and because you're one of the owners of the corporation, you get to vote. This means that once in a while you receive something in the mail called a proxy statement. The proxy statement allows you to give your vote to the people who are paying themselves enormous bonuses. Either that or you can travel to the corporation's annual meeting (held in Indonesia this year) and stand up in the back and ask shrill questions like some Ralph Nader nutfudge.

You rarely buy common stock for the dividend and almost never (unless you're buying 1,000,001 shares) for the voting rights. You buy stock because you have one of those opinions mentioned earlier. You think other people will think this stock is worth more later than you think it's worth now. Economists call this—in a rare example of comprehensible economist terminology—the Greater Fool Theory.

Speaking of folly, you can also invest in the commodities market. This is where you buy thousands of pork bellies and still don't know what you're going to have for dinner because, in the first place, you're broke from fooling around in the commodities market and, in the second place, you're not completely insane. You didn't actually have those pork bellies delivered to your house. What you did was buy a "futures contract" from a person who promises to provide you with pork bellies in a couple of months if you pay him for pork bellies today. You did this because you think pork-belly prices will rise and you'll be able to resell the delivery contract and make out like a . . . perhaps "make out like a pig" is not the appropriate simile in this case. Of course, if prices fall, you've still got the pork bellies, and won't your spouse be surprised?

The reason you go broke in the commodities market—or die from the cholesterol in sausage—is because you're betting you know more than the actual producers and consumers of the commodity. Take the less-risible example of feed-cattle futures. Ranchers have a pretty good idea of how their cattle raising is going: They can count the calves. If it looks like a good year, the ranchers will sell cattle futures early so they don't suffer from weak prices when all that beef comes on the market at the same time. Burger King has a pretty good idea how the hamburger business is going. And they know how many cattle it takes to make all their burgers (about two). If it looks like a bad year for Whoppers, Burger King will put off buying cattle futures to take advantage of the coming beef glut.

This leaves you to buy high and sell low*. The producers and consumers of a commodity know a lot about that commodity's market, and you know your investment portfolio is filled with rotting meat.

When you buy a "future," you're actually making a third kind of investment that's neither debt nor equity. That is, nobody owes you money, and you don't really own anything yet. What you've bought is one type of those allegedly supercomplex and supposedly ultradangerous items called derivatives.

You remember how in 1995 a semieducated young wanker in Singapore, fiddling with derivatives, brought England's noble, ancient Barings Bank to its knees, and now everyone in the House of Lords is selling fish and chips. And you heard how in 1994 the treasurer of

---

*There are exceptions, of course. Hillary Clinton made $99,517 trading cattle futures between October 1978 and July 1979. This could lead to tasteless jokes about Mrs. Clinton getting inside information from the cows at NOW, if one were inclined to that type of coarse, sexist humor.

Orange County, California, picked up a derivative hitchhiking on Sunset, drove around the corner for a little fiduciary slap and tickle, and the next morning an entire suburb of Los Angeles awoke to find that its streets and sewers had been sold at a bankruptcy auction.

Considering the way things turned out for England, Orange County, and you in the commodities market, derivatives do seem daunting. But, in fact, all that the three of you did was make deals with other people in the market.

A derivative is a deal *about* buying or selling rather than the buying or selling proper. When you own a derivative, what you own is a bargain that you've made. You've promised to pay or charge a certain price for a certain thing to be received or delivered at a certain time. Where it gets confusing is that this promise itself can now be bought and sold.

Derivatives are so-called because they "derive" their value from other more straightforward investments, such as just plain owning cows, Orange County, Singapore Slings, or whatever. These things are known as the underlying commodities. The derivative is the deal. The underlying commodity is what the deal's about.

Derivatives are risky. But risky is the point. Derivatives are a way to buy and sell risk. Big risks mean big rewards. Some people can afford more risk. Some people like more risk. And some people are as chicken as I am.

You're into derivatives whether you like it or not. Your adjustable-rate mortgage is a derivative: You got a deal on a loan that was cheaper, at that time, than a fixed-rate mortgage. In return, you're taking a risk. Your risk is that the amount of interest you'll pay in the future will be derived from a formula involving the prime rate, T-bills, and the chairman of Chase Manhattan's boxer-shorts-waistband size. In this case, the underlying commodity is banker fat.

Now that we've become experts on every kind of investment, we can figure out what the triumph of free-market capitalism really means. What it means is euphoria and panic. If investments are okey-dokey, we're all making a fortune selling Pfizer shares to each other. Convenience stores put twenty-dollar bills in the TAKE ONE/LEAVE ONE tray. The World Bank gives toasters to Africa. If investments are not-so-hotso, we throw up our hands and declare bankruptcy. Jobs get so scarce we have to pay to baby-sit for other people's kids. And the Salvation Army goes up and down the Bowery taking soup back from bums.

The investment business is based on people being able to do what they want with their money. They may want to do some odd things. "People put their money where their thoughts are," said one investment banker I interviewed. This means that there are a lot of men who are, so to speak, in financial topless bars, sticking millions of dollars into the G-strings of lap-dancing debts and equities. "If a thing can move freely, it can move stupidly," said another investment banker.

This is how booms and busts develop in the marketplace. And these booms and busts can have larger consequences, such as in 1929 when stocks were crashing, banks were collapsing, and President Hoover was hoovering around. Pretty soon, you could buy the New York Central Railroad for a wooden nickel, except nobody could afford wood. People had to make their own nickels at home out of old socks, which had also been boiled, along with the one remaining family shoe, to make last night's dinner. So the kids had to walk to school with pots and pans on their feet through miles of deep snow because no one had the money for good weather. My generation has heard about this in great detail from our parents, which is why we put them in nursing homes.

Our own kids will probably be shunting us off to the senior care facility when we start telling them about the Asia crisis. Back in 1997 there'd been a bull market in stocks since the apatosaurus roamed the earth. Inflation scares were limited to newspaper stories about silicone breast implants. The unemployment rate was so low that if your dog wandered into a McDonald's, it would wander out wearing a TRAINEE badge. And Asian economies were even stronger than ours. They had some kind of "Asian values" thing going on, involving hard work, thrift, respect for the family, and fortune cookies that read, "Confucius say: Do your homework." Plus, countries in Asia had smart government policies, such as "Export everything." The world was getting calcu-lators, stereos, and VCRs. Asians were getting rich. Everything was wonderful.

Then somebody attacked the baht. Currency traders snuck up behind Thailand's legal tender and stabbed it with a chicken-satay skewer. They hit it so hard, it thought it was a Mexican peso. They tore it into little pieces, wadded them up, and started a huge spitball fight on the Bangkok stock exchange that caused all of Thailand's stocks to go running home to Mother.

What the traders really did to the baht was sell it. Investors in international currency markets started looking at Thailand's economy. Maybe the world had as many calculators, stereos, and VCRs as it wanted. But the Thais were borrowing money overseas to produce more—borrowing so much money that Thailand had a balance of payment deficit even though it was exporting everything. Some of those smart government policies turned out to include, "You'd better loan money to a certain general's son if you're smart." Thais couldn't buy calculators, stereos, and VCRs—they'd all been exported—so Thais bought overpriced real estate and cockeyed stock issues. Thailand had risky debt, bad debt, and worse equities. Maybe owning baht wasn't such a good idea.

Currency traders sold baht. The government of Thailand bought baht, using the foreign currency it had from exporting calculators, stereos, and VCRs. Thailand did this to keep the baht from being "devalued." Devaluation simply means admitting that your currency is worth less compared with other currencies, but no government likes to do it. When a currency is devalued, imported raw materials—stereo ore and barrels of unrefined calculator numbers—become more expensive. Inflation rises. Foreign investments—VCR farms—lose value. Stock prices fall. Everything goes in the toilet.

The whole 1970s experience in America was essentially the story of the dollar being devalued. We can't blame the Thais for wanting to avoid a situation that could lead to disco and Jimmy Carter. Anyway, currency traders were glad to sell baht, so they sold some more. Aggressive currency traders even sold baht they didn't own. They borrowed baht to sell, hoping to repay the loan later with cheaper baht. (This is called selling short. You can do it with stocks or, for that matter, with the car you borrowed from your neighbors, if you think you can pick up the same Saab for less before they get back from the Bahamas.) Traders figured that eventually the Thai government would run out of foreign currency. The Thai government ran out of foreign currency. Everything went in the toilet.

When the currency traders were done with Thailand, they started looking at other economies in Asia. Maybe owning Indonesian rupiah, Malaysian ringgit, and South Korean won wasn't such a good idea, either. Malaysian prime minister Mahathir Mohamad blamed the ringgit's devaluation on "Jewish speculators." (You may remember how everyone in New York was going around saying, "Oy vey, sell the ringgit.")

By October 1997, the currency-dumping spree had reached Hong Kong, and, although the Hong Kong dollar wasn't devalued, the Hong Kong stock market took a TWA Flight 800. The Hang Seng index fell 1,211 points on October 23, with its shares losing $42 billion in value. This scared the pants off the Japanese market. The pantsless Japanese shocked the European markets, which took it out on the markets in Mexico and Brazil (on the theory, I guess, that undercapitalized wogs are undercapitalized wogs no matter where you find them). By Monday, October 27, the terror had reached the New York Stock Exchange. The Dow Jones Industrial Average went down 554 points because . . . because everyone else was doing it. It was the largest dollar decline in history and the largest percentage drop in ten years.

Then the market recovered. "Monday was very, very scary," said David the floor broker. "We were worried about Tuesday. But after the Tuesday rally started, it was all forgotten."

It turns out that on October 28, the American economy was still there. None of America's factories or malls had been abducted by space aliens. American workers hadn't forgotten how to flip burgers during the night. The market soared.

But was this just a "dead-cat bounce"? On Wall Street, they say— "Even a dead cat will bounce once if it drops from high enough." The market skidded.

But Asian devaluations could be good. Imports will be cheaper. Inflation will stay low. The market jumped.

But Asian devaluations could be bad. Exports will cost more. Trade will suffer. The market plummeted.

What if Japan gets dragged down? The market plunged some more.

Who cares? All we sell Japan are *Seinfeld* reruns. The market leaped.

What about China? The market slid.

What about my beach house? The market bounced back.

"We're rich!" I told my wife. "Get a Range Rover and a pasta machine!"

"We're poor!" I yelled. "Sell the dog."

"We're rich again!"

"We're poor."

"We're really poor."

"Rich! Rich!"

"Poor! Poor!"

And on like that for several weeks, until my wife pointed out that our entire investment portfolio consists of ten shares of Eastern Airlines inherited from my uncle Mel.

The investment industry creates euphoria and panic. It moves astonishing amounts of cash around the world at startling speed with shocking results. Then it pays itself fantastic amounts of money. Companies registered with the United States Securities and Exchange Commission charged their customers $27.8 billion in brokerage fees in 1996. They made $30.7 billion trading for their own accounts, $12.6 billion underwriting stock issues, $10 billion selling mutual fund shares, and $84.3 billion doing things classified as, to use a technical SEC term, "other." People on Wall Street don't consider themselves seriously employed unless they're "making a phone number." Kids fresh out of business school are building indoor golf courses and dating Anna Nicole Smith. There's an old stock-market joke about your investments: "The broker made money. The firm made money. Two out of three's not bad."

Is the investment industry just a bunch of pirates in neckties?

"Most of them are," said a sales representative for a brokerage house.

"What makes you think they're not?" said a financial analyst.

"I wish," said a man who manages $2 billion of other people's money. He was staring morosely at the yard-high stacks of annual reports and research materials on the credenza next to his desk. "I was out of town for two days," he explained. "My secretary FedEx'ed me some other stuff."

"The work hours are horrible," explained the Irish specialist broker. "Tons of hours. It takes speed, concentration. There's a big burnout factor. A lot of 'I want a life.'"

But the same can be said of delivering Domino's pizzas. The professionals in the world of money seem to make so much of that money themselves. How can anybody justify the size of the paychecks?

"I don't," said the $2 billion money manager.

"I can't defend it," said David the floor broker.

"They shouldn't be making it," said the specialist.

Why do we put up with this? The whole business of international finance is dumbfounding. These damn business cycles—we don't know whether to lie around the Riviera, clipping the coupons on bonds, or sit around the kitchen table, clipping the coupons in newspapers. Investments cause us to act silly. One minute we're loading our possessions on top of the Ford and fleeing the dust bowl. The next minute we're buying dust futures on the Chicago Commodity Exchange.

This shit-shower of money flying around the world . . . This fiscal El Niño blowing certificate-of-deposit droughts to one place and no-load mutual fund floods to someplace else . . . These cash storms lofting *Hindenburg* high-techs into the sky . . . These speculatory lightning strikes sending transportation and utilities down in flames. What's in it for us?

We ordinary toilers at the cubicle farm: Why don't we rise up? Why don't we get rid of the capitalist system and replace it with something that's nicer and more predictable, and gives everybody an even break? "What," I asked all the Wall Street people I interviewed, "does the investment industry give to society?"

But this time they had an answer.

"Liquidity," said the $2 billion money manager.

"Liquidity," said the investment banker who'd described how men's thoughts were on pecuniary B-girls.

"Liquidity," said the other investment banker who'd told me things could move stupidly.

"Liquidity," said the Irish specialist broker.

"It provides liquidity," said David.

Liquidity is the Wall Street word for having things you can do with your money and being able to do them. Liquidity is the essence of the free market. Men with more time to explain themselves might have said something like, "We hold these truths to be self-evident, that all men are created equal, that they are endowed by their Creator with certain unalienable Rights, that among these are Life, Liberty, and Ka-ching!, Ka-ching!, Ka-ching!"

If we're going to have freedom and the money to enjoy it, we have to put up with the stuff in this chapter. At least that's what the people who run the stuff in this chapter say. Which brings me to the only reason anybody ever reads a chapter like this: What should *you* do with *your* money?

And I actually happen to know. In the course of researching the investment industry, I had drinks with Myron S. Scholes and Robert C. Merton, who had just won the 1997 Nobel Prize in economics. They won the Nobel by creating a mathematical formula for pricing derivatives.* They've made a pile of money Sir Edmund Hillary couldn't climb. And they are two of the smartest people in the world—the Nobel committee says so. I asked them what you should do with your money. (Actually, I asked them, "What *I* should do with *my* money" but . . .) They said the same thing: "Asymmetrical information."

You should trade on asymmetrical information. The commodities-selling ranchers counting their calves, the Burger King executives calculating their burgers—these are examples of asymmetrical information. When somebody in a market has (or thinks he has) information that the rest of the people in the market don't have, that's asymmetrical.

$$*C = SN\left(\frac{1n\left(\frac{S}{k}\right)+\left(r+\frac{\sigma^2}{2}\right)^t}{\sigma\sqrt{t}}\right)-Ke^{(-rt)}N\left(\frac{1n\left(\frac{S}{k}\right)+\left(r+\frac{\sigma^2}{2}\right)^t}{\sigma\sqrt{t}}-\sigma\sqrt{t}\right)$$

Where: C, S, N, 1n, and K = things you don't understand
And r, σ, t, and e = things you don't want to know

There wouldn't be much of a market otherwise. If everybody believed what everybody else believed, everybody would set the same price
on everything. The middle-aged men on the stock-exchange floor could
quit hollering and go have lunch. *The Wall Street Journal* would become
The Wall Street Shopping Mall Giveaway.

Asymmetrical information shouldn't be confused with "inside information" because it's exactly the same thing. Inside information is just
the part of asymmetrical information that it happens to be illegal to use.
If you're a highly placed executive at Seagram and know about the up-
coming Disney takeover and the new Scotch-and-Water Park, you can't
buy Disney stock in anticipation of the premium that Seagram is going
to pay for Disney shares. But if you're the janitor who empties the highly
placed executive's wastepaper basket, and you know that scotch tastes
terrible with inner tubes in it and that drunk people in mouse suits are
not to be trusted, you can do anything you want.

The problem is, you aren't either of those people. And neither am
I. This is why we shouldn't be investing in stocks. We should invest in
mutual funds. Mutual funds have multitudes of ex-indie-filmmaker
M.B.A.s searching out asymmetrical information.

The problem is, there are too many M.B.A.s discovering the same
asymmetrical information, which makes the information all symmetri-
cal again. This is why we should invest in index funds.

The problem is, index funds contain the same stocks that make
up the Dow Jones Industrial Average or the like. Index funds will go
where the stock market goes. And where the hell is that?

This information is so asymmetrical, nobody knows it.

(What you should really do with your money is watch me. That is,
watch what the baby boom does. We baby boomers have caused everything since 1946. We'll keep buying stocks until we retire. But when
we hit sixty-five, we're going to sell stocks. And the stock market is going
to go down. And we're going to wet ourselves. The math is simple: 1946
+ 65 = 2011. Buy stocks until 2011, and then buy Depends.)

There are alternatives to the free market. Congress could pass stricter
investment-industry regulations, more orders and directives like the New

York Stock Exchange's rule against running. Investment-industry professionals probably hate all those limitations. Except they don't. "I think the mix is perfect," said David. "The rules are rigid and strict."

"There are things you take for granted in our market—rule of law," said the B-girl investment banker.

"It's mostly disclosure rather than regulation per se," said the move-stupidly investment banker.

SEC requirements and NYSE bylaws are there to make sure that investment trading is fast and confident and the O. J. jury doesn't have to be brought in every time somebody says "at" instead of "for." These kinds of restrictions aren't concerned with how much money goes to which place, just with how it gets there.

On the other hand, we could have the government take over the investment industry. The government would consider what's best for us all. If Americans wanted to buy stock, the government might, for example, look at the Coca-Cola Company. Coca-Cola was selling for $1.54 a share in 1982, and, as of mid-1998, it went for $78. That would have been a good buy. But Coca-Cola is not a product that provides social benefits. It causes cavities, is a factor in the increasingly dangerous nationwide obesity health threat, and contains caffeine, which harms fetal development in unwed mothers. The government would buy shares in the Studebaker corporation instead.

Studebaker is heavy industry. Heavy industry provides high-paying jobs to semiskilled workers. Studebaker made important contributions to America's defense efforts during World War II. And Studebaker automobiles produce very little air pollution, because there are only about 200 of them left on the streets. True, Studebaker is out of business, but the government could leave a box of investment money in the empty lot where the Studebaker factory used to be, and semiskilled workers could come by and take what they need.

Plus, if the government controlled the investment industry, those pirates in neckties would be replaced by civil servants on modest salaries. Your investment decisions would be made by government employees, people like, in Arkansas for instance, Paula Jones. You could have your whole retirement fund tied up in a failed lawsuit about the president's dick.

Maybe we should leave government out of it. Maybe we should select a committee of wise and principled individuals to guide the global investment markets—Mario Cuomo, Toni Morrison, Václav Havel, Oprah, the Dalai Lama, Alec Baldwin, and Kim Basinger. The committee would consider such matters as product safety, environmental impact, social justice between rich and poor nations, and whether a corporation has a "glass ceiling" for women executives. Then the committee would allocate capital accordingly. Kim can be very persuasive on the subject of animal rights. Now your retirement fund consists of a thousand bunny rabbits that have been rescued from medical testing.

Or we could leave the investment industry pretty much alone and just divide its profits evenly. Bill Gates heads an enormous corporation in Redmond, Washington. You teach data processing at a community college in Akron, Ohio. At the end of the year, Bill and you—and everybody else—divvy up. Once. After that, Bill may decide that running Microsoft is an awful lot of work. For the same money, he might as well swipe your job teaching data processing. He certainly has the clothes for it.

Or we could all just move to North Korea and eat tree bark.

Wall Street's free-market capitalism is doubtless a wonderful thing and a boon to humanity, but it scared me. The free market scared me even when I watched it function under the rule of law. Capitalism scared me despite the fact that I was seeing it operate within a well-defined set of rules understood by all the players. And I liked the players. Capitalists are at least as honest and nice as the people I know who don't have capital. But I was still scared.

Free-market capitalism was terrifying under the best circumstances. What it was like under the worst circumstance, I couldn't imagine. And because I couldn't imagine it, I needed to go someplace that had no rules and was full of crooks. I considered Washington, D.C., but Albania looked like more fun.

3

BAD CAPITALISM

❖

ALBANIA

Albania shows what happens to a free market when there is no legal, political, or traditional framework to define freedoms or protect marketplaces. Of course there's lots of violence—as you'd expect in a situation where the shopkeepers and the shoplifters have the same status under law. And, of course, there's lots of poverty. Theft is the opposite of creating wealth. Instead of moving assets from lower- to higher-valued uses, theft moves assets from higher-valued uses to a fence who pays ten cents on the dollar for them. But capitalism conducted in a condition of anarchy also produces some less-predictable phenomena. Albania has the distinction of being the only country ever destroyed by a chain letter—a nation devastated by a Ponzi racket, a land ruined by the pyramid scheme.

A pyramid is any financial deal in which investors make their money not from investing but from money put into the deal by other investors, and those investors make money from the investors after that, and so on. It's the old "send five dollars to the name at the top of the list, put your own name at the bottom of the list, and mail copies to future ex-friends." If I want to make fifty dollars from my five dollars, ten new dupes must be recruited. If each of them hopes to make fifty dollars, a hundred suckers will be needed, then a thousand, and hence the "pyramid" name. If a pyramid scheme grows in a simple exponential manner—10^1, 10^2, 10^3, etc.—it takes only ten layers of that pyramid to include nearly twice the population of the earth. And 9,999,999,999 of these people are going to get screwed because the guy who started the pyramid has run away with all the five-dollar bills.

When communist rule ended in Albania, in 1992, the nation was broke and was kept from starving only by foreign aid and remittances from Albanians in Italy, the U.S., and elsewhere. But the people of Albania still managed to scratch together some cash. Like American baby boomers, they were worried about the future. So, like baby boomers, they invested. The Albanians invested in pyramid schemes. The pyramids grew. People were getting rich, at least on paper. And then, in 1997, the pyramids collapsed.

Albanian reaction to the financial disaster was philosophical—if your philosophy is nihilism. Violent protests occurred all over the country. The Albanian government banned public meetings. The protests became more violent. The government reacted to this by authorizing the military to shoot at crowds. The military responded to that by deserting in droves. Soldiers had money in the pyramid schemes, too, and were just as mad as anyone else. The violent protests turned into armed rebellions. The government lost control of every military base in the country. By spring the Albanian army was reduced to perhaps one intact unit, numbering a hundred soldiers. The entire defense arsenal was looted.

There'd been plenty to loot. Albania's Communists had required every man, woman, boy, and girl to undergo military training. Estimates of the number of weapons loose in the country ranged as high as 1.5 million. And the Albanian defense ministry admitted that a whopping 10.5 billion rounds of ammunition had been stolen—more than 3,000 bullets for every person in the nation. Heavy weapons were also pilfered—artillery, missile launchers, and high explosives. Some of these were taken by local Committees for Public Salvation, but most wound up in less-responsible hands. The National Commercial Bank in the city of Gjirokaster was robbed with a tank.

Korce, near the border with Greece, was terrorized by gangs of masked men. Outside Fier, on the seacoast plain, twenty people died in a shoot-out between criminals and armed villagers. The southern port of Vlore was taken over by a gangster chief named Ramazan Causchi, who preferred to be called "the Sultan."

At least 14,000 Albanians tried to escape to Italy by commandeering boats. One thousand two hundred people squashed into a single purloined freighter. The president of the country himself, Sali Berisha, stole a ferry to send his son and daughter to Brindisi, Italy. Prison guards deserted and 600 inmates broke out of Tirana's central prison. Among the escapees was the head of Albania's Communist Party, the splendidly named Fatos Nano. (Nano exhibited the pattern of recidivism common to ex-convicts by campaigning hard during Albania's elections in June 1997. He is now prime minister.)

U.S. Marines and Italian commandos evacuated foreign nationals by helicopter. Humanitarian aid ceased. The International Committee of the Red Cross threw up its hands. "This is almost like Somalia," said an ICRC official. In four months more than 1,500 people died and tens of thousands were injured. Theft slipped into pillage. The railroad to Montenegro was stolen—the track torn up and sold for scrap. Pillage degenerated into vandalism. Schools, museums, and hospitals were wrecked. And vandalism reached heroic scale. Bridges were demolished, water-supply pumping stations were blown apart, power lines and telephone wires were pulled down. Albania came to bits.

I went to Albania in July 1997, and I know a country is screwed up when I can tell something is wrong with its history and social organization from 20,000 feet in the air. Flying over the Albanian Alps on the trip from Rome to Tirana, I noticed that the villages are not tucked into the fertile, sheltered valleys the way the villages of Austria, Switzerland, or even Bosnia are. The villages of Albania are right up on the treeless, soilless, inconve-

nient mountaintops. Before ski lifts were invented, there was only one
reason to build homes in such places. A mountaintop is easy to defend.

The Tirana airport had one runway and a small, shabby, white-
washed concrete terminal building with a random planting of flowers
outside. There were no visa or immigration formalities. Presumably, few
people were trying to sneak into Albania to glom welfare benefits. Customs agents did run my bag through an X ray, however. With all the
ordnance available in Albania, it's hard to imagine what they were looking for. Pro-gun-control literature, maybe.

I'd found a translator and driver by calling the Hotel Tirana and
hiring the front-desk clerk's boyfriend. I'll call him Elmaz. He met me
in the airport parking lot in his uncle's worn-out Mercedes. Elmaz said
Tirana was thirty minutes away. We drove toward town on a four-lane
turnpike that—"Five kilometers long," said Elmaz—promptly ended.
"Is only highway in country," said Elmaz. The buckled, pitted two-lane
road that followed was full of cars, trucks, and horse carts—an amazing number of them for such a supposedly obliterated economy. Scores
of wrecked trucks and cars lined the road. Albania has so many wrecks
that all the horse carts are fitted with automobile seats, some with center consoles and luxurious upholstery.

The landscape was the Mediterranean usual, a little too sunbaked
and scenery-filled for its own good. But the fields were only half-sown
in midsummer, and out in those fields and up along the hillsides were
hundreds of cement hemispheres. Each dome was about eight feet across
and had a slit along the base. All the slits faced the road. It seemed to be
a collection of unimaginative giant penny banks.

These are self-defense bunkers. Elmaz said there are 150,000 of them
in the country. They're everywhere you look. They are Albania's salient
visual feature. The shop at the Hotel Tirana sells alabaster miniatures as
souvenirs—model igloos, though the gun slots seem to indicate floun-
der-shaped Eskimos. In the cities, some of the bunkers have cement flower
planters molded onto their tops, a rare conjunction of war and gardening. Larger bunkers appear along the beaches and at other strategic spots.
The mountains are riddled with fortified tunnels, and even the stakes in
Albania's vineyards are topped with metal spikes so that paratroopers will
be impaled if they try to land among the grapevines.

Albania's longtime communist leader, Enver Hoxha (pronounced Howard Johnsonish: "Hoja"), ordered all this after the Soviet Union's 1968 invasion of Czechoslovakia. He was sure Albania was going to be invaded next. Hoxha called for ". . . war against imperialism, against the bourgeoisie, social democrats, national chauvinists, and modern revisionists. . . . They hurl all sorts of foul invectives on us. This gladdens us and we say: Let them go to it! Our mountains soar up higher and higher!"

But who'd want to invade Albania? Or so I was thinking as Elmaz and I drove past Albania's Coca-Cola bottling plant. There, peeking out from behind a ten-foot fiberglass Coke bottle on the roof, was a sandbagged machine-gun nest. Maybe Hoxha wasn't crazy.

In the event, the pillboxes were no use against the force that actually invaded Albania, which was the force of ideas—though not exactly the same ideas that sparked the Declaration of Independence, to judge by what Elmaz showed me over the next week. Elmaz was studying to be a veterinarian. Everything had been stolen from his school: books, drugs, lab equipment, even parts of the buildings themselves. "We are without windows, without doors," said Elmaz. "We study with only desks and walls." The desks had been stolen, too, but the faculty had found them in local flea markets and bought them back. "All the horses we have were shot," said Elmaz.

Across the road from the veterinary school was a collective farm that once had 5,000 cattle. "They stole five thousand cows!" I said, amazed at the sheer get-along-little-doggy virtuosity needed to rustle a herd that size in Albanian traffic.

"No, no, no," said Elmaz. "They could never steal so many cows in 1997."

"How come?"

"Because they were all stolen in 1992 when communism ended."

How could mere confidence games lead to total havoc? And why did pyramid schemes run completely out of control in Albania? It took about an hour to find out. Elmaz drove me to see Ilir Nishku, editor of the country's only English language newspaper, *The Albanian Daily News*.

"Why were the pyramids so popular in Albania?" I asked Nishku. "Were people just unsophisticated about money after all those years of communist isolation?"

"No," said Nishku, "there had been pyramid schemes already elsewhere in Eastern Europe, and they had collapsed before the Albanian ones were started. People in Albania knew about such things as the failure of the MMM scheme in Russia."

"Then how did so many Albanians get suckered in?" I asked.

And the answer was simple. "People did not believe these were real pyramid schemes," Nishku said. "They knew so much money could not be made honestly. They thought there was smuggling and money laundering involved to make these great profits."

The Albanians didn't believe they were the victims of a scam. They believed they were the perpetrators—this being so different from the beliefs of certain Wall Street bull-market investors in the United States.

"My family had two thousand dollars in the pyramid schemes," said Elmaz. It was their entire savings.

Nishku told me the first Albanian pyramid scheme was started in 1991 by Hadjim Sijdia. Sijdia Holdings offered 5 percent or 6 percent interest per month, 60 percent to 72 percent a year—way too much, especially considering that Albania was then in a period of low inflation. But Sijdia Holdings had some real investments, and although Hadjim Sijdia was jailed in Switzerland for fraud, he managed to get out and somehow repay his debts.

Following Sijdia Holdings, however, came schemes with a primary business of scheming. There were about nine large pyramids in Albania. Three of them—Sude, Xhaferri, and Populli—had no real assets at all. By 1993 small-business owners had gotten the idea and began creating minipyramids all over the country. Free enterprise can be free of all sorts of things, including ethics, and competition drove the promised rates of return high and higher. At one point the Sude pyramid was offering interest of 50 percent a month.

"The pyramid schemes," said Ilir Nishku, "created the idea that this is the free market and just four years after communism, we could get rich. They created the wrong idea that *this* is capitalism."

"Everyone was sitting in cafés," said Elmaz.

Albania's economic statistics looked great: 9.6 percent growth in 1993, 8.3 percent in '94, 13.3 percent in '95, 9.1 percent in '96.

"Albania's economy chalks up the fastest growth rate on the continent," chirped the slightly clueless *Bradt* travel guide.

The very clueless *United Nations 1996 Human Development Report* for Albania declared, "The progress in widespread economic well-being reported in the *1995 Human Development Report for Albania* has continued, forming a social basis for [here's where our UN dues really go to work] human development."

Something called the *Eurobarometer Survey* said the Albanians were the most optimistic people of Eastern and Central Europe.

Even Enver Hoxha's ancient widow, Nexhmije (pronounced . . . oh, who cares), waxed positive on capitalism. Released from prison in December 1996, she had a new bathroom installed in her apartment. Jane Perlez of *The New York Times* interviewed the communist crone: "'This is the good thing about the consumer society,' [Nexhmije] said, showing off some pink Italian tiles. 'Though it's very expensive, you can find everything.'"

The glory days lasted until February 1997. Then five of the big pyramids collapsed, and all the little ones did. Four other major pyramid schemes quit paying interest and froze most accounts, which is to say they went kerflooey, too. An estimated $1.2 billion disappeared, more than half the Albanian gross domestic product; that is, more than half the value of all the goods and services produced in Albania that year.

"Where did all that money *go*?" I asked Nishku.

He began ticking off possibilities: Swiss banks? The Albanian government? Money-laundering operations in Cyprus? Turkish Mafia? Russian Mafia? Mafia Mafia? "We don't know," he said.

I asked Nishku if there was any possibility that people would get their money back.

He said, "No."

The capitalism I'd encountered on Wall Street was, said its proponents, all about freedom. Albania has lots of freedom. Everyone admires freedom. And, indeed, one of the best places in the world from which to admire freedom of every kind is the Hotel Tirana's balcony bar overlooking Skenderbeg Square in the center of Albania's capital city.

Sheshi Skenderbej is an all-concrete piazza the size of a nine-hole golf course. A dozen streets empty into it. From each street come multitudes of drivers going as fast as they can in any direction they want. Cars head everywhere. Cars box the compass. They pull U-ies, hang Louies, make Roscoes, do doughnuts. Tires peel and skid. Bicycles scatter. Pushcarts jump the curbs. Pedestrians run for their lives. No horn goes unhonked. Brakes scream. Bumpers whallop. Fenders munch. Headlight glass tinkles merrily on the pavement. There's lots of yelling.

Until 1990, Albanians were forbidden to own motor vehicles. They didn't know how to drive. They still don't. Every fourth or fifth car seems to have an AUTOSHKOLLE sign on the roof, and not a moment too soon. Now there are 150,000 automobiles in Albania. If you've ever wondered why you don't see beaters and jalopies on Western European streets, why there are no EU junkyards, it's because the junk is in Albania. Elmaz said, "When we were first open to Europe, we bought used cars. Very used cars. After one year . . ." He pursed his lips and made the Mediterranean "kaput" noise.

The bad cars of Europe are in Albania. And the hot cars. An unwashed Porsche 928 lurching inexpertly through the square just out of range of my highball ice cubes seemed a probable example. Its huge V-8 was being gunned to piston-tossing, valve-shattering rpms. Even a mid-1980s model 928 would cost an average Albanian sixteen years' of salary.

An American wire-service reporter was teasing Elmaz about used-car shopping: "I'd like to get a Renault Twingo, maybe. A '95 or '96. For about a thousand dollars? One that hasn't been rolled."

"Ha, ha, ha," said Elmaz in the kind of laugh that indicates nobody's kidding. "I know someplace."

The wire-service reporter, who seemed to be rather too well-informed on various matters, said that pot cost thirty dollars a kilo in Albania. And The Economist magazine's business report on Albania said that in March 1997, a fully automatic Kalashnikov assault rifle could be bought on the streets of Tirana for as little as three dollars.

"*Everyone* is surreptitiously armed," said the wire-service reporter. Or not so surreptitiously. I saw a middle-aged man in civilian clothes walking along what used to be Boulevard Stalin, holding his five-year-old son by one hand and an AK-47 in the other.

Such are Second Amendment freedoms in Albania. And First Amendment freedoms lag not far behind in their extravagance. Each evening during the first weeks of July 1997, a couple hundred royalists would march into the chaos of Skenderbeg Square, bringing traffic to a new pitch of swerve and collision.

I watched the royalists set up podium and loudspeakers on the steps of a Soviet-designed cement blunder that used to be the Palace of Culture. They unfurled the heart-surgery-colored Albanian flag, bearing the image of what's either a two-headed eagle or a very angry freak-show chicken. The royalists shouted into the microphone such things as, "We will get our votes, even by blood!" The volume was enough to drown out the loudest car crashes. Then, at greater volume yet, they played the Albanian national anthem, which is as long as a Wagner opera and sounds like the Marine Corps band performing the *Ring* cycle while falling down all the stairs in the Washington Monument.

The royalists were demonstrating on behalf of one Leka Zogu, who thinks he's the king of Albania. He'd just gotten his butt whipped (80 percent of the voters said, "*jo*") in a national referendum on restoring the monarchy. Not that Albania ever had a monarchy. The country wasn't even a country until the twentieth century. It was a backwater of the Ottoman Empire from the 1400s on and a back-further-water of the Byzantine Empire before that.

Leka Zogu's father, Ahmed Zogu, was a putsch artist from the sticks who overthrew what passed for the government in 1924, crowned himself King Zog I in 1928, pimped the country to Mussolini, and Airedaled it into exile one step ahead of Axis occupation in 1939. Leka was two days old at the time. Since then the younger Zogu has sojourned in Rhodesia and South Africa, been thrown out of Spain over an arms-dealing scandal, and spent a brief jail stint in Thailand for gunrunning—at least as good a preparation for the throne as having your ex-wife martyred by paparazzi.

After an hour or so of royalist racket, Leka Zogu's motorcade arrived, flashing the kind of suction-cup roof lights that people buy when they want you to think they belong to the volunteer fire department. This sloppy parade of Mercedes sedans shoved into the rumpus of Skenderbeg Square, and the royal himself popped out in one royal beauty of a leisure suit. Leka (in the Albanian language the definite article is a suffixed u or i so "Leka Zogu" translates as "Leka the Zog") stood at the microphone like a big geek—six feet eight inches tall, chinless, and bubble-bellied. He mumbled a few words. (His unmajesty's command of Albanian is reported to be sketchy.) Then he booked. Wide guys patted lumpy items under their clothes. All the Benzes tried to turn around at once, creating still worse traffic mayhem, if such a thing is possible.

And it is. A few days before I got to Albania some of Leka's supporters became so enthusiastic that they started a gun battle with the police. The shooting went on for fifteen minutes. Although only one person was killed, because the two sides weren't actually near each other. The police were in a soccer stadium several blocks from the demonstration.

Anyway, Albania is fairly pissabed with freedoms. Free enterprise not least among them. Capitalism is pursued in Albania with the same zest—not to mention the same order and self-restraint—as driving, politics, and gun control.

Hundreds of cafés and bars have opened, most of them whacked together from raw timber with the same carpentry skills used by Oregon Rasta-Sufis when converting old school buses for Lollapalooza excursions. The rude structures are built on any handy piece of open ground and "have occupied even school yards in the capital," says *The Albanian Daily News*, old copies of which, along with every other form of litter, carpet the city streets in NYSE-floor profusion. Private garbage collection is not yet up and running in Tirana, but private garbage disposal is fully operational. Every public space is covered with bags, wrappers, bottles, cans—and the booze shacks and pizza sheds that sold them.

Gardens have been obliterated by jerry-building, monuments surrounded, paths straddled, soccer pitches filled from goal to goal. The Lana River is walled from view, not that you'd want to look. The squat-

ter construction companies tossing up chew-and-chokes on its banks
have used pickaxes to make haphazard connections with waste pipes
and water mains. Hydrohygienic results are the predictable. The Lana
has crossed the lexicological line between *river* and *open sewer*. And what
used to be Youth Park, a huge area of downtown greenery, has become
the world's first dining and leisure shantytown, a brand-new cold-
brewski slum with extra cheese.

But it's gambling that's the real meat and drink. It's done on the
same confounding electronic video-card-playing devices that the Pequot
Indians are using to reconquer Connecticut. Albania is a country that,
from 1986 to 1990, imported a total of sewing machines, electric stoves,
and hot-water heaters numbering zero. And Tirana is a city with electricity as reliable as congressional-committee testimony on campaign
contributions. But there they are: the very latest examples of wallet-
vacuuming technology from America, available everywhere and, through
some miracle of Mafia-to-Mafia efficiency, functioning smoothly all day.

Albania is also a country where the poverty line is $143 a month
for a family of four. Eighty percent of Albanians are living below that
line. And what looks like 80 percent of Albanians are standing in front
of bleeping, blinking games of chance feeding 100-lek coins—fifty-cent
pieces—into the maw. The most-common commercial sign in Tirana is
AMERICAN POKER.

The second most common sign is SHITET. Appropriately. Although it
actually means "for sale." Appropriately. Or perhaps it should be "up for
grabs," whatever that is in Albanian. Maybe it's "Amex." I went to an
American Express office to get some money, and they were completely
taken aback. They would never have anything so grabbable as money right
there in an office. For money you go to the Bank in the Middle of the Street.
Here—everyone being surreptitiously armed—great wads of money are
being waved around, some of it peculiar. I got a few greenbacks with the
green on the backs more of a pants-at-a-Westport-cocktail-party shade
than usual and a twenty with something dark and odd about the presidential portrait. Was Andrew Jackson in the Jackson 5?

The thousands of tape cassettes being sold in the middle of the street
are counterfeit, too. At least I hope they are. I'd hate to think anyone
was paying royalties on Bulgarian disco and Turkish rap. The Marlboros

are real, however, and cost less than they do when they fall off the back of a truck in Brooklyn. The clothes fell off a truck, too, I think, though not, unfortunately, a DKNY semi. Albanians have the Jersey Dirt Mall mode of dress figured out. Like everything else, these duds are sold intra-avenue, from racks mingled with car accidents, royalists, money, guns, and automated five-card draw.

Reading over what I have written, I fear I've made Albanians sound busy. They aren't. Even their gambling is comparatively idle—exhibiting none of the industry shown by the old bats in Atlantic City with their neatly ordered Big Gulp cups of quarters and special slot-machine yanking gloves.

The Albanian concept of freedom approaches my own ideas on the subject, circa late adolescence. There's a great deal of hanging out and a notable number of weekday, midafternoon drunk fellows.

There are lots of skulking young men in groups on Tirana's corners and plenty more driving around in cars with no apparent errand or evident destination. It's not a mellow indolence. I saw one guy cruising in his Mercedes, an elbow out the window, a wrist cocked over the steering wheel, riding cool and low. But his trunk lid was open, and chained in the boot was a barking, gnashing, furious 150-pound German shepherd.

Men in Albania hold each other's hands too long in greeting, a gesture that seems to have less to do with affection than disarmament. They kiss each other on the cheeks, Italian style, but more Gotti than Gucci. Everybody stares. Nobody steps out of your way.

The Albanians have a Jolly Roger air. You could give an eye patch and a head hankie to most of the people on the street and cast them in *Captain Blood.* Not to demean a whole ethnic group or anything, but like most Americans, the only Albanians I'd ever heard of were Mother Teresa and John Belushi. A entire country full of Mother Teresas would be weird enough—everybody looking for lepers to wash. But imagine a John Belushi Nation—except they're not fat, and they're not funny.

"They'll rob you," said the wire-service reporter as we—pretty idle and indolent ourselves—ordered another round at the Balcony

Bar. "Don't carry your wallet." Then a neophyte television producer walked up and announced that he'd gone out to tape some local color and hadn't made it to the city limits before he lost a car, a TV camera, and $5,000 in cash.

A whole family lived in front of the Hotel Tirana, doing nothing. Between the hotel entrance and Skenderbeg Square was a quarter-acre patch of what used to be grass. Therein camped, from dawn to dark, a very big and fat woman; a very small and bedraggled woman; several skinny, greasy men; and approximately a dozen seriously unkempt children. The big woman spent all day spraddle-legged on a tablecloth, playing cards with the skinny men. The small woman spent all day wandering back and forth across the packed-dirt lot. Every time a hotel guest stepped outside, the children descended upon him or her, begging in a horde, or if begging was to no avail, thrusting little hands into pockets and purses, and grasping at whatever the hotel guest was carrying. Otherwise the children swatted and kicked each other. Sometimes the children would go over to the big woman, who'd also give them a swat. And if the tykes obtained money, they'd return to the big woman, and she'd snatch it.

The family had a puffy, sallow baby with the scorched blond hair that is a sign of malnutrition. The infant seemed to be eight or ten months old but didn't appear to be able to hold its head up. It never cried. A ten- or eleven-year-old boy was the principal caretaker. He squeezed the baby to his chest with one arm while he chased the other children around, giving them karate chops and kung-fu kicks. Meanwhile, the baby's appendages wagged and jiggled in all directions—a floppy tot.

Between martial-arts exhibitions, the baby was left alone on a sheet of cardboard on Skenderbeg Square's tumultuous sidewalks. Passersby were supposed to leave coins. Occasionally they did.

"They are Gypsies," said Elmaz. But *Gypsy* is the preferred local bigotry epithet, the N-word of the Balkans, with the added advantage that it can be used on anybody darker than Kate Moss.

The translator who worked for the wire-service reporter said he'd questioned the child-care boy about the baby. The boy had said, "His mother was going to throw him away. But she gave him to us. Now we're taking care of him."

There is not, so far as I was able to discover, an Albanian Child Abuse Hotline. "That's because it would be jammed with how-to calls," said the wire-service reporter.

"What the fuck is with this place?" said someone else at the bar. And I do not have an answer for that.

All of Albania's rich and varied manifestations of freedom, however, came to a halt promptly at 10 P.M., when the shoot-to-kill curfew began.

It seemed the Albanians had had a bit *too* much freedom, so much freedom that the Organization for Security and Cooperation in Europe had sent an Italian-led contingent of some 7,000 troops to keep the lid on.

The OSCE troops arrived in April 1997 in their scout cars and personnel carriers. The situation in Albania was so bad that having Italians tooling around in armor-plated vehicles actually made the streets safer. Now, after 10 P.M. in Tirana, everything was quiet. No, not quiet. There was continual gunfire coming from the maze of Tirana's backstreets. And the gunfire set off Tirana's dogs. As a result I spent the night thinking, first, about stray Kalashnikov slugs and the Hotel Tirana'a floor-to-ceiling windows: "Gosh, I wish I had a room on a lower floor." Then thinking about what a really large number of loud dogs Tirana has: "Gosh, I wish I had a room on a higher floor." I ended up back at the balcony bar, fully exposed to both the bullets and the barking, but at least I had gin.

Tirana was not quiet at night, but it was invisible. Nothing moved on the main streets. And most of the town's electricity was out so I couldn't see it moving, anyway. I gazed into a stygian void with just an occasional tracer shell arcing across the night sky. Make a wish?

Why is freedom in Albania so different from freedom in the United States? This would take a lot more than an hour to find out, if it could be explained at all.

Albania is a little place the size of Maryland, with a population of 3.25 million. Albania is little, and Albania is out of the way, blocked from the rest of the Balkan Peninsula by high, disorderly mountain ranges, and, until this century, cordoned from the sea by broad, malarial swamps. Seventy-five percent of the land is steeps and ravines. In the north, the Albanian Alps rise in such a forbidding confusion of precipices that they are known as the *Prokletije,* or Accursed Mountains. In the eighteenth century, Edward Gibbon called Albania "a country within sight of Italy which is less known than the interior of America." (Although Gibbon hadn't heard about Whitewater and Arkansas politics in general, so perhaps he was being unfair.) As late as 1910, geographical authorities were saying that certain districts of Albania "have never been thoroughly explored." And considering the neophyte TV producer's experience, they won't be explored soon.

This isolated, outlandish place emerged from World War II run by the isolated and outlandish communist guerrilla chieftain, Enver Hoxha. In 1948, Hoxha broke his alliance with Tito because Yugoslavia wasn't being pro-Soviet enough. In 1961, Hoxha broke his alliance with Khrushchev because the Soviet Union wasn't being pro-Soviet enough. In 1978, Hoxha threw out the Red Chinese for having played Ping-Pong with the U.S. And by the time Hoxha died in 1985, Albania wasn't on speaking terms with anyplace but North Korea and maybe the English Department at Yale. Hoxha's successor, Ramiz Alia, stayed the loony course for a while, but in 1990, with communism going into a career slump all over the globe, Alia tried some reforms. Wrong call.

The Albanians' response to a sudden introduction of personal autonomy and individual responsibility casts an interesting light on the human psyche. They ran like hell. According to Balkans expert James Pettifer, "Over 25,000 people seized ships moored in Durres Harbor and forced them to sail to Italy." Thousands of others fled to Greece or occupied the grounds of Western embassies in Tirana. University students pulled down the gigantic gilded statue of Enver Hoxha in Skenderbeg Square, and the Alia government had to dismantle and hide the nearby statues of Stalin and Lenin. There was repeated food rioting, widespread destruction of public property, and extensive looting of everything owned by the government—and everything was.

Then things got better. Dr. Sali Berisha, whom Pettifer calls a "leading cardiologist" (Albania *has* a leading cardiologist?), was elected president. The Communists were jailed. In Pettifer's words, "The new

government . . . embarked on a program of privatization and the construction of a free-market economy."

But life got too much better. This privatization being programmed
and this free-market economy being constructed were based on only
one industry: pyramid schemes.

Although Albania seems inaccessible, it has been, over the past three
millennia, repeatedly accessed. Albanians have had the misfortune to
live too close to the kind of folks who can't seem to resist invading
things—even things like Albania.

Albania has been invaded by various Greek city states, Macedonia,
Rome, Byzantium, Slavic hordes, Byzantium again, Bulgarian hordes,
Byzantium one more time, Normans, Christian Crusaders, Charles I of
Anjou, Serbs, Venetians, Turks, and Fascists. Durres, historically the
principal city of Albania, has changed hands thirty-three times since the
year 1000.

Albania has been invaded, yes. Conquered, no. While the rest of the
Balkan Peninsula was being hellenized, latinized, Slavofied, or Turkey-
trotted, Albanians stayed Albanian. Their language is the last extant
member of the Phrygo-Thracian family of tongues once spoken by
peoples from the far side of the Black Sea to the eastern Adriatic.

The highland areas of Albania have been claimed by various nations but governed by none. Authority has always rested with the *Mal*,
the Albanian word for tribe and also—to give some idea of the cozy
interaction among Albanian clans—the Albanian word for the mountain that each village is on top of.

The tribalism that has disappeared from the rest of Europe (or been
reduced to what tartan you wear on your golf slacks) is still a prime fact
of existence in Albania. Tribal identification transcends the theological
hatreds so avidly pursued in the rest of the Balkans. There are tribes
with both Christian and Muslim members. "The true religion of the
Albanian is being an Albanian," said nineteenth-century nationalist
Pashko Vasa.

Tribal identification transcended atheism, too. In the 1960s,
twenty-eight of the fifty-two members of the Albanian Communist Party's
central committee were related by blood.

Blood being the key word. Albania is remarkable for the number and persistence of its blood feuds. As soon as a boy is of age, he is liable to become a Lord of Blood, a *Zot i Gjakut,* with responsibility for killing members of the clan who killed members of his clan, who killed members of their clan, and so forth—a sort of pyramid scheme of death, if you will.

Men who are "in blood" can spend years shut up inside their fortified houses. Girls, however, are let off the hook unless they swear to be virgins and wear men's clothes. Lest anyone accuse the Albanians of utterly eschewing all rule of law, this takes place under the auspices of the *Kanun Lek Dukagjini,* the Law of Lek, a voluminous compendium of tribal custom and practice dating back at least to the 1400s, copies of which may be purchased at book stalls in Tirana.

According to James Pettifer, who wrote an essay on the subject for the *Blue Guide* to Albania, anthropologists estimate that there are some 2,000 blood feuds going on in Albania and that as many as 60,000 people are involved. (The *Blue Guide* is one of the few tourist manuals with a good section on the ins and outs of vendetta killing.) In 1992, a man was beheaded with an ax in a Tirana hotel lobby—revenge for a murder his father had committed in a northern village more than forty years before.

The Albanians certainly have preserved their culture. Whether this is a good idea is a question that can be decided only, of course, by Albanians. But in these times of multiculti zeal, it may be worth noting that the Albanian language did not have a proper alphabet until 1908. The country didn't get a railroad until 1947. The first Albanian university was founded in 1957. And there is an Albanian proverb to the effect that a woman must work harder than a donkey because a donkey feeds on grass, while a woman feeds on bread.

Culture is an important factor in determining the economic success of a nation. But, that said, what else is there to say? Germany got rich with a culture as barbaric—a couple of world wars and a Holocaust prove it—as anything ever seen. Tibet stayed poor with a culture so wonderful that half of the movie stars in America want to move there. And how do you change a culture anyway? We could wire Albania for cable and let its citizens see how the rest of the world lives. Jerry Springer should give them some good ideas.

† † †

Albania did not improve upon inspection. Even the animals in the Tirana zoo had been stolen. The monkeys were gone from Monkey Island. The aviary was empty of birds. All the large ruminants had been "eaten," said Elmaz. Only two lions, a tiger, and a wolf remained in captivity. No one had had the guts to steal them—although several young men seemed to be gearing themselves to the task. The bars on the wolf's cage had been pried back. One young man stuck his hand inside, shouted, and snatched the hand back. The wolf ignored him, and the men went down the hall to tease the tiger and lions.

In the middle of downtown Tirana, 200 yards from Skenderbeg Square, is a block-long hole in the ground. Garbage fires smolder at the bottom. This is where Sijdia Holdings was going to build Albania's first Sheraton hotel with pyramid-scheme investments. Only a portion of the cellar was completed. The basement staircase rises above ground level on one side of the hole. There's a door into the stairwell with a neon sign above it: CLUB ALBANIA. Entirely too symbolic

The nearby apartment buildings that housed the country's communist elite were built in the clean, austere International style of twentieth-century cities everywhere, but they're crumbling. Where big chunks of stucco have fallen away, primitive rubble-wall construction is visible, ready to explode with the structures' weight in the eastern Mediterranean's next little earthquake.

Apartments for the common folk were built much worse. Elmaz's mother had had the unenviable job of teaching geography to students who, as far as they knew, would never be allowed to leave the country. She lived in a block of flats with four stories of haphazardly laid masonry courses. Flaking mortar oozed from every joint. The bricks looked like they'd been dug from beds of clay with canoe paddles.

The Hotel Tirana, which went up in 1979, was so badly designed that the Italian entrepreneurs who took it over had to add a separate tower as a fire escape. Short gangways lead from the tower to an emergency exit on each floor. This outside stairway created security problems, however, so the tower was encased in steel mesh. Now if there's a fire at the Hotel Tirana, the result will be hundreds of guests in an enormous fry basket.

Near the Lana River is a neighborhood called the Block, once reserved for Enver Hoxha's inner circle. Their idea of luxury was semi-
suburban, the kind of semi-suburb you're trying to convince your parents
to move out of before their car gets stolen. But the Hoxha residence looks
like the house of a really successful Chicago dentist. There's something
of the Chicago prairie style to its broad but ill-proportioned windows,
clumsy, deep-eaved roof, and dumpy fieldstone terracing—call it Frank
Lloyd Left.

Hoxha's daughter Pranvera is, in fact, an architect. I don't know if
the Hoxha homestead was her work, but other evidence indicates she's
at least as addled as her dad was. She designed what used to be the Enver
Hoxha Memorial a couple of streets away. It's an immense concrete Pluto
Platter of a building with conical walls used these days for daring card-
board-under-the-butt slides by local preteens. It once contained, says
the *Blue Guide,* "more or less everything that Hoxha ever touched or
used." It now contains the USAID office, dispensing foreign aid. Which
of these constitutes the greater foolishness, I leave to the reader.

Elmaz and I drove forty kilometers west of Tirana to Durres, passing a complex of greenhouses from which both houses and green had
been removed. We saw two summer palaces King Zog had built for himself, completely ransacked. Someone had tried to take the very paint off
the walls.

Durres was, at the time, Albania's only working port. And in that
port were exactly two ships. One was a Chinese-built destroyer that had
been "bought" from the Albanian navy. At any rate, $6,000 had changed
hands. Now the *Khajdi* was a discotheque, paneled inside with the same
rough wood used in the beer halls and gambling hells of Tirana's Youth
Park. Something had gone wrong in the bilge, however, and the *Khajdi*
was listing so far to starboard that you felt you'd had more than enough
to drink the moment you stepped inside. Business was bad, the propri-
etor reported.

The other ship was a beached freighter missing hawsers, hatches,
portholes, and anything else that could be filched, including anchors.
A couple of men had shinnied up the foremast and were trying to pry a
brass knob off the top. A gang of boys ran around the deck playing pi-

rates or, if you think about it, not actually playing. Technically speaking, they *were* pirates.

Elmaz said the looting had pretty much stopped, at least in the thirty or forty kilometers around Tirana. I asked him whether the OSCE force had imposed law and order. He didn't think so. "They are just driving around and sitting in cafés like everyone else," he said. I asked him if the government had managed to quiet things down. It didn't have an army anymore, but it still had the secret police, actually the too-well-known police, the Sigurmi, left over from the Hoxha regime and now renamed, with euphemistic masterstroke, the National Information Service. But Elmaz didn't think the police had done much except pester Sali Berisha's political opponents.

"Then what stopped the looting?" I said.

"They were finished," said Elmaz.

A little before curfew on my last night in Albania, I was sitting in a café with the wire-service reporter and a couple other fellow stateside hacks. "Albanians are just like anybody else," I was saying.

"They're crazy," said the wire-service reporter.

"No, they're not," I said. "They just have a different history, different traditions, a different set of political and economic circumstances. They're acting exactly the way we would if we . . ."

There was an Albanian family at the next table: handsome young husband, pretty wife, baby in a stroller, cute four-year-old girl bouncing on her dad's knee. The girl grabbed the cigarette from between her father's lips and tried a puff. Mom and Dad laughed. Dad took the cigarette back. Then he pulled a pack of Marlboros from his shirt pocket, offered a fresh cigarette to the little girl, and gave her a light.

4

GOOD SOCIALISM

❖

SWEDEN

Nobody was teaching four-year-olds to smoke in Sweden. Nobody was doing anything bizarre there. I was walking through Gamla Stan, the Old Town in Stockholm, when it struck me that Sweden was the only country I'd ever been to with no visible crazy people. Where were the mutterers, the twitchers, the loony importunate? Every Swede seemed reasonable, constrained, and self-possessed. I stared at the quaint, narrow houses, the clean and boring shops, the well-behaved white people. They appeared to be Disney creations—and not from the new, hip, PG-13 Disney rumored to be opening a Scotch-and-Water Park. This was the Disney of the original Disneyland. Gamla Stan had the same labored cuteness, preternatural tidiness, and inexhaustible supply of courtesy from its denizens. I half-expected to turn around and see someone dressed as Donald Duck. Instead, I turned around and saw someone dressed as the king of Sweden. Which, in fact, he was. King Carl XVI Gustaf was riding, in a gilded coach-and-four with footman in knee breeches holding on behind, right down the middle of the street in a country renowned the world over for its utter egalitarianism.

† † †

I'd gone to Sweden in February 1996 to find a socialist paradise. I was looking for someplace that had the prosperity of Wall Street without the chaos of Albania, someplace where wealth was better spread around than a free market tends to spread it, and where economic life had fewer shocks and alarms. And I'd gone to Sweden in February on the theory that anyplace can pass itself off as paradise on a balmy summer weekend, especially a place where nude volleyball was pretty much invented. But let us look at paradise when the days are so short that if you take an afternoon nap, you not only wake up in the dark, you miss sunrise. And as for the temperature: "It's not so cold," say the Swedes. "We're right on the water here, so it never really gets that . . . Darn it, hand me the hammer, Rolf. The Mr. Coffee has frozen solid again."

But a socialist paradise was what, indeed, I found—"*folkhemmet*," as it's called, "the people's home." This sounds like the latest sensitive renaming of the local poorhouse, but the word has perhaps more charm in the original language. Sweden is a welfare state from cradle to grave, and further than that. Between elaborate sex education and the constitutional status of the Lutheran Church, Sweden provides for its citizens from, as the Swedes put it, "erection to resurrection."

Medical care is available to everyone in Sweden at nominal cost, even to tourists, though I was not personally lucky enough to have an accident or disease while I was there. A visit to the doctor costs between fifteen dollars and twenty dollars. A specialist gets five dollars more. Hospital stays cost about twelve dollars a night for anything from a twisted ankle to cancer.

Unemployment insurance is 75 percent of your pay, and there's unlimited sick leave at the same rate of compensation. If you're completely disabled, you get your whole paycheck. (During a brief period of nonsocialist rule in 1991, a one-day waiting period for sick-leave benefits was instituted. An enormous drop in Monday and Friday worker illnesses resulted—one of the medical miracles of the twentieth century.)

Day care is available for all children from infancy until who knows when. Maybe until they get senile, because I have an official Swedish government report (which I never quite summoned the patience to read) titled *The Old Are Youngsters Who Have Grown Older*. Parents pay about

10 percent of day-care costs. Eighty-four percent of women work—most of them in day-care centers. No, it just seems that way. A very large proportion of women are employed in the public sector, however. Some of them are in Parliament.

Swedes get five weeks of legally mandated paid vacation. If you have a baby, parental leave lasts 450 days, at up to 80 percent of salary, and either the mother or the father can stay home. An additional 120 leave days can be had to care for a sick child. Thus some Swedes are able to take 570 days a year off from work. And teenage girls who become pregnant can presumably get fifteen months off from school with good grades.

Actually, there isn't any grading in Sweden until high school, and education is free through the Ph.D. level, with additional "study assistance" money available, plus cheap student loans. This should pretty much carry you through to retirement, which comes at age sixty-five, when you'll get an annual pension equaling two-thirds of the average income from your fifteen best earning years. And all benefits are indexed to inflation.

Sweden has managed to do these fine things without the usual side effects of collectivism. It didn't invade Poland and France, or send any of its citizens to Siberia. Sweden's per-capita gross domestic product is a hearty $20,800. Swedish life expectancy is 78.2 years, even if they do call in sick a lot. That's versus seventy-six years in the United States. And infant mortality is 4.5 per 1,000 live births, compared with the American rate of 6.5 per 1,000. There's no poverty worth mentioning in Sweden, and no great wealth. Well, there is great wealth, but they play it down. A Volvo limousine is something to see. Seventy-two percent of Swedish households have a washing machine. Ninety-seven percent have a television set. There's a car for every two adults. The Swedish system works.

Except the Swedish system is broken. In recent years the Swedish government's budget deficit has been as high as 12 percent of the gross domestic product. By comparison, at the end of the Reagan-Bush era, when America's budget balancers had let all the spinning plates fall on their heads, the U.S. deficit was less than 5 percent of GDP. We in America consider our body politic to be perilously in hock, but the

Swedish national debt is, proportionately, 40 percent greater than ours. Sweden's national debt is nearly equal to its GDP—to all the things made and all the work done in Sweden annually. To get even, the Swedes would have to move next door and mooch off Finland for a year. Just paying the interest on the national debt takes 7 percent of everything produced in Sweden. And this despite the Swedes taxing the hell out of themselves. The tax burden is the highest in the developed world. More than half of the GDP goes for taxes. So living in Sweden is like getting a divorce every April 15—a divorce with dependents. And these dependents never outgrow their need for child-support payments; quite the contrary: *The Old Are Youngsters Who . . .* , etc. Of an adult population of 7 million, 2.7 million are not working. Most of these people are living off some form of social benefits. Another 1.6 million are employed by the government or in government service agencies. And only 2.7 million are actually paying the bills by working in real businesses.

Public spending in Sweden is equal to nearly 70 percent of the GDP, and the Swedish economy is doing about as well as ours would be if seven out of ten of our economic decisions were made by political types. Would you send Newt Gingrich and Ted Kennedy to do your grocery shopping? How many of those groceries do you think would make it home? For twenty-five years, Sweden's economic growth has been lagging behind that of other industrialized nations, and between 1990 and 1993 the Swedish economy shrank by 5 percent.

There's been a small upturn since, but the Swedish Institute (government funded and hence prone to sunny outlooks) admits, "The majority of households have seen their financial circumstances deteriorate in recent years." For Swedish industrial workers, aftertax earnings adjusted for inflation have stagnated since 1975. And rightly so, since Swedish labor productivity has increased by only 74 percent since 1970, compared with a 700 percent increase in labor costs—many of those costs resulting from government-mandated employer contributions to . . . well, to the government.

As the 700 percent figure might indicate, inflation has been a problem in Sweden. There have been only a few years since 1979 when Sweden's inflation rate was below the average for other prosperous countries. Government deficits are partly to blame, but Sweden is also a small country moshed up against the Artic Circle. Unless Swedes want their material circumstances limited to wood pulp, livestock, and cod, they have to import a lot of things. The Swedish krona is one of the weakest currencies in Western Europe, Western Europeans being no fools. "Do you want that in deutsche marks, Swiss francs, or day care, family leave, and fifteen-dollar doctor visits?" Thus, imported goods are expensive in Sweden. In fact, everything's expensive in Sweden because, on top of the other government exactions, there's an astonishing 25 percent national sales tax on almost all goods and services. Every time you order a burger, you buy the government fries and a Coke. No, actually just a Coke, since the tax on food and restaurant meals is a mere 12 percent. At least tipping is minimal. The Swedish attitude seems to be that all services, even drink orders, should be provided by the government, and the government's been tipped already.

One thing not causing Swedish inflation is an overheated job market, although full employment has been a principle of Swedish government since the 1930s. (Full employment is not one of my own personal goals in life, but it seems to be important to socialists.) Until 1990, Sweden had an unemployment rate of less than 3.5 percent, which is amazing, considering that 3.5 percent of my bum friends wouldn't take *any* job, even if it paid $100 an hour and involved doing inventory for a blind liquor-store owner. But now Sweden's unemployment rate is 7.6 percent, and, if you add the people in various do-little government programs with names like Youth Training Scheme and Working Life Development, the figure is closer to 13 percent.

Nor is the situation likely to change soon, since net investment in the Swedish economy has gone from about 16 percent of the GDP in 1970 to less than nothing recently. People have been going around to businesses, taking their investments back: "Give me that drill press." In Sweden you can get a better return on your money from government bonds than you can from corporate stocks, and you don't have to read the financial pages every day to see if the government's still there. Believe me, it is.

So the Swedish system works, and the Swedish system is broken. This left me with a lot of questions about Sweden. And I wasn't the only one.

"What is Sweden like?" I was asked. A reasonable query, except it was posed by a Swede, and I'd only been in the country for a week. The foreign visitor's thoughts are always of interest, I suppose. "How do you like Australia?" ask Australians. "Are you having fun in Italy?" ask Italians. "When are you leaving?" ask the French. But never in my travels have I had a native say to me, "Who are we, and what are we doing?"

I didn't think it would be diplomatic to mention Disneyland. "It's like Minnesota," I said. "You know, wholesome, hygienic, polite, cold climate, everything works, and it's full of, um, Swedes." (Also, the radio programs are as dull as Garrison Keillor's, at least if you don't speak Swedish.)

Actually, Sweden isn't like Minnesota *or* Disneyland, but then again, it isn't much like Sweden, either. The people aren't all that tall and blond, they don't talk orgy-borgy talk, the women are no more beautiful than women generally are, and as for the vaunted Scandinavian lubricity, there was exactly one naughty-type Swedish magazine available at newsstands. It had the promising title *Slitz,* but the only nude photos were of an underfed young lady in appalling eye makeup, and the accompanying copy began with a sentence about *"legendariske visionaren och chefredaktoren Hugh M. Hefner."* You don't need to be a linguist to know where the hot stuff comes from in Sweden.

There is, in fact, formal censorship. I was at a dinner party having one of the precisely two drinks that Swedes have before the meal, when a guest arrived late. This is something no guest ever does in Sweden, not even if he died en route, though sometimes it can be hard to tell. The guest apologized sincerely. "I had to finish watching movies," he said.

"Jurgen is a film censor," said his dinner companion, also sincerely. Jurgen reassured me. "We're only looking for violence," he said. So *Showgirls* was okay, but *Hamlet* was out? "No, no, I don't believe anything should be censored," said the censor. "I'm looking for real violence—porno films where women are actually injured. And child pornography." Wasn't that more a matter for the police? And it was. But for some reason these moviemakers needed to be censored as well as arrested.

I'm sure I received a logical explanation. And I'm sure I don't remember it. This is, after all, a country that maintains an entire national state-supported religion, complete with bishops, a synod, and pastors in every parish, and only 5 percent of the population goes to church.

There are huge, splendid, empty, idle houses of worship everywhere. I went to the Storkyrka (Great Church) behind the royal palace. The Storkyrka was consecrated in 1306. It was the site of coronations until 1907, when the Swedish monarchy decided that formal coronations were too la-di-da. Inside is a very big statue of St. George killing the dragon. This was carved from oak by Bernt Notke in 1489 in a manner extremely lifelike, right down to a well-whittled horse anus. (One can only speculate about the shoptalk among the apprentice sculptors to whom this task no doubt fell.) The dragon is rather more lifelike than necessary: a scale-armored, talon-freighted, fang-brandishing spiny reptoid frozen in midslither. It is a fine reminder of the high artistic skills of the Nordic Renaissance and also of Sweden's strict attitude about drugs. Only 4 percent of Swedish high-school students have tried drugs even once, although the percentage may have been higher in 1489.

The only indication that the Storkyrka was used, other than by us tourists, was a little red table and six or eight wee plastic chairs. A day-care center had been set up right beneath the place where St. George's lance was popping dragon slime, and you can hardly blame the tots if they never set foot in a church again.

But the dragon isn't real. It isn't consequential. It isn't in earnest, and Sweden is an earnest country. A new storm sewer was being dug in Stockholm's Kungstradgarden. Posters had been mounted around the site showing the engineer's drawings and giving details of the costs, building technique, and future benefits of this large drain. At Stockholm's tourist-information center, a main feature is the Swedish Institute, "a government-financed foundation established to disseminate information about Sweden." Picture a tourist-info booth in Rockefeller Center stocked with books and pamphlets about labor relations, social insurance, public procurement, and the domestic chemical industry, half of them in Swedish.

I gathered heaps of Swedish self-seriousness. One tome was called *Love! You Can Really Feel It, You Know!*, a title I can only hope lost something in translation. *Love!* is "a body of reference material produced by Skolverket (Sweden's national agency for education) for use in Swedish schools . . . to provide an overview of how education in the arena of sexuality and human relationships works today." The chapter headed "The Adolescent Years—Questions to the World" contains these "Questions from Boys": "How big is the average dick?" and "How many holes does a girl have?" And under "Questions from Girls": "When will my breasts stop growing?"

When will my breasts *stop* growing?

Not that the Swedes possess no sense of humor.

"What does Norway have that Sweden doesn't?

"*Good neighbors.*"

I heard that joke several times. But in Stockholm there's a whole museum of not getting it. The *Vasa* was, as a guidebook put it, "the mightiest royal warship of her times." The *Vasa's* wreck was discovered in 1956, and she was raised almost intact after five years of work by diving crews. The hull was enclosed in a shed and sprayed with wood preservative for another seventeen years. Then restorations began, and finally, in 1990, the Vasamuseet opened, a noble, copper-sheathed, tent-shaped structure housing the ship and seven floors of displays and exhibits. Which is all well and good. However, the *Vasa* was launched on August 10, 1628, sailed 1,400 yards, and sank like a brick. "The mightiest royal warship of her times"—her times being August 10, 1628, from 4:30 until 5 in the afternoon.

The day after I visited the Vasamuseet, a crane was set up in front of my hotel. The crane was mounted on a truck bed and extended sixty or eighty feet. It was supposed to hoist some air-conditioning equipment onto the roof. The truck driver was maneuvering the crane in a slow, methodical Swedish manner. And the whole thing tipped over— *Plopp* (the name, incidentally, of a popular Swedish candy bar).

The crane fell across four traffic lanes, through the roof of a shuttered kiosk, over a breakwater, and into the harbor. And I . . . I'm an American. I can't help it. I laughed. The hotel manager was standing next to me in the lobby. She said, "It isn't really funny." Of course, if anybody had been hurt or a row of cars had been creamed or a bunch of tourists had been standing in line at the kiosk to buy sea-cruise tickets, then . . . then it would have been hilarious.

† † †

Maybe Sweden is simply incomprehensible to an American. There is no discernible evidence of the economic problems in Sweden, or of a conflict between private and public economic aims. The Swedes, left wing though they may be, are thoroughly bourgeois. They drive Saabs like we do, know their California chardonnays, have boats and summer cottages, and vacation in places that are as much like home as possible, which is to say at Disneyland.

Stockholm is one of the more attractive cities in the world, somber beauty division. It sits on a paisley map of islands, inlets, peninsulas, and bays dividing the freshwater of Lake Malaren from the Saltsjon arm of the Baltic Sea. The city is modern in all the things that should be modern (phones, roads, cars, toilets), while all the things that should be old (royal palaces, battle monuments, trees in the parks) are as old as they're supposed to be.

Any shortcomings seem to be problems of affluence rather than want. The sidewalks are slushy. Even with 13 percent unemployment, no one deigns to take so humble a job as shoveling snow. And when it comes to such very modest business ventures as shoe-shine stands (do not bring your best cap-toed oxfords to Stockholm in the winter), there are none.

Sweden is cozy, and Sweden is safe. Baby carriages are routinely left outside shops. Of course, we can't be sure of the Swedes' motives in this, and I did see more baby carriages than I saw toddlers or school-age children. But the children I observed were well-behaved despite a Swedish law—this is not a joke—against spanking your kids. "Behave or I'll reason with you," however, is, from a Swede, a fairly terrible threat. The teenagers weren't too rotten acting, either. They had plenty of snot rings and *dummkopf* haircuts and wore those European sweaters the color and shape of spilled porridge, but actual rebellious behavior seemed limited to looking mopey. I guess when the entire object of your society is to make everything as swell as possible for everybody, the only way you can lash out is by bumming.

Sweden's litter situation is non-NYSE and un-Albanian in the extreme. There is graffiti in Sweden, but it is neatly confined to bridge abutments and the cement embankments along certain canals. There are no street vendors or annoying public musicians (though perhaps it wasn't the season). There are no woebegone panhandlers or newspaper-wrapped transients (it was certainly the season for that). The modern structures are maintained. The old structures are restored. The Swedes must levitate their garbage. I never saw a bin or can. When the crane fell over, it was cut apart with torches and whisked away by supper time.

I asked Janerik Larsson—executive vice president and director of communications at a media conglomerate with the conglomeration of a name Industriforvaltnings AB Kinnevik—why Swedes still worked. If they don't work, they get almost what they would get if they did work. And if they do work, their raises and bonuses are all taxed away. Give Americans a situation like that, and we'd be putting all our economic energy into playing extra cards at the bingo hall. But there was nothing visible in Sweden to indicate much national goldbricking. Mr. Larsson pointed to the window: "You see how it is outside? It's *always* like that here." Over the centuries the Swedish gene stock has been culled. The lazy ones froze.

I asked Dr. Carl-Johan Westholm—the president of the Federation of Private Enterprises (in Sweden, even opposition to central planning is centrally planned)—why Sweden still worked. If Sweden is so poor, where is the poverty? Why aren't there people at stoplights offering to clean my windshield? Or, more to the point, my shoes? "We don't have income, but we still have wealth," said Dr. Westholm. "You may live in a big house, and the neighbors think you're wealthy. And they're right in a sense. But they don't see you going to the bank to take out a second mortgage." He explained that more than 46 percent of the Swedish government budget is spent on transfer payments—giving cash to people. The budget shortfall is equal to about a third of that 46 percent. To give out three kronors, the government has to sponge one of them. "Sweden is borrowing its prosperity," said Dr. Westholm.

What happens to Sweden when nobody's willing to lend it more money and the Swedes finally realize that they really can skip work for four months if the kid pukes? The people of Sweden—like Damocles—are set down to a sumptuous feast, and overhead, suspended by a hair is . . . not a sword, this is too prosaic a country . . . a gigantic wet blanket.

† † †

According to the Swedish Institute's booklet *On Sweden,* "The overall aims of the social welfare system are to redistribute income more evenly over each individual's life cycle, narrow the gaps between social classes, and provide everyone with a broad selection of public services." An American reads that sentence and hears, "We're putting half your allowance in the bank because you'll no doubt want to buy some Rage Against the Machine CDs and a skateboard when you're eighty." Then the American starts thinking about social status. True, Yanni, Marv Albert, and Jenny McCarthy are part of the underclass, but is it because they're poorer than John Updike? And is this a gap we want to close? And "broad selection of public services" seems to be another way of saying: "To get downtown, you can take the bus. Or the next bus. Or the bus after that."

But one understands the impulse behind the Swedish ideas. Nobody can contemplate America's notorious wealth and renowned poverty without thinking, at least once, "Why can't we fix this?" Give your cell phone to the lady talking to herself in the park—let her talk to someone else for a change. Many underprivileged youths never get the benefits of a college education. The next time you see a deprived adolescent, why not present him with your old bong, fuzzy snapshot taken on San Pedro Island, and tattered copy of Monarch Notes for *Bleak House*? Impoverished Americans exist in very depressing circumstances, so *share* your Prozac.

The Swedes can almost make you believe in this. In the first place, they are nice—nicer even than the people in Anaheim who spend all day in Donald Duck masks. At shops, in restaurants, on the streets, everyone is so helpful and pleasant that it frightens an American, since nobody in the U.S. behaves this way unless he's trying to sell you mutual fund shares. Cabdrivers get out and open the door for you. One night my taxi was cut off in traffic, and my driver rolled down his window, leaned toward the offending vehicle, and said—I quote verbatim—"*Tsk-tsk.*" Even the hotel manager who told me that the crane falling over wasn't really funny caught herself and a moment later said, "Maybe it is funny, a little."

Every businessperson, academic, or politician I called made time to see me (always for precisely one hour, by the way).

The American ambassador Thomas Siebert and his wife, Deborah, are as nice as everyone else in the country. They came by the hotel for drinks, invited me for tea, and were full of information and suggestions. I actually found, to my horror, this niceness infecting me. Ambassador Siebert was Bill Clinton's roommate at Georgetown, and Mrs. Siebert is a good friend of Hillary's. I went into a deep funk over the nasty things I've written about those blathering highbinders, the president and first lady. (I got over it.)

Hardly an evening passed without hospitality of the full-blown seated-dinner kind. Although this was a mixed blessing. There are many delightful things about Sweden, but almost none of them are meals. The Swedish idea of spicy falls somewhere between Communion wafers and ketchup. Cream sauce is everywhere. I went to an Italian restaurant that had on its menu spaghetti Bolognese with cream sauce, linguini al pesto with cream sauce, and fettuccine Alfredo with cream sauce, even though fettuccine Alfredo is nothing but cream sauce, anyway. The city guide in my hotel room noted these "typical Swedish dishes": anchovy au gratin, nettle soup with eggs, baked eel. And here are some suggested entrées from a Swedish cookbook called *A Gastronomic Tour of the Scandinavian Arctic:* smoked reindeer heart with seasonal salad, noisettes of young reindeer with creamy green-peppercorn sauce, and reindeer tongue with a salad of early vegetables. What's that, Blitzen? I can't understand a thing you're saying.

Maybe the problem with Swedish food has something to do with the almost obsessive Swedish interest in fairness. Maybe if fairness is a society's most-esteemed value, then "average" becomes a great compliment. Mmm, honey, that was an *average* dinner. In fact, this is nearly the case. The word in Swedish is *lagom,* which translates, more or less, as "just enough" or "in moderation" or "sufficient." And *lagom* really is used as a compliment.

I went to interview two Swedish leftists, a cabinet minister in the ruling Social Democratic Party government and the chief economist for the Landsorganisationen, or LO, the principal Swedish trade union. And they both harped on fairness, though in the nicest way.

The lobby wall in the big art-deco LO headquarters is covered with a mural depicting a blond, shirtless buff dude wielding a glowing ingot of pig iron. There is an art history dissertation waiting to be done about the connection between Calvin Klein ads and socialist realism. The economist, Per-Olof Edin, told me, "Inequality creates violence and crime in the United States." And it probably does, although one can only wish it would create more violence toward Donald Trump. Nor did this explain why, in Sweden, where there's little inequality, crime has increased fourfold since 1950. Mr. Edin said, "Enormous differences in income, wealth, and power push people toward communism." And maybe so, but the only people it pushed toward communism in America were '60s college students who already had income, wealth, and power—or at least their fathers did. And Mr. Edin went on at some length about the social problems and economic inefficiencies caused by competition. Which means, I suppose, that basketball would be a better game if all ten players were on the same side and we lost those stupid hoops.

The cabinet minister was Marita Ulvskog, whose last name translates as "timberwolf" and whose portfolio was Minister for Consumer, Religious, Youth and Sport Affairs, and why not just keep going with a title like that and make her Minister of Hobbies, Boardgames, Gardening and Affairs Among Middle-Aged Married People? Mrs. Ulvskog could see I was alarmed at her business card. "I am dealing with the things that politicians shouldn't deal with," she said with a laugh. And then, without a laugh, she said, "At the same time, there is lots of legislation on this." And in Sweden you can bet there is.

"We don't want a society," said Mrs. Ulvskog, "with large differences—in income, in social welfare, in regions, in men and women." And good luck to the Social Democrats. Try this with animals, and everything would be a cow. Which may explain why the zoo in Stockholm does, in point of fact, have cows in it.

I asked Mrs. Ulvskog if the differences among people in Sweden could be made narrower than they already are. "No, not really," she said.

"And in creating the egalitarianism you do have," I asked, "is it the Swedish political system or Swedish society that works so well?"

"Perhaps," said Mrs. Ulvskog, "it is the society."

So the Swedes have come up with a wonderful trick to make everyone equal, but it can only be performed by Swedes. Also, it isn't working very well anymore.

But Sweden did work for a long time. From 1870 to 1970, Sweden had a higher rate of economic growth than any country in the world except Japan (and Japan was cheating—using the statistical dodge of starting with a nearly Paleolithic baseline). By the 1950s, Sweden was among the richest countries on earth, with a per-capita GDP—an amount of gross domestic product per person—that was twice the European average.

Several things turned this hayseed country in the unheated attic of Europe into a wealthy modern state. Land-reform laws in the early nineteenth century allowed farmers to exercise property rights by enclosing common space, thereby increasing production, though at the expense of landless rural laborers. The medieval guilds, which gave comfy local monopolies to artisans, were abolished in 1846, and business freedom was guaranteed by law in 1864. Craftsmen could now succeed—or fail—at anything they wanted, anywhere they liked. Sweden also had supplies of timber, iron ore, and other minerals. Since these were export commodities, a policy of free trade was instituted. Thus, Sweden's prosperity was the result of the very deregulation that a socialist government would be expected to abhor.

A socialist will tell you that these policies lead to economic disparities and social dislocations. And the socialist is right. During the late-nineteenth and early twentieth centuries, almost one-million Swedes, nearly a quarter of the population, left Sweden. Fortunately they had someplace to go: Minnesota. Dislocated and disparity-ridden as they may have been, the Swedes did pretty well there.

A Scandinavian economist once proudly said to free-market advocate Milton Friedman, "In Scandinavia we have no poverty." And Milton Friedman replied, "That's interesting, because in America among Scandinavians, we have no poverty, either."

A very different kind of Scandinavian economist, Peter Stein, tried to explain to me the Swedish Model or Swedish Miracle, the so-called

Middle Way, which is supposed to deliver all the houses, cars, and nuisance calls from competing long-distance carriers that America has with the perfect social equality of, say, Sweden. Mr. Stein is one of a small group of Swedes willing to believe in complete economic liberty. It is a group so small that I think I met all of them in a room at Stockholm's free-market-oriented City University, an institution itself so small that it's housed on a couple of floors of an office building. Mrs. Ulvskog had told me, "A conservative politician in Sweden is closer to a United States liberal than to Newt Gingrich."

Mr. Stein pointed out that for sixty-two of the one-hundred years of splendid growth, the Swedish socialist welfare state contained no socialism and hardly any welfare. The left didn't take power until 1932, and when the Social Democrats did get in office, they made socialism work by the novel expedient of not introducing any. Very few industries were nationalized. The Social Democrats may have believed in such things in principle, but they were Swedish and logical. They decided to let the capitalists go ahead and make money, tax the wages and profits, and use those taxes to buy social benefits. They would "nationalize consumption, not production." But even with these social benefits, the leftists were *lagom*. In 1960 the notorious Swedish tax burden was about the same as the burden is now in the United States: Swedish government spending was 31 percent of GDP, and the deficit hardly existed.

Growth continued, unemployment was minimal, and inflation was low. It was a left-wing Eden, albeit with an occasional stock-and-bond-owning serpent in a Volvo limousine. Most social benefits were tied to having a job, so the Swedes kept working. And they worked cheap. Approximately 90 percent of Sweden's blue-collar workers and 80 percent of its white-collar workers are unionized. The unions sat down with the Swedish Employers' Confederation and colluded in centralized wage negotiations. The pay rate was based on productivity and world price levels. As Per-Olof Edin told me, "For fifteen to twenty years it's been the LO that has been saying wages must be kept low." This would hardly make for a rousing speech at an AFL-CIO strike rally.

A policy of "solidaristic" wages was pursued, meaning the same pay for the same kind of work, regardless of the employer's ability to cough up. This favored the most efficient and productive (and largest) companies, though it screwed small businesses and start-up entrepreneurs. Companies were allowed to fire workers for any material reason. Featherbedding was forbidden. Labor mobility was encouraged by government emphasis on retraining and placement instead of unemployment checks. Free trade was maintained. No attempt was made at centrally planned production or marketing. The Swedes may have pestered their barnyard fowl, squeezed it, jiggled it, and poked it in the bottom, but they did not kill the goose that laid the golden egg.

Then something went wrong. The Swedish government started granting entitlements that weren't dependent on holding a job and were often dependent on *not* holding one. At the same time, the concept of full employment was extended to sectors of the population that didn't even necessarily want to be fully employed, such as the handicapped and mothers of young children. Likewise, an attempt was made to maintain full employment in failing industries where employment previously would have been discouraged. Steel mills, shipyards, and textile factories were nationalized to "preserve" jobs. Public-sector employment grew from 20 percent to 30 percent of the workforce between 1970 and 1983. Taxes rose to stinking heights but not high enough to cover costs. Social services continued to expand without regard for budgets.

As more people worked at government jobs where productivity was hard to measure, if not actively discouraged, centralized wage negotiations broke down. "Same pay for same kind of work" was replaced by "same pay for any kind of work." Peter Stein, in his bluntly titled monograph *Sweden: From Capitalist Success to Welfare-State Sclerosis,* wrote, "Swedish doctors work an average of only 1,600 hours a year, compared to 2,800 worked by U.S. doctors. It pays doctors to stay home and paint their own houses rather than spend their time practicing medicine and hire painters." A society is only slightly better off with its doctors painting houses than it is with its housepainters performing liver transplants.

Until 1976 the Social Democrats had ruled alone or in coalition for forty-four years. They were socialists, so they figured Sweden's success must be the result of socialism. The Social Democrats forgot that the Swedish Miracle was the result of fragile and elaborate compromises and also of, as Marita Ulvskog called it, "standing outside the war." Nice phrase.

Politicians had achieved control over the Swedish economy, but they were now trapped by their own power. The free market quit following the rules of economics and began following the rules of universal suffrage. The Social Democrats confess to it. "A 'political market' then emerged," Mrs. Ulvskog said. "You had to give something to the voters. We couldn't tell the voters we were going to cut." The electoral process turned into a vote auction, with both socialist and nonsocialist parties upping the ante. "Going once . . . going twice . . . SOLD to the Social Democrats for free Ph.D.s and 100 percent disability benefits. Do I hear any bids for the next Parliament? Yes? The gentleman from the Liberal-Moderate coalition says lower taxes and more police." Under such circumstances, even the best people, even the Swedes, could not resist the temptation to vote themselves more goods and services for less cost and bother.

This may have been more naive than cynical. The Swedes seem to have no natural distrust of government. There is in Scandinavia a long tradition of communal decision making. The Vikings had an assembly of all adult males that met once or twice a year and was called the Thing, surely the best name ever for a legislative body. Swedish peasants always had some land-ownership rights, and they usually maintained friendly relations with their king. Class distinctions existed, but pesky nobles made their money more by war and trade than by gouging the rustics. The Swedes never had feudalism to build a real Magna Carta hatred of central power. The Swedish constitution is long and so detailed that somewhere in it is probably a schedule for trimming the hedges, but it doesn't contain checks and balances. There is no Supreme Court, no federalism, no Tenth Amendment. The Parliament can do anything it wants, including change the constitution (by voting to do so twice with one parliamentary election between votes). Not that the Swedes are alarmed by this. "We think of the government as one of us," they say. The government is part of the community, and a very strong sense of community have the Swedes.

Perhaps too strong. Dr. Westholm, of the Federation of Private Enterprises, said, "There are no Swedish moral scruples about taxes." Otherwise a marvelously honest people, the Swedes have a blind spot about taking certain property that isn't theirs, as long as the loot is fairly divided.

And come to think of it, the Vikings were the same way. It makes you wonder what was going on in those longboats. Maybe discussions of political economy, Viking style. "Yah. We pillaged Ireland. Good. But Sven had seven rapes, and Nils only had one, so we all get to rape Sven."

Sweden is no longer the homogeneous herring-choicer back-forty that it was when the Swedish model was invented. More than 12 percent of today's Swedes were born abroad or have at least one foreign parent. They've come to Sweden for the same reason that Swedes went to Minnesota: to find a better life. They've also come to escape oppression. Sweden has a generous refugee policy and gives political asylum to some 20,000 people a year.

Thomas Gür, a Swede of Turkish descent and the author of a book about the problems of immigrants in Sweden, offered to show me Rinkeby, one of Stockholm's "toughest" neighborhoods. We left from the subway station at Sergels Torg, a large sunken plaza from the *Brady Bunch* architectural era and one of the few truly ugly spots in downtown Stockholm. It's known as the "declining square" both because the terrazzo paving has a distinct slant and because of the people who hang out there. This is the gritty heart of the metropolis where drugs are sold and youth gangs roam. Or are supposed to. The gangbangers and dope pushers seemed to be on one of their five weeks of legally mandated vacation when Mr. Gür and I walked through.

Swedish subway stations are each decorated by a different prominent contemporary artist and raise the question, Which is worse: vandalism or modern art? We took a very long subway ride, a ride that even in the largest American city would have carried us to the realms of golf and polo (the brand if not the ponies). But when we emerged, we were in a housing project.

The residents were mostly Middle Eastern, Turkish, Kurdish, Azerbaijani, a few Somalis—"new Swedes" as they're called—plus one old Swede, age about twenty-five, drunk in the middle of the day. He was the only dirty or disorderly element in the suburb. Everything else was a perfect grid of apartment house boxes without ornament or identifying feature, all built in 1960s crap-colored bricks, each the same distance from all the others with nothing but a vacuum of snow between, except here and there a tree standing foolishly by itself.

And that was it. There wasn't anything else to see except three or four shops, a dusty café, and a windowless mosque in a drab cement commercial square. The people on the sidewalks—sidewalks laid out straighter than people have ever walked—looked gray, sad, cold. Of that great marketplace which is the Middle East, with all its hawking and haggling in items and ideas, its idling, conniving, its news, gossip, and, indeed, its crime, there was nothing. Only two old Kurdish men selling sweaters out of a box. The sprawling new Swede families were crated up in the dinky flats designed for a working class with 1.9 children per cohabitational unit. "Some of these buildings were even built without windowsills," said Mr. Gür, "because people would put ugly things on them." I saw one woman in a chador lean out a sill-less window and spit. And that's all I saw of humanity.

Swedes do not seem particularly prejudiced against the immigrants. There are a few Swedish skinheads, who sometimes gather in numbers of about a hundred at the statue of King Carl XII in Stockholm's Kungstradgarden. They are regularly beaten up by about a thousand antifascist activists who then break store windows to protest the skinhead outrage.

The Swedish government pursues a confused—but fair!—policy of multiculturalism, encouraging immigrants to assimilate themselves into Swedish society while also encouraging immigrants to maintain customs they may not want anymore. "Kids are doing Turkish folk dances that they never would have done in Turkey," said Mr. Gür.

The multicultural policy isn't working. Unemployment among Turkish Swedes is 25 percent. And that's of those seeking jobs. Thomas Gür says that as many as 50 percent of Turkish Swedes aren't seeking them. The number of newer immigrants, such as Somalis, who are looking for work is even fewer. They have discovered, for instance, that they don't have to learn Swedish to get paid. Thanks to government programs, they can get paid to learn Swedish.

Of course, the immigrants are assimilating in their own fashion. There was a poster on the wall of the mosque that was so multicultural it doesn't even need translating:

Kung-Fu Dans & Fighting
Med Afrikansk Musik
(Bakom Pizzeriet Parma)
For mer information till ABDUL

It's interesting how—level society as you will—someone always turns out on top. I was thinking this as I was sitting in the office of the Minister for Consumer, Religious, Youth and Sport Affairs. It wasn't a lavish office by U.S. cabinet secretary standards, but it was *lagom*— two big, joined suites on a corner looking down the street to Lake Malaren. The walls were painted fashionable teal. The furniture was hip and blond. All salaries in Sweden may come out, after taxes, somewhat the same. But who gets the room with the view? Who flies off to European Union cheese-food milk-fat-content subcommittee negotiating sessions on the sunny isles of Greece? And opera tickets are heavily underwritten by the Swedish government. What a relief to the working stiff. "Bundle up the kids, Helga, we're all going to see Claude Debussy's *Pelleas et Melisande!*"

I had dinner that night in another expensive restaurant, and in the men's room, there was a rack of reading material, all of it annual reports. I don't think anyone had ever been in there who wasn't—like me—on an expense account, except, of course, for the fellow, probably an immigrant, who cleans the toilet.

The Swedish welfare state is based on redistribution of the most thoroughgoing kind. Everybody pays high taxes; even poverty benefits are taxed. And the taxes are returned to everybody in the form of "social goods." "We have tried to build a system where everybody gets something out of the state," said Marita Ulvskog. "Our position is that the millionaires must get something out of the state, i.e., a health system good enough for millionaires."

The Swedish Model assumes that citizens agree on what they want and that government can tell what this is. But what if the government is run by someone from Albania? And in return for your high taxes, the social goods you get are American Poker and a crate of rifles? The residents of Rinkeby looked about that satisfied with their bargain.

As for redistributing material things, all societies do it. But mostly they keep it in the family. I've got one already, and one's enough. Anyway, a modern government is not a family, not even metaphorically. Imagine a family where the kids and the dogs could vote. What would the food be like? Depends on the number of dogs. It might be reindeer tongue.

All this taking and giving back puts enormous power in the hands of government. Thus the Swedish Model also assumes that the government is good, that the government won't decide that what Sweden really needs is to conquer Denmark. And since Sweden is a democracy, the voters must be good, too, and not decide to support that government in return for free wedges of looted Jarlsberg. World history is not full of good governments, or of good voters, either. One of the great things about the U.S. Constitution is that it outlines a republic limited in scope and able to operate in spite of damnable officials and a chowderhead electorate—as 222 years of American history prove.

And what about the fairness so dear to the Swedish heart? Is it fair? Should we all get the same pay and privileges? Then why shouldn't we all get the same love and respect, the same health and happiness, the same cute little butt and big boobs?

Secure and *lagom* though Sweden may be, there is nonetheless something frightening about socialism, something that scared me as much as a close look at capitalism had. And the last time I walked through Gamla Stan, I didn't wonder where the crazy people were. In Sweden the craziness is redistributed fairly. They're all a little crazy.

5

BAD SOCIALISM

❖

CUBA

What could go wrong in theory with an overpowerful government like Sweden's had gone wrong for real in Cuba—very wrong. I got my first look at Havana at dawn in March 1996, from the window of my room in the Hotel Nacional. The city was gray with the grizzled markings particular to tropical desolation. Bright colors were bleached to dirty pearl. There were ashen streaks from leaking roofs and dark whorls left over from stagnant puddles. Mildew spread across walls like a living soot.

Even from ten stories up, I could see holes in everything: holes in roofs, holes in streets, holes where windows ought to be. There were holes in everything, and chunks missing from everything else. Chunks had fallen from balconies, cornices, porticoes, marble and granite facades. The city blocks were missing chunks of buildings. Some of the remaining buildings were missing so many chunks I thought they were abandoned until I saw the hanging laundry. And the laundry was full of holes.

Cuba looked like it had lost a war. And it had—the cold war. But Albania had lost the cold war, too, and Tirana, as I'd see a year later, was a colorful, noisy place this time of day: Cafés were full, cars collided, street vendors shouted their wares. Havana was silent.

I watched enormous breakers tumbling against the seawall of the Malecon, Havana's oceanfront boulevard. Thousands of gallons of gray brine sloshed over the holes and chunks in its concrete pavement. Torrents of dingy sea foam flushed against the Malecon's paintless old town houses. Very few *tuberos,* those brave souls who try to escape from Cuba aboard tied-together inner tubes, would be out today. They'd be washed right back into somebody's living room. And a very crummy living room, to judge by what I could see.

I was feeling pretty crummy myself. I'd arrived the previous midnight and gone straight to the Nacional's bar and started drinking *mojitos.* This was Cuba-fan Ernest Hemingway's second favorite drink, after the wake-up slug out of a hidden gin bottle. A *mojito* is made by mixing too much sugar with too much rum in not enough soda water and adding crushed mint leaves and lime juice. It sounds disgusting, and believe me, the next morning it is.

The walls of the bar were decorated with black-and-white photographs of celebrities visiting the Nacional, all of them, except a couple second-string European intellectuals, before the Castro era. Bad rumba music boomed from the girlie show in the hotel nightclub.

After five or eight *mojitos* I went to the john. If you were designing a socialist system—a nation in which everyone had the same social status—wouldn't eliminating rest-room attendants be the first thing you'd do? And if I were designing a socialist system (what a hobby), I'd at least let the masses visit the hotel that they all supposedly own in common. But ordinary Cubans can't enter the Nacional or its several acres of seaside gardens unless they are, for instance, rest-room attendants.

A few Cubans manage to sneak in. When I went upstairs at 3 A.M., there was a North American–type fellow in the elevator with a young woman, a girl, really, maybe sixteen years old. She was clean and clean-cut, soberly dressed, without jewelry or makeup, wholesome of manner and apparently a prostitute. At least the elevator operator thought so. He ordered her out. She was not a hard-looking girl, but a hard look crossed her face as she left.

I rented a car for an exorbitant amount of money. The car-rental company's manager spoke at length about Cuban-American friendship and how the citizens of both countries desired peace and mutual cooperation, "except for a few fascists such as Barry Goldwater and that Oklahoma bomber." The manager seemed to have done pretty well in the revolution. "According to my Rolex . . . ," he said, noting the time on my rental contract. And I got to hear about how he liked women with large bottoms.

He gave me the keys to a dirty and dented Japanese sedan. It had a Toyota nameplate, but, looking at the fit and finish, I'd say it was manufactured by that Studebaker corporation our government is going to buy stock in if we reform the investment industry.

I drove through Habana Centro. In 1991, Fidel Castro told Mexican journalist Beatriz Pages, "The other Latin-American countries have tens of millions of beggars; Cuba has none. In other Latin-American countries, you see children cleaning car windshields, running among the cars to do that." I stopped at a red light. Children ran among the cars, cleaning windshields.

Not that there were many windshields to clean. Traffic in Havana was mostly a matter of bicycles and pedestrians who had grown so used to empty streets that someone who looked both ways before crossing was probably a paranoid schizophrenic. People dawdled along, peddling at four miles an hour in the passing lanes and pushing baby strollers down highway exit ramps. Old ladies stood in the middle of the avenue puzzled that there should be someone who wanted to get by.

There were, however, still traffic police, hundreds of them, one on almost every corner doing God knows what all day. And traffic rules were completely in force, though stoplights were burned out and street signs were illegible with corrosion. It was, for instance, almost impossible to make a legal left turn in Havana, and all the streets in the city seemed to go one way to the left. These streets are numbered odd east-west and even north-south. I was inclined to give up *mojitos* when I found myself at the corner of Tenth and Eleventh streets.

Habana Centro looked like 1960 Cleveland after a thirty-seven-year strike by painters and cleaning ladies. But the old city, La Habana Vieja, was beautiful. Cuba's Spanish-colonial architecture is classical and restrained, less Taco Bell influenced than Mexico's. And unlike the rest of the Caribbean, Cuba's old buildings are made of stone. The island has, during its history, suffered various periods of neglect, such as the present one. Maybe the Cubans were trying to design things that would look good as moldering ruins.

The tourist areas of the old town had been cleaned up, and somewhat more cleanup was in progress. A number of museums and government-owned restaurants were open and were, as *Fodor's* Cuba guidebook says of one such, "decorated with antique furniture recovered from the great mansions of the local bourgeoisie." Tactfully put. Outside of the tourist areas, however, there was a fair danger of experiencing some freelance socialism; you might find that *you* were the local bourgeoisie from which something got recovered.

Later in the morning, Havana's streets grew crowded, but not with a madding crowd. Nobody was doing much of anything or going anywhere in particular. Thousands of people were just hanging around in the middle of a weekday in a country where, by law, there's no unemployment. Some people were walking dogs. All the dogs were old and small, the kind kept by rich women for purposes of baby talk. Maybe the dogs had been left behind when the rich women fled the revolution—thirty-seven-year-old miniature schnauzers forced to pawn their costume-jewelry collars and have their fur clipped at barber colleges.

The dogs didn't look happy. The kind of meat that goes into dog food would be eaten by people in Cuba if there were any of it to be had. The people didn't look happy, either. There was an edge and an attitude among the idling mobs in Havana. They gave out lots of hard looks, grabbed their testicles, and made those Latin sounds—hisses and sucky lip noises—especially at foreign women.

But when I actually met the Cubans—and I met a lot of them at a gas station after I drove the Toyota into a big hole, causing a front wheel to fold like a paper plate with too much potato salad on it—they were swell. They were pleasant, helpful, cheery, polite. They all had relatives in Union City, New Jersey. And an American woman told me that when she went out alone, the noises ceased. Or nearly ceased. The men grabbed their testicles in a formal and courtly manner.

The gas station was one of the few visible instances of anybody doing anything for a living. The Cuban government has not only eliminated the concept of unemployment, it's eliminated the concept of jobs, if you don't count begging or pestering strangers to buy "genuine Cohiba cigars" that "a good friend of mine sneaks out of the factory." Either the fellow who sneaks Cohibas out of the factory has an unusual number of good friends, or Cohiba-sneaking is Cuba's largest industry.

There was even less honest economic activity on the streets of Havana than on the streets of Stockholm—no roving food vendors or knickknack merchants, and only occasional kiosks selling cigarettes and newspapers, which they were mostly out of.

At a few prescribed spots in the city, there were arts-and-crafts markets. The arts and the crafts looked like they were made by accountants, lawyers, university professors, and other famously unhandy types who'd been out on the patio with dull tools trying to turn pieces of scrap wood into Che Guevara wall plaques and cigarette boxes with CUBA IS BEAUTIFUL carved on the lids in a desperate attempt to get U.S. dollars.

The dollars were provided by a few tourists watched over by more than a few tourist police. Membership in this august branch of the constabulary being proclaimed, in English, on the breast pockets of their uniforms. The tourist police did not, however, enforce fashion law. The tourists wore NBA balloon shoes on noodle legs, pie-wagon-sized jogging shorts, and idiot logo T-shirts.

The Cubans, poor as they were, looked much better. Not that their clothing was good. It seemed to be from American relatives who had gone to Price Club and put together large boxes of practical duds. But the Cubans wore that clothing well—tight where tight flattered, artfully draped where artful draping was to the purpose, and when all else failed, the clothes were simply absent. There were bare midriffs, wide skirt slits, buttons undone to the navel.

Cubans are stylish. Cubans are even glamorous, especially the women. And some of the women were entirely too glamorous for the middle of the day. Because there was one kind of economic activity on the streets of Havana, and lots of it. Flocks of women stood along major roads plying the trade just as it's plied in L.A. "Why is that girl hitch-hiking in her prom dress?" I heard a tourist ask.

The whores were budding in Cuba, and everything else was old, with-ered, blown, used up. Even the Young Pioneers, solemn kids in red kerchiefs doing calisthenics in the park, seemed to be obsolete children, products of some musty, disproven ideas about social hygiene. Tired, stupid slogans—SOCIALISM OR DEATH—were painted everyplace. The paint on the signs was peeling. All the paint in Cuba was peeling. Half an hour in Havana was enough to cure a taste for that distressed look popular in Crate & Barrel stores. Crumbling and rot abounded.

Of course, there was a good neighborhood in Havana. There al-ways is in these places. Miramar is on the beach to the west of down-town. The streets were lined with royal palms and also with new BMWs. The cheerful mansions had been built in the style that's called Spanish if you live in Pasadena. These were perfectly maintained and lavishly gardened, and every one of them was owned by a Cuban government institution, a foreign corporation, or an embassy, and so were the cars. In between the cheerful mansions were mansions of little cheer. The Castro government "recovered" these and turned them into housing for "the people." It was part of the liberty, equality, and fraternity espoused by the Cuban revolution. The fraternity in question must have been the one portrayed in *National Lampoon's Animal House*. Much of Miramar looked like the Deltas had been living in it for the past seventy-four semesters. They'd all gotten crabby and gray. And they'd run out of beer.

Nighttime was better in Havana. The city had so few lights that after dark, I hardly noticed the electrical blackouts. It looked like nobody lived there. Since hardly anybody wants to, it was a fitting look.

There were some privately owned restaurants. The food was good, and I could get a meal for five dollars. However, it did have to be dol-lars. No one in Cuba was interested in pesos. Even beggars checked to see if the coin being offered was American. The private restaurants were allowed no more than twelve seats, and only family members could be employed. This was as far as the Cuban government had been willing to go with capitalism among its own citizens. It will be interesting to see how this model works if it's applied to other free enterprise undertakings, such as airlines. Mom will begin beverage service as soon as Junior gets the landing gear up.

The big restaurants were nationalized, and in a nation that's suffering severe food shortages, this meant that only rice and beans were available to foreigners who had dollars. Ha, ha, ha. Hard-currency joke. I could get anything I wanted—lobster, steak, Cohiba cigars actually made by Cohiba, and rum older than the prostitutes sitting at all the other tables with German businessmen. The catch was, not only couldn't Cubans afford these things, neither could I. In the Floridita, where the daiquiri was invented and where the New York City price of drinks was apparently also invented, cocktails cost five dollars—more, at the black-market exchange rate for dollars, than most Cubans make in a week. I was also in constant danger of being serenaded. Guitar players roam Cuba's restaurants in packs. They know one song, "Guantanamera." The complete lyrics are:

> "Guantanamera, Guantanamera,
> Guan-tan-a-meeeeera, Guantanamera."

This unofficial national anthem was popularized by noted Cuban patriot Pete Seeger.

Was I missing something? Cuba is famous for its charm. I decided to hire a guide. Maybe he could find me some. Roberto, as I'll call him, took me to Hemingway's house in the village of San Francisco de Paula. It's a white stucco plantation-style manor on a hilltop with twenty-two acres of land, a guest cottage, and a swimming pool. I must remember to write harder. There's a three-story tower with a den at the top where Hemingway could go and think big thoughts. ("Where is that gin bottle?") And in the toilet off the main bedroom, there's a pickled lizard on a shelf. The lizard got into a fight with one of Hemingway's cats. The cat won, but the reptile fought so bravely that Papa felt the need to immortalize it. The liquid in the container was low. It looked like somebody had taken a few nips out of the lizard jar. And on second thought, I'm not sure I have what it takes to be a major author.

Hemingway's widow donated the house to the Castro government. And Britain donated Hong Kong to China.

Roberto was chatty, full of official, government-approved information. On the way to San Francisco de Paula, we passed the dirty, bedraggled worker housing that everywhere mars the Cuban landscape. The buildings are nothing but concrete dovecotes: six-story-high, hundred-yard-long stacks of tiny apartment boxes open on one end. They must have staircases, but I couldn't see any. Maybe the government comes along at night and plucks up people and puts them in their pigeonholes. "The workers made these!" said Roberto. Though, if you think about it, workers make everything. "The government gives them the construction material," he said. "Then they rent for twelve years. And then they own them!" In other words, you get a free home in Cuba as long as you build it and pay for it.

When we drove into La Habana Vieja, Roberto pointed at a gutted hotel: "These are special worker brigades, doing this construction. They can work sixteen hours a day." This must have been one of the other eight. Everyone was sitting around smoking cigarettes. "They get extra rations," said Roberto, "a big bag with soap, cooking oil, rice, beans . . ." Roberto sounded as if he was describing the contents of a big bag from, say, Tiffany's.

"In 1959 there were six-thousand doctors in Cuba," said Roberto, apropos of nothing. "Three thousand of them left after the revolution. Yet we are training new doctors. By the year 2000 there will be sixty-thousand doctors in Cuba!" But Roberto could only talk government talk so long. He couldn't stay off the real subject, what was on every Cuban's mind all the time: the economic mess. "You see these cabdrivers?" he said, pointing to a line of tourist-only taxis. "People need to earn dollars. These drivers may be doctors."

"In Cuba," said Roberto, "anything you want is available—for dollars." But people are paid in pesos, even if they work for foreign companies, which Roberto, in fact, does. The national tourist service isn't owned by the nation anymore. It's been sold to overseas investors. These people pay $300 a month for Roberto's services. But they don't pay Roberto. They pay the Cuban government. The Cuban government then pays Roberto 150 a month, in pesos.

Figuring out what the Cuban peso is worth is a complex economic calculation. To put it in layman's terms, a pretty close approximation is nothing. Pesos are of use almost exclusively for buying rationed goods. The Cuban rationing system is simple: They're out of everything. Although you can get a really vile pack of cigarettes for ten pesos. Think of Roberto's salary as a carton and a half of smokes.

Roberto was able, however, to earn dollars through tips. Cadging these being, of course, the subtext to his economic discourse. He used to be a teacher but couldn't live on the pay. His wife is a chemical engineer, but her chemical plant shut down three years ago. While we were walking around the old town, Roberto met another engineer, now working as a carpenter for dollars—building the table under which he'd get paid.

"Just to feed ourselves," said Roberto, "we have to go to four markets. The ration store for, maybe, rice. Then the government dollar store—this is very expensive. Then the dollar market where farmers can sell what they grow if they grow more than the government quota. And then the black market."

We drove down Avenida Bolivar, through what had been Havana's shopping district. Hundreds of stores stood closed and empty, the way they've been since 1968, when the last small businesses were nationalized. "That is where the Sears store was," said Roberto, pointing to the largest empty building. "But now we have nothing to sell."

Every so often Roberto would snap out of it and resume the official patter: "Over there is a memorial to Julius and Ethel Rosenberg. Perhaps you have a monument to them in North America?" I said I didn't think so. But mostly, Roberto wanted to talk about free enterprise. He and his wife were sleeping on the mattress his mother bought when she got married: "It has been repaired over and over. We get the TV sometimes from Miami—oh, the 'Beatty Rest' mattresses! And what good prices!"

Roberto was optimistic. He kept showing me new family owned restaurants. "Look, there's one!" He pointed to a pizza parlor. "There's more!" He pointed to several pizza parlors. In Cuba, capitalism's thin edge of the wedge comes plain or with pepperoni.

Roberto thought small private retail shops would be opening soon. He thought the government's new "convertible peso," which is pegged 1:1 to the dollar, would become the national currency. He was even enthusiastic about the fees the Cuban authorities were beginning to charge, such as highway tolls. "Maybe we will get better service," he said. Roberto told me that the economy had "come back since the low point of '94, a little," and that this was due to the private businesses. "The only thing the government controls now is the taxes," said Roberto.

He was wrong. Fidel Castro, in his 1996 year-end speech to the Cuban National Assembly, described the economic reforms thus: "We legalized robbery." Castro then did, indeed, announce an income tax on the self-employed. But worse is probably to come. Raul Castro, Fidel's brother, addressed the Communist Party Central Committee, ranting at economic changes, foreign influences, and petty entrepreneurs trying to get rich. The Communist Party newspaper, reporting on the committee meeting, said, *La sicologia del productor privado . . . tiende al individualismo y no es fuente de conciencia socialista.* However that's translated, it doesn't sound good for business. (The Party paper, by the way, is named for the yacht aboard which Castro sneaked into Cuba in 1956. The yacht was bought from an American who had christened it after a beloved relative. Castro didn't get it. This is why the official organ of the Cuban Communist Party is called *Granma.*)

That night, after Roberto had been sufficiently tipped, I went to a bar on the east side of Havana harbor with a European reporter who's lived for years in Cuba. He thought economic reform was over. He said the authorities were "still emphasizing that outside investment is 'not vital,'" and that they "still think the state sector can be made 'more efficient.'" He quoted a Canadian diplomat: "The pace of economic reform in Cuba is determined by the learning curve in economics of Fidel Castro. And he's a slow learner."

As we talked, a young Cuban woman came out on the terrace. She ignored us in a very unprostitutional way, chose a chair just within earshot, and began avidly appreciating the city skyline. "I'd buy it if she were a tourist," whispered the reporter, "but Cubans do not go to dollar bars for the view."

There is one vibrant, exciting, and highly efficient sector of the official Cuban economy: the police. I was driving through the Vedado neighborhood in western Havana absolutely desperate to turn left. Finally, I just went and did so. Almost a mile away, in an entirely different section of town, a policeman walked out into the street, flagged me down, and wrote me a ticket for the transgression. There's a space provided for this on the rental-car papers, and the fine comes out of the deposit.

The traffic-cop omniscience was creepy enough, but I happened to be on my way to visit a dissident couple. Well, "dissident couple" is a little dramatic. They hadn't actually dissented about anything. They just wanted to leave Cuba. They went to Sweden and applied for asylum. But the generous Swedish refugee policy does not extend to refugees from progressive, socialist countries to which Sweden gives millions of dollars in foreign aid. They were sent back. And now they were in permanent hot water.

They lived in a shabby tower block with a ravaged elevator, piss stink in the stairwells, bulbs filched from the lobby light fixtures, and even the glass stolen from the hallway windows. And in Havana, this was a good place to live. The apartment had been inherited from a parent, a parent who had been an official in the revolutionary government. "Come on Friday," the couple had said. "We don't have power outages then."

There were five rooms—small rooms (you couldn't flip a pancake in the kitchen without standing in the hall), but five rooms nonetheless—and a bathroom (when the water was running). And not too many of the louvers in the jalousie windows were broken. Carlos and Donna—not their real names of course—come from families that had been prosperous (families that now, incidentally, won't speak to them). The low, narrow-walled living room was filled with too much big, dark furniture from a more expansive age, like a Thanksgiving dinner for twelve put in the microwave. I felt claustrophobic although I was five stories in the air and could see the ocean shining in the distance.

Carlos and Donna are not allowed to hold jobs, but they each speak four languages and so are able to get work as guides and translators with the various groups of academics, philanthropists, conference delegates, and film-festival attendees who are forever traipsing through Cuba looking for international understanding and a tan.

"You have to earn dollars anyway here," said Carlos. "'Dollars or Death' is what everyone says." He showed me their ration books, which have categories for everything from tobacco to clothing. So far in 1996, only one liter of cooking oil per family had been available. Eggs were plentiful at the moment—fourteen a month for the two of them. Carlos and Donna also got two bars of soap a month, some months. There was virtually no meat, and it was inedible, besides. "All red meat has been nationalized," said Carlos by way of explanation. Cuban nationalization does to goods and services what divorce does to male parents—suddenly they're absent most of the time and useless the rest. Cubans can't even get real coffee from the ration stores. They get coffee beans mixed with the kind of beans you get in tortillas. This tastes the way it sounds like it would and gives everyone stomach cramps.

The few legitimate delights of Cuba—coffee, rum, cigars—require not just dollars but lots of dollars. And even this doesn't always work. The Monte Cristo coronas I bought in a government shop had the flavor and draw of smoldering felt-tip pens.

Carlos and Donna had had one other brush with the law. Besides committing the heinous crime of trying to move, they were also caught with dollars. Until mid-1993 it was illegal for Cubans to own dollars. Given what the peso was worth, that meant it was illegal for Cubans to have money. Carlos and Donna found sixty dollars tucked in a book they'd inherited. They dressed in their best clothes and, being fluent in French, tried to pass themselves off as foreigners at a beachfront hotel. "To get a decent cup of coffee," said Donna. But the hotel waiter wasn't fooled. Perhaps the two bars of soap a month was the giveaway, this being more than most French tourists use. As Carlos and Donna walked home, they were arrested.

They escaped any serious jail time, maybe because of their foreign-diplomat connections. But they were threatened with six- or seven-years imprisonment. And a year later the block captain—the government snitch who resides on every Cuban street—called them in and threatened them with imprisonment again. "When dollars became legal," said Carlos, "everyone was happy. I wasn't so happy thinking about all those people who were locked up for years sometimes, just for having one or two dollars.

"Still, I don't have any hatred against the system," he said. "But this is just for myself, for my own sake—I don't want hatred to destroy me."

"When we couldn't leave," said Donna, "we were in despair for a while. Then we became involved in the charity work of the church, in their hospitals. This created new meaning."

"We're happy now," said Carlos.

But they don't have children. They felt too cut off from Cuban society for that. Carlos doesn't even know if his parents are still alive. And Cuba isn't exactly the future most of us have planned for our kids. Unless we're really mad at the little buggers.

"The revolution brought some benefits," said Carlos, "at least at first. There was better housing, but it was gotten by giving away what had been stolen from others. The health care is free—and worth it. I can go to the doctor, but he can do nothing for me. This is why the Catholic Church must have its own hospitals. The education is free, too. But it's indoctrination. This is not a real education. Then they make the students work on the sugar harvest. Of course, the students wreck the agriculture. They don't care. They don't know what they're doing."

Carlos and Donna thought it was important that people know what a disastrous and terrifying place Cuba is. "Not for the sake of future revenge," said Donna, "but because of the frailty of memory. People will forget how bad it was, the way they're already forgetting in Russia. But more important, they'll forget why it became that way."

It will take a lot of forgetting. Socialism has had a nasty reign in Cuba. Hundreds of low-level supporters of the ousted Batista regime were executed, and thousands were jailed. Homosexuals, Jehovah's Witnesses, and people with AIDS antibodies have been sent to concentration camps. Critics of the government are forced into internal exile or confined in mental hospitals. The Americas Watch human-rights group has said that Cuba holds "more political prisoners as a percentage of population than any other country in the world." Freedom House, a pro-democracy organization whose board of trustees is an ideological gamut running from Jeane Kirkpatrick to Andrew Young, says, "There is continued evidence of torture and killings in prison and in psychiatric institutions. . . . Local human-rights activists say that more than 100 prisons and prison camps hold between 60,000 and 100,000 prisoners of all categories." (This is about twice America's generous rate of per-capita incarceration.) How many of those categories are political? Well, from a socialist point of view, all of them. And any normal Cuban is probably going to wind up in jail sooner or later anyway, because, according to Amnesty International, serious offenses in Cuba include "illegal association," "disrespect," "dangerousness," "illegal printing," and "resistance." Castro himself was in jail for a while under the previous administration and in a 1954 letter from his cell he wrote: "We need many Robespierres in Cuba."

I knew that the potential for disaster lurked in socialism, but what had caused this potential to be realized in Cuba and not in Sweden? I asked Carlos and Donna, Was there something fundamentally different about Cuba's socialist ideology? Or had evil people simply taken control of socialism in Cuba?

"Neither," said Carlos. "It's because of power. They have total power. Think what you yourself would do if you had total power over everyone."

Not a pretty picture, I admit. And I'm not even a socialist. Socialists think of society as a giant, sticky wad. And no part of that gum ball—no intimate detail of your private life, for instance—can be pulled free from the purview of socialism. Witness Sweden's Minister for Consumer, Religious, Youth and Sport Affairs. Socialism is inherently totalitarian in philosophy.

The Swedish socialists have exercised some degree of self-restraint. The Cuban socialists haven't bothered to. In Cuba, the authorities have a Ken Starr grand-jury-like right to poke into every aspect of existence, no matter how trivial. Imagine applying marxist theory to rock and roll, this being what the *Union de Escritores y Artistas de Cuba,* or UNEAC, the official labor organization for creative types, is supposed to do. Karl

Marx said in *Das Kapital,* "Nothing can have value without being an object of utility. If it be useless, the labor contained in it is useless, cannot be reckoned as labor, and cannot therefore create value." Roll over Beethoven, and how.

Professor Dr. Jose Loyola, who was, according to his business card, "*Compositor y Musicologo*" and "*Vice Presidente Primero*" of UNEAC, talked to me about utility. Specifically, he talked about trying to get Cuban elements into rock and roll to offset imperialist U.S. influences. Sex, drugs, and cha-cha-cha? Professor Dr. Loyola's office was in a splendid nineteenth-century town house, the kind of digs that should belong to a rock star. Although I had visited an actual Cuban rock star, Santiago Feliu (who I assume is a major genius because I couldn't find any of his cassettes or CDs, and the good things are always missing from the shops in Cuba). Anyway, Feliu lived in what looked like a graduate student's off-campus apartment.

The UNEAC town house had been spoiled by the cheap partitions and wobbly chrome-leg chairs loved by bureaucracies everywhere, and by photographs of Fidel where art used to hang. While we sat in the part of the former dining room that was now the professor-doctor's stuffy office, the power went out repeatedly.

I asked how musicians got into this union. They submit an application with *curriculum vitae* listing their important concerts, the rewards and prizes they've won, and the recordings they've made. Then a commission made up of three or four "prestigious musicians" meets and decides upon acceptance or rejection. Which is just the way people get into the business everywhere.

> LEAD GUITAR WITH BAND, "THE DRIVEWAYS"
> PLAYED: STEPMOM'S REC ROOM; OPEN-MIKE NIGHT,
>   THE PATHETIC BEARD COFFEE SHOP
> MANY CITATIONS, MOSTLY FROM SEATTLE POLICE
> ATTACHED: INDIE DEMO CUT, "LIFE SMELLS"

Mick? Elton? Do we let him in?

I asked what UNEAC did for its members. "The prestige of the organization opens many doors," said Professor Dr. Loyola. "It promotes the work of the artists and takes care of some of their, ah, material problems." In other words, you starve if you aren't in UNEAC.

"What if you aren't a member?" I asked.

"Oh, most artists aren't members," said Professor Dr. Loyola. "There are fourteen thousand professional artists in Cuba. Only four thousand are members. The other ten thousand have the government's Ministry of Culture to promote their work." The way our government's National Public Radio plays "Life Smells" by The Driveways on *All Things Considered.*

"What kind of problems do musicians face in Cuba?" I asked.

"Material problems."

"Material problems?"

"Maybe," said the professor doctor, "if we had stores where they could buy their instruments, it would be better."

"Could be," I said.

"Some people get musical instruments from the Ministry of Culture," he ventured and changed the subject. "Before, there were many empirical musicians in Cuba. Now they have formal training. Now there is a kind of upgrading school for empirical musicians." And what a shame this wasn't the practice in America's rural South during the time of Huddie Ledbetter and Lightnin' Sam Hopkins. They wouldn't have been so "downbeat" if they'd been able to get work in the New York Philharmonic orchestra.

"What does UNEAC do," I asked, "if an artist gets in trouble with the government?"

"If he is right, we will help him out. And if he is not right, we will help orient him in the correct direction," said Professor Dr. Loyola with a perfectly straight face.

Since 1959 the Cuban government has been "orienting" everybody in "the correct direction," thereby making a total mess of the Cuban economy. And one of the things that's so messy about it is that there's no way to measure how messy it is.

There are simply no reliable Cuban economic statistics. Perhaps one of the things that keeps Sweden from turning into Cuba is that, when it comes to publishing honest reports about everything government is doing, the Swedes can't stop themselves. The Cubans have resisted this temptation. The Cuban government realizes that it has no motive to tell the truth about economic conditions, even to itself. And as for measuring Cuba's black-market economy, criminals don't issue annual reports.

Everybody, Cuban officialdom included, agrees that Cuba's economy has shrunk by at least a third since the 1980s. But a third of what? Cuba's per-capita gross domestic product for the year 1995, for example, has been calculated at $2,058 by dissident Cuban economists, $2,902 by the Cuban government, $3,245 by wishful-thinking pinko American academics and—the highest estimate of all—$3,652 by the U.S. Department of Commerce. Now the per-capita GDP in Cuba is about $1,200, according to the National Bank of Cuba, or $1,480, if you believe the CIA, while the *Columbia Journal of World Business* thinks the figure may be as low as $900. Nobody knows. Just as nobody knows what the peso is worth.

The official exchange rate for the peso is the same as that for the new *peso convertible:* one peso equals one dollar. Not even the Cuban government pretends to believe this. The black-market rate in March 1996 was 21 pesos per dollar. But there was something wrong with that also. Just two years before, the rate was 150 pesos per dollar. And dollars hadn't gotten any less necessary or much more available. Latin-American scholar Douglas W. Payne thinks the Cuban secret police took over the black market. Or maybe the Cuban government was using the convertible peso—which, though printed in bright tropical hues, is essentially counterfeit U.S. money—to flood the currency exchanges. Odd things can happen when the government is more corrupt than you are. The real answer to the exchange-rate conundrum may be that there is no exchange rate. Only a lunatic would trade a U.S. dollar for anything the Cuban government prints, except exit visas. "There will arrive the day when money will have no value," Fidel Castro once said in a fit of marxist utopianism. But apparently he meant it.

More was to be gleaned by looking around in Cuba than by trying to do imaginary math. I went into the Ministry of Trade's product showroom, and there, offered for wholesale export to the world, were coconut shells painted to look like turtles, baskets that seemed to have been woven by people wearing catcher's mitts, posters for obscure brands of rum, pictures of Che Guevara, and Aunt Jemima rag dolls in half a dozen sizes.

The Cubans may not be good with their hands, but they're very skillful with blame. They blame the Soviet Union. And not without reason. When the Soviet bloc collapsed, the Cubans lost somewhere between $4 billion and $6 billion a year in grants, subsidies, and trade concessions. Taking the low figure, that's a dollar per person per day for everyone in the country. You can live for less than that in Cuba, and almost everyone has to.

Of course, the Soviets got something in return for this aid. They got sugar and cobalt and nickel. Which is why it was always easy to get a plate of sugared cobalt and nickel at Moscow restaurants in the 1980s. Plus, the Soviets got to be a huge pain in the ass to the United States. But what the Cuban government got was the luxury of perfect shiftlessness. The Castro government took boatloads of money from the Soviet Union and took all the businesses, industries, and land in Cuba, too. Sweden may be borrowing prosperity, but Cuba tried to beg and steal it.

So the Soviet Union is to blame for Cuban poverty because the Soviet Union fell apart, which means that everything is really America's fault. Everything usually is. Cubans have been blaming their troubles on the United States at least since independence in 1902 and probably since Columbus set course too far south and missed becoming an American citizen. Even as José Marti was leading the struggle for freedom from Spain, he was denouncing the United States as a "monster." And he was living in the United States at the time.

My tour guide Roberto told me that the explosion of the battleship *Maine* was just an "American pretext to get into the Cuba-Spain war." No matter that's how Cuba won.

On the other hand, the United States has been less than an ideal next-door neighbor. "Just at the moment I'm so angry with that infernal little Cuban Republic that I would like to wipe its people off the face of the earth," said Teddy Roosevelt in 1906. American armed forces occupied Cuba from 1899 to 1902, and from 1906 to 1909. There was further military intervention in 1912 and threats of plenty more, plus an invasion by proxy at the Bay of Pigs in 1961. And a U.S. trade embargo, in force since that year, certainly looks to the Cubans like a "wipe its people off the face of the earth" gesture.

The Cubans estimated that as of 1996, this embargo had cost them between $38 billion and $40 billion. That happens to be much less than they'd received from the Soviets for doing the things that got them embargoed. But no quibbles. We're talking politics here, not sense. Then in 1996 came the Cuban Liberty and Democratic Solidarity Act, or Helms-Burton Act, as it's called, after its respective sponsors in the U.S. Senate and House. This passed by whopping majorities because Cuba had just shot down two private planes carrying anti-Castro exiles who had a habit of dropping leaflets on Havana. Probably the leaflets contained dangerous information about the price of mattresses in Miami. Helms-Burton tightened the embargo by imposing sanctions not only on those who trade with Cuba but on those who trade with those who trade with Cuba and those who date them and their friends and pets. Or something like that. It's harsh.

And the Cubans were steamed. All over Havana, walls had been painted with six-foot cartoons depicting Senator Jesse Helms as Hitler and Uncle Sam as Hitler, and Jesse Helms as Hitler again. The Cubans didn't seem to know what Rep. Dan Burton looked like. Come to think of it, I don't, either.

Of course the embargo is stupid. It gives Castro an excuse for everything that's wrong with his rat-bag society. And free enterprise is supposed to be the antidote for socialism. We shouldn't forbid American companies from doing business in Cuba, we should force them to do so. Bring them ashore with Marines if necessary. Although I guess we've tried that.

And the Cubans are stupid for rising to the bait. There's another little island next to a gigantic, powerful country that threatens to invade and enforced an embargo for decades. And Taiwan has done okay.

I went with two American newspaper reporters to interview a Cuban economist, Hiram Marquetti, a professor at the University of Havana and an industrial-planning consultant to various state companies and government agencies. I wanted to see what it was like talking to an "expert" who wasn't allowed to tell me the facts and maybe wasn't allowed to know them.

Marquetti, looking grave, said the U.S. embargo had cost Cuba $42 billion, upping the amount a couple of billion dollars from what Cuban Foreign Ministry advisor Pedro Prada said in his book, *Island Under Siege* (available in English in hotel gift shops and complete with an appendix: "Opponents of the Blockade," listing Danny Glover, Cindy Lauper, and Cheech Marin).

Marquetti, looking graver, admitted things were lousy. Malnutrition was evident in some sectors of the population. During the last few years, he said, the average Cuban's intake of vitamin A was down 35 percent, iron down 40 percent, and vitamin C down 15 percent. The last item is interesting in a country where citrus trees are basically weeds. Marquetti, looking graver yet, said, "The highest percentage of disposable income goes to food, usually more than 50 percent. We need the free market to complete the supply." But he also said that this free market and the dollars that make it work "do not necessarily have to do with the opening of the economy." He claimed that "dollarization" was about Cuba acquiring "new technology, expertise in company management, and access to new markets." It was not about any actual Cubans acquiring any actual money.

"Total foreign investment, including contracts, has been $2 billion since 1992," said Marquetti, now looking proud. Though my European journalist friend thought only about $750 million had ever really been spent, and a *New York Law Journal* article cited estimates as low as $500 million. "Nickel mining provides $50 million a year in salaries alone, though such figures are not usually released, for security reasons," said Marquetti, looking sly and confidential.

The newspaper reporters were getting bored. "What effect is dollarization having on families and society?" asked one of them. Said Marquetti, looking bureaucratically oblivious, "Number one: foreign investment. Two: intensive development of tourism. Three: opening to foreign trade." Sis has been out hitchhiking and someone made a foreign investment in her. It's all part of Cuba's intensive development of tourism. And, boy, is she open to foreign trade.

"What about the prostitutes?" said the other reporter, more or less reading my mind. "There are rumors that the government turns a blind eye because of the dollars they bring in."

All at once, Marquetti looked human and, indeed, rather enthusiastic. "They are very inexpensive," he said. "They are very educated. They are very young and very pretty. Cuba is a country that attracts tourism for cheap sex," he said, stopping just short of a wink. Marquetti tried to look grave again. "Since the crisis there has been a negative social impact, but you can't eliminate it through repressive means." It's not like these girls are scattering mattress-price leaflets. "We have to look for other solutions, such as education." But he'd just said they *were* educated. "Some sectors of Cuban youth, they view prostitution as a solution to their economic problems."

As for Hiram Marquetti himself, he was selling his report on the Cuban economy—five dollars per copy.

Before the revolution, annual per-capita income in Cuba was $374; that's about $1,978 in current dollars. So Cuba is poorer than it used to be, although the poverty is spread around a little more. Castro's government is as dishonest as the prerevolutionary government was. The modern corruption involves more greed for power than passion for lucre, but that's actually worse. And the depraved sex is still available if you can sneak the whores past the elevator operators.

Getting more people to sneak whores past elevator operators was, so far, the best the Cuban government had been able to do in terms of a plan to improve the economy. Tourism was supposed to be the salvation now that Soviet aid had vaporized and sugar was selling for less per pound than garden loam. About 700,000 tourists a year were visiting Cuba, an increase of more than 100 percent since 1990. The Cuban government expected foreign companies to invest an additional $2.4 billion in tourist facilities by the year 2000. This would double the number of hotel rooms on the island. And every one of those rooms will be occupied, I predict, by somebody as ticked off as I was.

Because Cuba does not quite have the tourism thing figured. When I checked into the Hotel Nacional, I was given the manager's room, in which he was living. I was given another room. The key card didn't work. The bellhop went to get another key card. Then the safe didn't work—no small matter since Americans can't use credit cards in Cuba and have to conduct all business in cash, an awkward lump of which I was carrying.

When I returned from the hotel bar bloated with *mojitos,* the key card didn't work again. I went down to get another. The elevator took ten minutes to arrive. The new key card didn't work. I went back. The elevator took another ten minutes. That key card didn't work, either. The maid let me in.

I was awakened at dawn the next morning by a series of chirpy phone calls from the government tourism service in the downstairs lobby. CubaTrot or Havan-a-Vacation or whatever it was called had a driver and a translator and a guide and something else, maybe a circus elephant, waiting for me, bright and early, ready and willing, all set to take me anywhere I wanted to go, except back to bed. None of which stuff I had ordered.

At dawn on the second morning the operator called saying I "must go to reception immediately." When I went downstairs the desk clerk said, "It was nothing." When I went upstairs the key card didn't work. At dawn on the third morning it was a wrong number. On the fourth morning it was someone jabbering expressively in French.

At least I was always awake in time for breakfast. Every day I ordered coffee, toast, and orange juice, and I never got the same thing twice. I traveled to a beach resort in Trinidad on the Caribbean coast, and at dawn the phone rang—a hang-up. I ordered coffee, toast, and orange juice, and got coffee, orange juice, and a cheese sandwich with ketchup on it. The next morning at about 7, a room-service waiter arrived at my door, unbidden, with a plate of dinner buns. As I was checking out, there was an irked Canadian couple at the front desk saying, "We got a message. You told us, 'Call from Toronto,' nothing else, eh? We're thinking there's maybe something wrong at home. So we try and we try, and we get through, eh? And it costs us fifty dollars. And nobody's called us at all."

I had driven to Trinidad on the *autopista,* which is a six-lane. . . a four-lane . . . sometimes a two-lane. . . . The Russians never got around to finishing it. And it's not like there are any divider lines painted on it anyway. The *autopista* runs from Havana southeast through the middle of the island. There was so little traffic that cows grazed on weeds coming up in the pavement cracks. I had stumbled into a radical ecologist's daydream. Or so it appeared until I'd pass some East German tractor trailer spewing a mile-long cloud of tar-colored exhaust.

You have to watch out when you drive in Cuba, but you never know what you're watching out for. It could be anything. Potholes, of course, some of them big enough for a couple of chairs and a coffee table. Then there are the people who leap out from the side of the road frantically, desperately, even violently trying to sell you one onion. Or a string of garlic. Or a pale, greasy-looking hunk of something. Lard? Flan? Pound of flesh? (It turned out to be homemade cheese.)

At every major road junction there were scores of hitchhikers, not the prostitute kind but regular folks, whole families among them. Cuba's national transportation system is in butt-lock. Says *Fodor's* guide, "Be prepared to wait three days for the next available bus." Standing among the people with their thumbs out were the traffic police. They stopped cars and trucks (though not those with *tourista* license plates) and made them take passengers.

Cops helping you bum a ride—now here was the revolution the way I had it planned thirty years ago when I was smoking a lot of dope. Except, not exactly. The reason so many people were hitchhiking in the middle of nowhere was that they'd been sent there to work on the sugar harvest. I don't recall that the workers' paradise of my callow fantasies contained any actual work.

That sugar harvest was going on all around me. Or, rather, not going on. I'm no agricultural expert, but I'm almost certain that leaning against fences, walking about with hands in the pockets, and sitting on stalled tractors smoking cigarettes are not the most efficient methods of cutting sugarcane.

Much work had been done, however, painting propaganda slogans. SOCIALISM OR DEATH appeared on almost every overpass. What if the U.S. government had slogans all over the place? I tried to come up with a viable campaign. My suggestion, AMERICA—IT DOESN'T SUCK.

As for "Socialism or Death," after a couple of weeks in Cuba, I was leaning toward the latter option. To which the Castro government's response is: Death? Yes. No problem. That can be arranged. But, *first,* socialism!

I turned off the *autopista* onto a raggedy strip of pavement through the Escambray Mountains. The sun went down, and suddenly traffic materialized—gigantic Russian trucks driven without sense, headlights, or any idea of keeping to the right on the road. I emerged from the mountains at Cienfuegos. Says *Fodor's:* "The people of Cienfuegos . . . constantly tout it as '*la Linda Ciudad del Mar*' (the lovely city by the sea)." They're lying. From here it was a thirty-mile drive through coastal mangrove swamps on a road covered with land crabs. Every time I went over one, it made a noise like when you were ten, and you spent two weeks making a plastic model of the battleship *Missouri,* and your dad stepped on it in the dark. I tried avoiding the crabs. They scuttled under the wheels. I tried driving at them. They stayed put. The road smelled like thirty miles of crab salad going bad.

It was almost 10 P.M. before I got to my hotel on the beach, the Ancon. But the buffet was still open. They were serving crab salad. I went to the bar.

In the morning the ocean sparkled, the sand gleamed, the cheese sandwich with ketchup arrived. Bright-pink vacationers frolicked in the surf or, rather, stood on the beach discussing whether to frolic in the surf, having seen large numbers of stingrays the last time they frolicked.

The Ancon was filled with middle-aged Canadians having the middle-aged Canadian idea of fun, which consisted mostly of going back to the buffet for seconds on the crab salad. The architecture was modernistic. The rooms were comfortablistic. The food was foodlike.

There are worse tourist facilities in Cuba, namely all of them. The Ancon is top of the line. I inspected the other beach hotels near Trinidad, and I had driven out to see those along the *playas del este* outside Havana. Most were stark. Some were dank and unclean. And one spread of tiny prefabricated cottages with outdoor sinks and group bathrooms looked like nothing so much as a Portosan farm.

Cuba serves the very lowest end of the international holiday market. When some waiter in Paris recites the *plats du jour* like he's pissing on you from a great height, you can extract your mental revenge by picturing him, come August, on Cuba's *Costa del Fleabag,* eating swill in a concrete dining hall.

I wandered around the Trinidad region. I went to see the Iznaga Tower, an early nineteenth century neoclassical structure with seven arched and columned setbacks tapering to 140 feet at the pinnacle— monumental but so delicately proportioned that the whole thing seemed about to take flight. It looked like a spaceship designed by Palladio. The purpose of this beautiful and subtle artistry, which took ten years to construct, was to keep the slaves from goofing off. The plantation owner would get up on top and give everybody the hairy eyeball. The tower was no longer in use. With the block-captain system, the chattel labor now spied on itself.

I drove through the Valle de los Ingenios (Valley of the Sugar Mills, as it's romantically called) and over the Escambray Mountains again. As late as 1967, anti-Castro guerrillas were extant here. The Cuban government prefers to call them "bandits." Back in Trinidad, in what used to be a church, there's the marvelously named Museum of the Struggle Against Bandits, which should certainly open a branch in the U.S., maybe in Dan Rostenkowski's old congressional office.

Not much was actually in the museum. The centerpiece was a beat-up pleasure boat supposedly captured from the CIA. Two suspiciously new and definitely Soviet machine guns had been mounted on its deck with unlikely looking half-inch wood screws. The rest of the displays were mostly devoted to photographs of Cuban soldiers "martyred by bandits." One of these poor soldiers was named O'Really.

Not much was actually in Trinidad, either. It's very old, if you like that sort of thing. Trinidad was founded in 1514 by Diego de Velazquez, the conquistador of Cuba. Although Cuba didn't really take much conquering. Confiscador would be more like it. The local heyday was in the eighteenth century, when Trinidad was a major slave port. Then better slave off-loading facilities were built in Cienfuegos. Not much has changed in Trinidad since, and this gets the guidebooks excited. *Fodor's* goes on at some length about how this "marvelous colonial enclave" has not been "polluted with advertising, automobiles, souvenir shops, dozens of restaurants and hotels, and hordes of tourists milling through the streets." Which, translated, means nobody's made a centavo here in 200 years.

The buildings around the main square were patched and painted. The buildings not around the main square weren't. Practically everything was one-story high and built flush against tiny, crooked streets paved in stones as large as carry-on luggage.

I got lost heading back to the hotel. The streets were becoming even tinier, and the people standing around in those streets were not looking full of glee that UNESCO had declared Trinidad a World Heritage Site. In fact, they looked depressed and mean. I was getting more than the usual number of cold stares and catcalls, and just when I'd thought to myself, "I wouldn't care to stop here," I stopped there.

The starter motor whined uselessly. The car was inert. A crowd of impoverished Cubans gathered around me. I was frantically looking up "Placating Phrases" in the *Berlitz* when I realized the rude noises and gestures had stopped. The people in the crowd were smiling. And not the way I would have smiled if I'd found a moneyed dimwit trapped in my barrio. "*El auto es busto,*" I explained, opening the hood in that purposeful way men have when we don't know what we're doing.

"*Mi amigo es mecanico,*" said a fellow in the crowd. He and two of his friends grabbed the fenders and pushed the car down the block and around a corner. A big guy about my age came out of a house, shook my hand, and removed the car's air filter. While the big guy probed the carburetor, the crowd went to work. One kid brought tools. Another kid sat in the driver's seat and worked the ignition on the big guy's instructions. Two young men rolled a barrel of gasoline up the street and tipped some into the tank. An old man came out of another house with a pitcher of water. He checked the level in the battery cells and filled the windshield-washer reservoir while he was at it. A second man removed the distributor cap and inspected the points. He pulled the spark-plug wires and looked into their sockets. A third man detached the fuel line and began sucking on it, spitting the gasoline into the street. The big guy took the fuel pump apart. The distributor cap man disappeared for a while and returned with some scavenged spark-plug sockets, which he spliced onto the old spark-plug wires. Other people checked the radiator and the oil. "I have an aunt in Union

City, New Jersey," said someone. That was the extent of anybody's English.

After an hour the big guy shook his head. It couldn't be fixed. Which was fine with me. The car smelled like dead crabs, and I'd get another one from FlubaTour at the hotel. But now I had a problem in diplomacy. My crowd of mechanics didn't want to take any money. I could, I gathered with some translating help from a cabdriver, pay for the gasoline. Gasoline was hard to get. But as for working on the car, well, they hadn't fixed it. But they should get some money for their time, I said. They shrugged. They looked at the ground. They were embarrassed, time being the only thing everyone's got lots of in Cuba. It was with negotiating effort worthy of Jimmy Carter fishing for a Nobel Peace Prize that I managed to get their price up to fifty dollars.

Che Guevara believed that socialism would create a "New Man," someone who worked not for personal gain but for the good of humanity in general. All the murders, imprisonings, harassments, and deprivations of Cuba have supposedly been aimed at creating this New Man— somebody who would act like the big guy. Except the big guy wasn't one of them. He had a handmade sign hanging over his door: PARKING 24 HOURS I CARE FOR YOUR CAR I DO SOME REPAIRS ON BICYCLES MOTORCYCLES AND CARS, written, with obvious hope of future capitalist imperialism, in English.

6

FROM BEATNIK
TO BUSINESS MAJOR

❖

TAKING ECON 101 FOR KICKS

After two years of wandering around in different economic locales, trying to look at various societies from an economic point of view, and
generally poking my nose into other people's business, I thought I should
make another attempt to answer the question, "What am I talking about?"
I went back to the books about economic theory and the college Econ
texts, and even Samuelson's dreadful *Economics*. And this time I was . . .
still bored, I'm afraid. And I was still overwhelmed. But the tedium had
become more interesting, if that makes sense. And my incomprehen-
sion was better informed.

Reading about economics after watching a lot of economic activity
is like reading the assembly instructions after the Christmas toy has been
put together. Certain significant patterns begin to take shape in the
mind—even though the instructions are still gobbledygook and the toy
doesn't work.

I make no claim to understand economics. But I have begun to
understand how economics is understood. This is how economics is
understood after two semesters at most colleges:

I. There are a lot of graphs.
II. I'd better memorize them.
III. Or get last year's test.

And this is how economics is understood after three drinks at most bars:

I. There are only so many things in the world, and somebody is taking my share.
II. All payment for work is underpayment.
III. All business is crime.
   A. Retailers are thieves.
   B. Wholesalers are pimps.
   C. Manufacturers are slave drivers.
IV. All wealth is the result of criminal conspiracy among:
   A. Jews.
   B. Japanese.
   C. Pirates in neckties on Wall Street.

That is also pretty much the way economics is understood by socialists. Perhaps the problems of socialism in this century have something to do with socialists stopping off for a snort before going to work running economies all over the world. Or maybe the socialists got fuddled by reading the works of professional economists. Here, for instance, is how economics is understood by followers of John Maynard Keynes:

THE KEYNESIAN EQUATION—SHOWING
THE RELATIONSHIP BETWEEN AUTONOMOUS
EXPENDITURES AND THE EQUILIBRIUM
LEVEL OF INCOME
Equilibrium level of income (Y) equals aggregate autonomous expenditures [Consumption (C) plus Investment (I) plus Government Expenditure (G) plus the total of Exports (X) minus Imports (M)] times 1 divided by the marginal propensity to save (mps)

where mps equals 1 minus the marginal propensity to consume
(mpc). Thus:

$$Y = \frac{[1] \ \ [C+I+G+ (X-M) \ ]}{1-mpc}$$

It's hard to imagine applying the above formula to any ordinary economic question, e.g., should I put my bonus in a certificate of deposit
or buy new stereo speakers?

When we look at economics in general terms, all of us—pirates in
neckties, Albanians, Swedes, Cubans—are daunted. It's worse than any
tricycle from Santa. We feel as though we're confronting an enormous
piece of machinery that we can't comprehend and don't know how to
operate. In fact, we feel like we're being run through that machinery.
We are wheat, rice, and corn being delivered to the Nabisco factory, and
we're going to come out the other end definitely toasted, possibly shred-
ded, and, maybe, we hope, coated with sugar.

Yet, although this is how we feel, this is not how we behave. When
we engage in any specific economic activity—when we buy, sell, mooch,
or work—each of us acts as if he knows what he's doing. Even Fidel
Castro does. In July 1997, *Forbes* magazine estimated Castro's net worth
to be $1.4 billion.

So we do understand economics. We just think we don't. And
sometimes, unfortunately, we're right.

Economists claim to study production, distribution, and consumption.
But production requires actual skills and so can't be taught by economics professors, because they'd have to know how to do something. And
consumption is a very private matter. Consider the consumption of toilet paper, condoms, frozen pizza-for-one eaten straight out of the microwave in the middle of the night, and cigarettes in the carport when your
spouse thinks you've stopped smoking. Therefore, economics tends to
concentrate on distribution.

When economists say "distribution," however, they mean the distribution of everything, not just the distribution of such finished products as the pizzas and the microwave ovens to thaw them. There is also the distribution of raw materials—the seeds and fertilizer needed to grow the pizza toppings and the petrochemicals necessary to make the wood-grain plastic laminates decorating the ovens. Then there's the distribution of labor—the effort required to freeze the pizza and round up all the microwaves. And the distribution of capital—the money required to buy plastic laminates and market pizzas that taste like them. There's distribution of ideas, too. (Whose idea was it to put pineapple chunks on a pizza?) And there's even distribution of space and time, which is what grocery and appliance stores really sell us. They gather the things we want in a place we can get to on a day we can get there and, voilà, a fattening midnight snack.

All these things that get distributed are called "economic goods." To an economist, anything is an economic good if it can be defined by the concept of "scarcity." And the economist's definition of scarcity is so broad that practically everything can be called scarce. Air is an economic good. If air gets polluted, we have to pay for catalytic converters and unleaded gasoline to make it breathable again. (And Woody Harrelson is reportedly opening an oxygen bar in Los Angeles.) Even if the air is free, we have limited lung capacity. The more so if we've been out in the carport huffing Camels. Air is an economic good for each of our bodies, and we hope that body is using the air economically—getting lots of O_2 into the bloodstream, or whatever, and not just making farts with it.

From an economist's point of view, everything is scarce except desires. Random sexual fantasies are not economic goods. But if we try to act on them, they rapidly become economic (or highly uneconomic, as the case may be). Goods are limited; wants are unlimited. This observation leads economists to say that the fundamental purpose of economics is finding the best way to make finite goods meet infinite wants (though it never seems to work with random sexual fantasies).

While trying to make finite goods meet infinite wants, economists spend a lot of time mulling over something they call "efficiency." Economists explain efficiency as being the situation where an economy cannot produce more of one good without producing less of another good. If you have two jobs, you've probably reached labor efficiency. You can't put in more overtime on job A without putting in less overtime on job B or the child-welfare authorities will come. You're efficient, although neither of your bosses may think so.

The example of efficiency that economists usually give is guns and butter. A society can produce both guns and butter, they say, but if the society wants to produce more guns, it will have to—because of allocation of resources, capital, and labor—produce less butter. Using this example you'll notice that at the far reaches of gun-producing efficiency, howitzers are being manufactured by cows. And this is just one of the reasons we can't take economists too seriously.

In fact, efficiency is a condition that's never been achieved, as you've seen from watching your job A and job B coworkers. Economists don't really know much about efficiency, and neither does anyone else. Doubtless the citizens of eighteenth-century England thought they were producing as many lumps of coal and wads of knitting as they possibly could. One more coal miner would mean one less stocking knitter. Then, James Watt invents the steam engine. Pretty soon, coal carts are hauling themselves, and knitting mills are clicking away automatically, and everybody has more socks and more fires to put wet, smelly stocking feet up in front of. Efficiency is constantly changing, and economists can't keep up with this because they have to grade papers and figure out what Y equals.

One thing that economists do know is that the study of economics is divided into two fields, "microeconomics" and "macroeconomics." Micro is the study of individual economic behavior, and macro is the study of how economies behave as a whole. That is, microeconomics concerns things that economists are specifically wrong about, while macroeconomics concerns things economists are wrong about generally. Or to be more technical, microeconomics is about money you don't have, and macroeconomics is about money the government is out of. These two concerns seem hopelessly meshed in real life, and therefore I've tangled them together in this book.

Economists also make a distinction—for no good reason I can figure—between "inputs" and "outputs." Inputs are the jobs, resources, and money we use in order to make the outputs we want, such as money, resources, and jobs. All outputs, even shit, heartbreak, and enormous illegal profits, turn out to be inputs: manure, movie plots, and capital investment in video-poker machines in Tirana.

Two additional unimportant economic terms are "supply" and "demand." Scarcity has already explained these. There's lots of demand and not much supply.

Economists measure supply and demand with curves on graphs. When the supply curve goes up, the demand curve goes down. But how true is this? Do I get less hungry because I know I have a freezerful of pizza? My experience with the microwave at 2 A.M. argues otherwise. And can we really know how much people want something? The kid "really, really, really" wants a snowboard. Does he really want it? Or after three times falling on his butt at Mt. Barntop, is he going to leave the thing propped in the carport for the next twenty years? As for the supply curve, the concept of efficiency shows us that we don't know how many snowboards can be produced, or how cheaply, and if we wait until next winter, they may be giving them out free with Burrito Supremes.

So far, from an examination of the basic principles of economics, we've learned that things are scarce. We knew that. Fortunately the less-basic principles of economics are more interesting.

TEN LESS-BASIC PRINCIPLES OF ECONOMICS

1. The Market Is Never Wrong.

A thing is worth what people will give for it, and it isn't worth anything else. If you have some shares of Apple Computer and you go into the NASDAQ market offering those shares for $1,000 apiece, you may be brilliant. Apple stock may be worth $1,000, easy. And all the NASDAQ customers may be idiots for buying Apple at a mere thirty dollars. A Macintosh is a much better computer than an IBM PC. But, smart as you are and dumb as everybody else is, the market says your shares didn't sell. And the market is right.

HOW TO READ A GRAPH

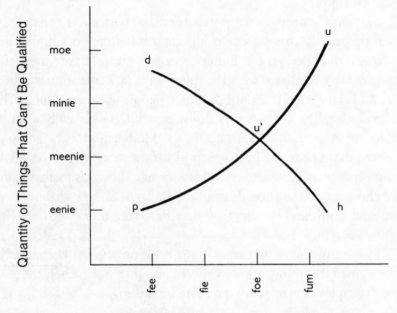

Where: pu = Number of pages of Econ text devoted to graphic analysis
         $du'h$ = Number of Econ students asleep in lecture hall

Also, a things may be "priceless." You'd rather die than trade your Macintosh for an IBM. But that's still a price, albeit a very high one.

2. So You Die. Things Still Cost What They Cost.

It's no use trying to fix prices. To do so, you must have a product that can't be replaced, and you must have complete agreement among all the people who control that product. They're greedy or they wouldn't have gotten into the agreement, and they're greedy so they sneak out of it. This is what was wrong with Paul Samuelson's idea about crop restrictions in Chapter I, and this is why the members of OPEC are still wandering around in their bathrobes, pestering camels.

Any good drug dealer can tell you that to ensure a monopoly, you need force. To ensure a large monopoly, you need the kind of force only a government usually has. And it still doesn't work.*

The government of Cuba, with force aplenty at its disposal, decided that beef cost too much. The price of beef was fixed at a very low level, and all the beef disappeared from the government ration stores. The people of Cuba had to hassle tourists to get dollars to buy beef on the black market, where the price of beef turned out to be what beef costs.

When the price of something is fixed below market level, that something disappears from the legal market. And when the price of something is fixed above market level, the opposite occurs. Say the customers at suburban Wheat Depot won't pay enough for wheat. The U.S. government may decide to buy that wheat at higher prices. Suddenly there's wheat everywhere. It turns out that people have bushels of it in the attic. The government is up to its dull, gaping mouth in wheat. The wheat has to be given away. The recipients of free wheat in the Inner City Wheatfare Program hawk the wheat at traffic lights, and what they get for it is exactly what people are willing to give.

3. You Can't Get Something for Nothing.

Everybody remembers this except politicians. Lately, it has been the fashion for American politicians to promise that government revenue—taxes—can be cut while government benefits—expenditures—remain intact. Benefits might even get larger. This will be done through effi-

*Unless Bill Gates buys the departments of Justice and Defense. In which case, watch out.

ciency, as if politicians are all going to invent the steam engine. Though, to the extent that steam is hot air, predictable jokes are invited.

Politicians have trouble giving up the idea of something for nothing; it's such a vote catcher. A government can give most people something for nothing by taxing the few people with money. This is how Sweden has gotten into trouble. There are never enough of those people with money. And the people with money are the people with accountants, tax lawyers, and bank accounts in Luxembourg, so they end up not paying their taxes. Or even if they do pay their taxes, like good Swedes, the people with money are also the people who know how to manipulate the system. Therefore, instead of the situation that Samuelson posited in *Economics* where "modern democracies take loaves from the wealthy and pass them out to the poor," we get a situation where loaves are taken from the wealthy and subsidized opera tickets are passed back to them.

A government can give all people something for nothing by simply printing more money. This doesn't work, because it makes all the money worth less, as it did in Wiemar Germany, Carter America, and Yeltsin Russia. Inflation is a tax on the prudent, who watch the value of their conservative savings-bond and bank-account investments disappear. It's a subsidy for the "big, swinging dicks" who can borrow money for harebrained speculative schemes and pay it back later with cheap cash. And it's a punishment to the old and the poor, who live on fixed incomes and who can't expect to get a big cost-of-living adjustment retrieving soda cans from trash baskets.

Finally, a government can give us something for nothing by running a deficit, by borrowing money from everybody and then giving everybody his money back, plus interest. This is obviously stupid and exactly what we've been doing for decades in the United States. Deficits are less immediately painful than high inflation or huge taxes, although eventually they lead to one or the other, or both. In the meantime, we're not getting anywhere. If all our investment money is tied up in loans to the government, that money is going to be spent on government things, such as financing the Inner City Wheatfare Program. Our investment money can't be spent on research and development to create a genetically engineered wheat-eating squid to turn that worthless wheat into valuable calamari.

4. You Can't Have Everything.

If you use your resources to obtain a thing, you can't use those same resources to obtain something else. That's called fraud (or having a credit card). In economics its called "opportunity cost." When you employ your money, brains, and time in one way, it costs you the opportunity to employ them in another. Opportunity costs fool people because they're unseen. When we observe money being spent, we're impressed. We gasp with awe at the huge new Federal Wheat Council headquarters in Washington, D.C. We don't admire the vast schools of squid feeding in our nation's wheat fields—because they aren't there. The main cost of government expenditure is not taxes, inflation, or interest on the national debt. The main cost is opportunity.

Sweden is a case in point. The Swedes like what their government does. They look around Sweden and see handsome government buildings, nice government programs, and generous government benefits. What they look around and don't see is what Sweden might have been if all that money had been invested in businesses and industries. From 1968 to 1969, before Sweden got carried away with its socialism, the country's per-capita gross domestic product grew by 5.7 percent. What if the Swedes had kept that up, or for the sake of mathematical simplicity, improved it a bit? As organized and self-disciplined as the Swedes are, why not? What if the Swedish per-capita GDP had been growing by 6 percent annually for the past thirty years? Swedes, who are now about 27 percent poorer than Americans, would be more than three times as wealthy as we are. They'd have a per-capita GDP of more than $66,000. They'd be richer than the people of any country have ever been. And Sweden, with a population of only 9 million, would be one of the world's great economic powers. Volvo would be winning the Daytona 500, Saab would have space stations, IKEA would furnish the homes of the Hollywood stars, and Swedish-massage therapy would be the most popular form of medical treatment on earth.

5. Break It and You Bought It.

Being fooled by hidden costs is the source of a lot of economic confusion. War is often spoken of as an economic stimulant. World War II "pulled America out of the Depression." Germany and Japan experienced "economic miracles" after the war. Somebody is not counting the cost of getting killed and wounded. Besides, if destruction were the key to greater economic productivity, every investor on Wall Street would be learning Albanian.

6. Good Is Not as Good as Better.

Almost as bad as costs that go unnoticed are benefits that get too much attention. It's great if everybody has a job. Computers are taking jobs away. We could guarantee full employment if we removed computers—and electricity, too—from the telephone companies and hired people to run all over town and fly around the world, telling our friends and business associates what we want to say.

When James Watt invented that steam engine, thousands of ten-year-old boys who had been hauling coal carts were put out of work. However, this left them free to do other things, such as live to be eleven.

7. The Past Is Past.

Another thing that gets too much attention is money that's already been spent. In economics this is called "sunk costs." It doesn't matter that you blew everything you made selling Apple at $1,000 a share on a scheme to genetically engineer squid. What matters is whether you can make any money off those squid now or convince people that the squid will make money in the future, so that those people will buy the fool company. This is called "marginal thinking," and on Wall Street it means almost the exact opposite of what we usually mean when we call someone a marginal thinker.

8. Build It and They Will Come.

Ralph Waldo Emerson was referring to better mousetraps, and the idea that the world would beat a path to your door for one tells us something about home hygiene in the nineteenth century. The underlying notion is stated formally in economics as Say's Law (after French economist Jean Baptiste Say, 1767–1832): "Supply creates its own demand." More is better. Any increase in productivity in a society causes that society to get enough richer to buy the things that are produced.

This works even in an economy as screwed up as Cuba's. The Cuban authorities allowed limited free-market sales of food, and this increased food production. Despite the extreme poverty of Cubans, that food did not sit around unsold.

9. Everybody Gets Paid.

People want to get something for what they do, although what they want to get may not be money—it may be sex or salvation or an opportunity to apply marxist theory to rock and roll. Everything is a business.

This is the "public choice" theory of economics. One of its founders, James M. Buchanan, won the 1986 Nobel Prize in economics for his work on understanding politics as an economic activity. Politicians don't measure profits in cash. The gain that they want is an increase in power. Thus the socialists of Sweden and Cuba are just as greedy as the pirates of Wall Street and Albania.

In order to increase their "power income," politicians have to pass more legislation, expand bureaucracies, and broaden the scope of government power. This power income is what the Swedish cabinet minister Marita Ulvskog was really talking about when she told me, "You have to give something to voters." Of course, that something can be, if you like, measured in money—*your* money, the money that government costs you in taxes, deficits, or currency inflation. Anyway, a politician who claims he's going to cut the size of government is saying he's going to creep up on himself and steal his own wallet.

10. Everybody's an Expert.

Of all the principles of economics, the one that's most important to making us richer (or more powerful or whatever) is specialization, or "division of labor." Milton Friedman uses a pencil as an example. A pencil is a simple object, but there's not a single person in the world who can make one. That person would need to be a miner to get the graphite, a chemical engineer to turn graphite into pencil lead, a lumberjack to cut the cedar trees, and a carpenter to shape the pencil casing. He'd need to know how to make yellow paint, how to spray it on, and how to make a paint sprayer. He'd have to go back to the mines to get the ore to make the metal for the thingy that holds the eraser, then build a smelter, a rolling plant, and a machine-tool factory to produce equipment to crimp the thingy in place. And he'd have to grow a rubber tree in his back-yard. All this would take a lot of money. Yet a pencil sells for nine cents. .

The implications of division of labor are surprising, but only if we don't think about them. If we do think about them, they are, like most eco-nomic principles, a matter of common sense. There are, however, a few things about economics that don't seem to make sense at all. Todd G. Buchholz, in his book *New Ideas from Dead Economists,* says, "An inso-lent natural scientist once asked a famous economist to name one eco-nomic rule that isn't either obvious or unimportant." The reply was "Ricardo's Law of Comparative Advantage."

The English economist David Ricardo (1772–1823) postulated this: If you can do X better than you can do Z, and there's a second person who can do Z better than he can do X, but can also do both X and Z better than you can, then an economy should *not* encourage that sec-ond person to do both things. You and he (and society as a whole) will profit more if you each do what you do best.

Let us decide, for the sake of an example, that one legal thriller is equal to one pop song as a Benefit to Society. (One thriller or one song = 1 unit of BS.) John Grisham is a better writer than Courtney Love. John Grisham is also (assuming he plays the comb and wax paper or something) a better musician than Courtney Love. Say John Grisham is 100 times the writer Courtney Love is, and say he's 10 times the musi-cian. Then say that John Grisham can either write 100 legal thrillers in a year (I'll bet he can) or compose 50 songs. This would mean that Courtney Love could write either 1 thriller or compose 5 songs in the same period.

If John Grisham spends 50 percent of his time scribbling predict-able plots and 50 percent of his time blowing into a kazoo, the result will be 50 thrillers and 25 songs for a total of 75 BS units. If Courtney Love spends 50 percent of her time annoying a word processor and 50 percent of her time making noise in a recording studio, the result will

JOHN GRISHAM AND COURTNEY LOVE EACH SPEND EQUAL TIME WRITING AND COMPOSING					
	THRILLERS		SONGS		BS PRODUCTION
John Grisham	50.0	+	25.0	=	75
Courtney Love	.5	+	2.5	=	3
					78 Total BS

JOHN GRISHAM SPENDS ALL HIS TIME BASHING THE LAPTOP KEYBOARD AND COURTNEY SPENDS ALL HER TIME CATERWAULING AND PLINKING GUITAR STRINGS					
	THRILLERS		SONGS		BS PRODUCTION
John Grisham	100	+	0	=	100
Courtney Love	0	+	5	=	5
					105 Total BS

be 1 half-completed thriller and 2.5 songs for a total of 3 BS. The grand total Benefit to Society will be 78 units.

If John Grisham spends 100 percent of his time inventing dumb adventures for two-dimensional characters and Courtney Love spends 100 percent of her time calling cats, the result will be 100 thrillers and 5 songs for a total Benefit to Society of 105 BS.

(Just to make things more confusing, note that Courtney Love loses 40 percent of her productivity by splitting her time between art and music, while John Grisham loses only 25 percent of his productivity. She has the "comparative advantage" in making music because her opportunity costs will be higher if she doesn't stick to what she does best.)

David Ricardo applied the Law of Comparative Advantage to questions of foreign trade. The Japanese make better CD players than we do, and they may be *able* to make better pop music, but we both profit by buying our CDs from Sony and letting Courtney Love tour Japan. And if she stays there, America has a definite advantage.

Comparative advantage is a rare example of the counterintuitive in economics. It's also unusual because it requires a little arithmetic to understand. We think of economics as strangled in math because of the formulas and graphs filling most economics textbooks. But you can (and I did) search the entire founding volume of economics, Adam Smith's *An Inquiry into the Nature and Causes of the Wealth of Nations,* without encountering a mathematical formula. In *New Ideas,* Buchholz quotes Alfred Marshall, the preeminent economist of the late nineteenth century (and a mathematician):

> (1) Use mathematics as a shorthand language, rather than as
> an engine of inquiry. (2) Keep to them until you have done. (3)
> Translate into English. (4) Then illustrate by examples that are
> important in real life. (5) Burn the mathematics.

We don't need to know math to understand economics, because economics isn't about abstract principles, it's about microwave ovens, cow howitzers, steam engines, wet knitting, snowboards, mousetraps, and Courtney Love on permanent tour in Japan. And this brings us to one more economic exception to common sense and a thing that requires all sorts of mathematics from us every day: money.

Why is this soiled, crumpled, overdecorated piece of paper bearing a picture of a rather disreputable president worth fifty dollars, while this clean, soft, white, and cleverly folded piece of paper is worth so little that I just wiped my nose on it? And what exactly is a "dollar"? If it's a thing that I want, why do I prefer to have fifty grimy old dollars instead of one nice new one? This isn't true of other things—puppies, for instance.

But money is not a puppy; it's not a specific thing. Money is a symbol of things in general, a symbol of how much you want things, and a symbol of how many things you're going to get. Money is a mathematical shorthand for value (and per Alfred Marshall, we seem to burn the stuff).

But what is value? The brief answer is "complicated." Value varies according to time, place, circumstance, and whether the puppy ruined the rug. Plus, there are some things upon which it is difficult to place a value. This is why we don't use money to measure all of our exchanges. Kids get food, clothing, and shelter from parents, and in return, parents get . . . kids. Important emotional, philosophical, and legal distinctions are made between sex and paying for sex, even if the socially approved sex costs dinner and a movie.

We need economic goods all the time, but we don't always need money for them, and it's a good thing, since for most of human existence, there wasn't any. Money didn't exist, or, rather, everything that existed was money. If I sold you a cow for six goats, you were charging it on your Goat Card.

Anything that's used to measure value, if it has value itself, is "commodity money." Societies that didn't have fifty-dollar bills picked one or two commodities as proto-simoleons. The Aztecs used cocoa beans for money, North Africans used salt (hence "salary"), medieval Norwegians used butter and dried cod, and their ATM machines were a mess.

Some commodities are better as money than others. Movie stars would make bad money. Carrying a couple around would be a bother, and you'd have to hack a leg off to make change. Precious metals, however, make good money and have been used that way for more than 5,000 years.

Metal commodity money is portioned out by weight. A coin is just a hunk of metal stamped to indicate its heft. From weighing money to making coins is a simple step, but a couple thousand years passed before the step was taken. Nobody trusted anybody else to do the stamping.

When coins *were* invented, the distrust proved to be well-founded. The first Western coins were minted by the kingdom of Lydia, in what is now Turkey, and were made of a gold-silver alloy called electrum. It's hard for anyone but a chemist (and there weren't any) to tell how much gold is in a piece of electrum versus how much silver. The king of Lydia, Croesus, became proverbial for his wealth.

In China, the weight of bronze "cash" was supposed to be guaranteed by death penalties. A lot of people must have gone to the chair. A horse cost 4,500 "1-cash" coins during the Han dynasty (206 B.C. to A.D. 220) and 25,000 cash during the Tang dynasty (618 - A.D. 907).

Kings, emperors, and, indeed, Swedish cabinet ministers have expenses. It is to a government's advantage to pay for those expenses with funny money. One reason that money violates common sense is that governments do tricky things with it.

Another reason that money violates common sense is that we don't have to use real commodities as money. We can use pieces of paper promising to deliver those real commodities. This is "fiduciary money," from the Latin word *fiducia,* trust.

In Europe, paper money developed privately in the thirteenth century from bills of exchange traded among Italian merchants and from receipts given by goldsmiths to whom hard money had been entrusted for safekeeping. We still use such private money when we cash a traveler's check.

Public fiduciary money was first printed, predictably enough, in Sweden. Swedish commodity money came in the form of copper plates. Thus, in Sweden, a large fortune was a *large* fortune. In 1656 the Stockholm Banco began issuing more convenient paper notes. The bank issued too many notes, and the Swedish government went broke—for the same reason that the Swedish government is broke today.

In 1716, Scotsman John Law helped the French government establish the Banque Royale, issuing notes backed by the value of France's land holdings west of the Mississippi. Banque Royale issued too many notes, and the French government went broke—for the same reason the French government is broke today. (Meanwhile, with the fates looking toward bank scandals of the distant future, John Law was created "duc d'Arkansas.")

But the most extensive Western experiment with paper money took place right here. In 1775 the Second Continental Congress not only created paper money but passed a law against refusing to accept it. The Continental Congress issued too many notes and . . . a pattern begins to emerge.

All fiduciary money is backed by a commodity, even if the backers are lying about the amount of that commodity. Historically the commodity most often chosen has been gold. By the nineteenth century, the major currencies of the world were based on gold, led by the most major currency: the British pound. This was a period of monetary stability and, not coincidentally, economic growth. There are people who think we should go back on the gold standard, and not all of them have skinny sideburns, large belt buckles, and live on armed compounds in Idaho. Money ought to be worth *something,* and gold seems as good as whatever.

But there's that endlessly perplexing relationship between money and value. The high value of gold is a social convention, a habit left over from the days when all bright, unblemished things (people included) were rare. Gold may go out of fashion. A generation may come along that, to the surprise of its parents, regards gold as gross or immoral, the way current twenty-year-olds regard milk-fed veal. And gold is a product. Different ways to get huge new amounts of it may be discovered. This happened to the Spanish. When they conquered the New World, they obtained tons of gold, melted it down, and sent it to the mint. It never occurred to them that they were just creating more money, not more things to spend it on. Between 1500 and 1600, prices in Spain went up 400 percent.

Presented with the enormous wealth of America's oceans, fields, and forests, Spain took the gold. It was as if someone robbed a bank and stole nothing but deposit slips.

Gold is an irrational basis for currency, but the real problem with fiduciary money—from a government standpoint—is that it's inconvenient. A currency that can be converted into a commodity limits the amount of currency that can be printed. A government has to have at least some of the commodity or the world makes a laughingstock out of its banknotes—"Not worth a Continental."

So if a government can lie about the amount of a commodity that is backing its currency—as the Stockholm Banco, Banque Royale, and Continental Congress did—why can't a government lie about everything? Instead of passing a law saying one dollar equals X amount of gold, why not pass a law saying one dollar equals one dollar? This is "fiat money" (from the Latin for being forced to drive a cheap, unreliable car), and it's almost the only kind of national currency left in the world.

Fiat money is backed by nothing but faith that a government won't keep printing money until we're using it in place of something more important, such as Kleenex. Concerning this faith, the experiences of Wiemar Germany, Carter America, and Yeltsin Russia make agnostics of us all. The only thing that protects us from completely worthless money is our ability to buy and sell. We can move our stock of wealth from the imaginary value of dollars to the fictitious value of yen to the mythical value of stock shares to the illusory value of real estate, and so forth. Our freedom to not use a particular kind of money keeps the issuers of that money—*honest* wouldn't be the word—moderate in their dishonesty.

I subjected myself to a large dose of economic theory because I'd finally realized that money was as important as love or death. I thought I would learn all about money. But money turns out to be strange, insubstantial, and practically impossible to define. Then I began to understand that economic theory was really about value. But value is something that's personal and relative, and changes all the time. Money can't be valued. And value can't be priced. I should never have worried that I didn't know what I was talking about. Economics is an entire scientific discipline of not knowing what you're talking about.

Trying to observe economic practice showed me that I needed to learn some economic principles, and trying to examine economic principles showed me that I'd better look at the practice again.

If I was going to continue trying to understand economics, I had to go back to reality—a remarkable example of which is Russia. In contemporary Russia, there are all kinds of economics, good and bad, capitalist and socialist. The economic activity is being conducted under conditions of anarchistic freedom and totalitarian restraint. The people who make the laws have too much power, and yet no power seems able to stem the lawlessness. Russia, as a case study, is wonderful. Unless, of course, you're a Russian.

7

HOW (OR HOW NOT)
TO REFORM (MAYBE)
AN ECONOMY
(IF THERE IS ONE)

❖

RUSSIA

At least with Russia, nobody even pretends to know what he's talking about. No economic textbook prepares a visitor for the Russian experience. No school of economic thought foresaw the Russian situation. Can a society that has had the full faith and credit of its government contradicting economic sense for generations become a free market and not blow up? Can a Cuban-type mess be turned into Wall Street pandemonium without causing Albanian bedlam? And is there some middle way like the ball-up in Sweden? All the world's Russia experts (and most of its Russians) are trying to figure these things out. But Russia is "a riddle wrapped in a mystery, inside an enigma, tied in a hankie, rolled in a blanket, and packed in a box full of little Styrofoam peanuts," said Winston Churchill, or something like that.

The Russians may adopt our ideas, our way of living, and our point of view. They may join the great international society of rights, law, and progress. Or their response may be, as graffiti I saw on a Moscow factory wall put it, FUCK YUO.

† † †

I came to Russia for the first time in July 1982, arriving at the twilight of the Brezhnev era and also, literally, at twilight. Dusk is prolonged and shining in midsummer at latitude 55°, but nothing shone in Moscow. Storefronts weren't lit, and there were very few storefronts. No headlights were visible. More to the point, no cars were. The city had street lamps, but as far apart as Patti Smith albums. The endless apartment blocks seemed blacked out. Could it be that no one lived in Russia? Or was there just not much living to be done? Red Square was shadowy. The Kremlin was dim. The Moskua River was an opaque trough beneath dismal bridges. The USSR was very dark, considering it was still daytime.

I came back to Russia in 1996 to find Moscow crowned in an arc of lights—Camel Lights. This being spelled out in tall letters atop a downtown high-rise. And the city below sparkled with ads for Sony, Coke, Levi's, Visa, Pizza Hut, Sprint, and Nike. Freedom had come to Moscow.

Well, one freedom anyway. Many human rights had been taken from the citizens of the old Soviet Union, and the first human right they got back seemed to be the Right to Outdoor Advertising. Maybe this was a minor liberty, but I don't know. Without advertising, human desires and intentions are invisible. What can people have? What do people want? Where are people going? They could be lining up to see *Titanic*. Or they could be lining up to tell on you. What succeeds with this public? What fails? A government could say the most popular flavor of ice cream is asparagus. How would you know? And what are all those buildings for? What's going on in them? (The answer to that question in 1982—in a country without profit or loss, with little to sell and less to buy—was "nothing.")

Now everything is going on in Moscow. Crowds load the sidewalks, moving briskly. The masses are actually massed. The masses are finally progressive. Except every member of the masses is progressing in a different direction. And he'd better be careful getting there. The pedestrian crosswalk is not yet an idea in Russia. Cars, trucks, and city buses approach intersections with the same speed and inclination to swerve as avalanches. Nor is this traffic the tinny, puttering, tacked-together output of the Soviet industrial pre-Cambrian age. You could have stood in

front of that stuff and watched it fall apart as it hit you. But now there
are Volvo semis and Mercedes sedans and solid little Opel coupes bar-
reling down . . . crash . . . into one of a hundred gaping holes in the
street, products of a flurry of construction that envelops Moscow in a
glorious aureole of mud, dust, bulldozer exhaust, and jackhammer
noises.

The place is hopping, happening, swinging, smoking. Factually
smoking. You can fire a butt anywhere in Moscow, and nobody fakes a
cough or pulls a C. Everett Koop mug on you. These people are busy.
They have lives. And this vast liveliness does something unlikely to
Moscow: It makes the city almost beautiful.

The Communists wanted to turn Moscow into a showplace and
couldn't get it right in seventy-four years of trying. From Stalin through
Khrushchev, most building was done in the style of TragiComic Classical. The architectural forms of the ancients were reproduced in badly
poured concrete and gross-out scale. Thus, poky offices are entered
through arches more fit to be sitting at the end of the Champs-Elysees,
and nasty warrens of slum housing are fronted with Ionic pillars as wide
as tennis courts.

The city's main streets are so broad that you can't hit to the far
curb with a three wood. Driving anywhere in Moscow is a half-day
excursion because the streets were laid out, not with a view to getting
anywhere, but according to what made the best parade routes. And
traffic signals are timed to let three battalions of crack airborne troops
and a hundred missile launchers through before the yellow caution
light comes on.

At least now there's something to do while you're waiting to cross
the street. You can have dinner. Moscow is engorged with good places
to eat. I spent my first night in the Hotel Metropol's restaurant, a Kubla
Khan's worth of stately pleasure dome with a fountain in the middle
and enough space to fly a radio-controlled model airplane. A full orchestra was playing (among the selections: an instrumental version of
Billy Joel's "Honesty"). You have heard of Tiffany lamps. The restaurant
at the Metropol has what looked to me like an entire Tiffany ceiling.
The cooking was French to such an exquisite degree that the garlic breath
from my escargots melted a hand towel when I got back to my room.

The next night I went to Uncle Gillie's, which had California cuisine in perfection. My chicken had not only been allowed to range free, it had been given aroma therapy and stress counseling. The night after that, I went to Il Pomodoro for Italian food authentic enough to satisfy the Corleone family, Russian versions of which were eating at several other tables. Then there was the Starlite Diner, built in America and shipped in modular sections to Russia. Here even the water was imported from the States. Great burgers—and it is the world's only diner filled with Republicans. International bankers in pinstriped suits crowded the booths, drinking milk shakes and bobbing up and down to the Four Tops.

"Tomorrow night I want caviar, blinis, and borscht," I said to my dinner companion, Dmitry Volkov, correspondent for the *Sevodnya* daily. "Where's a Russian restaurant?"

"There aren't any," said Dmitry.

And there aren't any Russian products in the stores, either, other than vodka, fish eggs, and a few tourist tchotchkes. There is a simple reason for this. The Russian stuff is no good. Even the smallest, simplest items stink. The way you use a Russian match is: After you strike it, you put it back in the matchbox. It's as likely to work as any of the other matches in there. In the old days the soda pop tasted like soap, the soap lathered like toilet paper, the toilet paper could be used to sand furniture, the furniture was as comfortable as a pile of canned goods, the canned goods had the flavor of a Solzhenitsyn novel, and a Solzhenitsyn novel got you arrested if you owned one. Now the Russians have discovered brand names. Easy to sneer at this. But there's a reason why, when we go to Florida, we don't drink Ocala-Cola.

Think what American shopping preferences would be if Sears were suddenly filled with wonderful products from the future—typewriters that could write things by themselves, safe cars that could go twice as fast as our own, shoes that made us sexually irresistible. The Russians are getting all these things.

Especially the shoes. Shoes are to Moscow what T-shirts are to Jimmy Buffet concerts. Shoes rule the store displays, particularly women's shoes—pumps, mules, sandals, boots—all of them with the highest possible heels, even the clogs and espadrilles. High heels and nude hose de-

fine the Moscow look and are worn with thigh-flaunting skirts so that
even policewomen and female army officers are tottering around, knees
in the breeze. The ensemble is not always chosen on the best of fashion advice. Often the effect is sausage on a stick. But what the hell.
This is a country where in 1988, when I was covering the Reagan-
Gorbachev summit, I saw a near riot in the shoe section of the GUM
department store. Scores of women were pushing and shouting for the
opportunity to buy Bulgarian sneakers.

Now, GUM is a mall, fully American, except for seventy-four years
of Soviet maintenance on the greenhouse roof, which leaks, and containing more than a hundred private stores. They sell everything from
high heels to nude hose.

Plus you can shop 24/7 in Moscow at thousands of Plexiglas and
plywood kiosks that have been built Tirana-fashion in parks, under
bridges, on railroad and subway platforms, and along every footpath
wide enough to walk a dog. A full half of these market the instant mini-
party with wares consisting of Marlboros, hooch, and pirated audio-
cassettes.

Unlike Tirana, however, Moscow had McDonald's. The McDonald's was
expensive. Everything in Moscow—except the thirty-cent subway—was
expensive. The drinks, meals, and hotel rooms were as costly as Monaco's.
And retail prices were no better than in most places on the value-added-
tax-plagued continent of Europe. Yet the average wage in Russia is $143
a month. Unless everybody is fibbing. Which they are.

Russia's businesses pay a 35 percent federal tax, plus a 20 percent VAT, plus local taxes that can be as high as 45 percent. That adds
up to 100 percent, so a tremendous amount of Russia's business is conducted via the "informal" economy. And it can be very informal. The
way you hail a cab in Moscow is that you don't. You hail any car, and
if the driver feels like it, he'll stop, negotiate a fee, and take you where
you want to go.

But some people in Russia don't have cars—or anything else. Re-
spectable grandmothers beg on the streets. The old folks are broke in

Russia. Increases in pension payments have been modest, while inflation has been indecent. In 1988 one ruble was worth $1.59. By mid-'96, one dollar was worth 5,020 rubles. And though money had been printed with abandon, the government ran out of it anyway. At the end of the first quarter of '96, pensions went unpaid. Then the panhandling golden-agers were all over the place.

Things have gotten somewhat better, but there's still gross poverty in Russia. I talked to economist Sergei Pavlenko, the director of the Working Center for Economic Reform of the Russian Government. He estimated the Russian poverty rate to be 25 percent. You can compare this with the 10 percent poverty rate claimed by the Communists before 1991. But don't. Pavlenko said that he had to wonder what the Communists considered poverty. The U.S. government sets the poverty threshold at $15,569 a year for a family of four. The Soviet government fixed the poverty line at seventy-five rubles per month. That was $119.05 at the official ruble exchange rate. But as in Cuba, the official exchange rate was a joke. The black-market rate back then varied from ten to fifteen rubles to the dollar, so seventy-five rubles was really something between $5 and $7.50. People were getting nothing under the Communists, too. It's just that they knew how much nothing they were going to get and when they'd get it.

But there's been more to the high price of freedom in Russia than high prices. You can be mugged these days or even shot if you put your mind to it. Moscow is no longer a town as safe as the tomb it used to resemble after 9 P.M. Random felonies, however, are still fairly rare. Russian crime is more likely to be the organized kind, and lots of it. The U.S. State Department estimates that there are 50,000 murders a year in Russia. More than half go unsolved. Sergei Pavlenko told me that four businessmen a day are killed in Moscow.

The key word is *businessmen*. Russia does not yet have an effective system of civil law. The only way to enforce a contract is, as it were, with a contract—and plenty of enforcers. What would be litigiousness in New York is a hail of bullets in Moscow. Instead of a society infested with lawyers, they have a society infested with hit men. Which is worse, of course, is a matter of opinion.

Moscow's English language weekly, *Living Here,* publishes a club and bar guide which had this to say about a typical *vorovskoi mir,* or "thieves' world" hangout:

Marika
Entrance: $20 for men, free for women
Why: Come here to gawk at Moscow's coked-up femme-fatale elite, none of whom will notice your existence; end your fun-filled evening by getting your date stolen and your life threatened by slobbering-drunk Mafiosi and their unshaven thugs.
Why Not: You still have dignity; you want to live.

The reliance on muscle means that criminals have a cut of everything mercantile or financial happening in Russia. This, combined with endless political wire-pulling and universal bureaucratic jobbery and graft, leads to an atmosphere that is . . . still a lot more fun than a KGB torture cell.

On my first evening in post-communist Moscow, after the lavish dinner, I ambled through the busy midnight streets to the Hungry Duck. An enormous circular bar occupied what looked like a trading pit from the Chicago Commodity Exchange. But there was no futures trading—or much future—in the old USSR. God knows the room's Soviet-era purpose, but the current purpose was clear. A thousand twentysomethings— Americans, Russians, Germans, British, French, Australians, Japanese; the foot-soldier employees of the corporations that have invaded Moscow, the Anne Kleined and Brooks Brothered sentinels who man the mouse pads and keyboards of capitalism's front lines—were having a Thursday night screen saver. Happy youth was pressed breast to pec in one raving mass while fifty people danced on the bar top and giggling waitresses passed out free vodka shots from some booze company promoting a new brand. Ties were yanked off. Blouses were unbuttoned. Beer spills were whipped to foam by flapping loafer tassels. Arms waved in the air. Legs waved in the air. Whole bodies fluttered in the smoky space above the crowd. And on the sound system, through speakers so big they would have done Stalin proud and played at volume enough to wake the old shit in his grave, Coolio sang "Gangsta's Paradise."

† † †

While I was visiting their country, the Russians were having an election. A momentous election. This was the first time in the 1,100–year history of the country that a national leader was being freely chosen by democratic means. And it might be a big election for everyone else in the world, too. Because running neck and neck were Boris Yeltsin, the man who almost single-handedly removed the Denver boot of bolshevism from the now freely spinning snow tire of Russian society (to coin a metaphor), and Gennady Zyuganov, a damned Communist.

Was the Soviet Union about to reunify? Was the Evil Empire coming back? Would the Russians vote themselves voteless? Would the tanks roll again? (The military commanders will have to pay some heavy bribes if they plan to park any armored vehicles near Moscow's more-fashionable restaurants.) Or would Russia continue on the straight and narrow path of modern political economy, eventually turning into a gigantic frozen Singapore? (Picture Lee Kuan Yew trying to cane a full-grown Russian.)

The only people who seemed to be unconcerned about the Russian elections were the Russians. When questioned about the vote, Russians, even loyal partisans, campaign volunteers, and candidate advisors, prefaced their answers with a shrug—the kind of shrug that can be delivered only with Russian-sized shoulders. I asked a Russian friend who would be the next president. He shrugged and said, "Yeltsin."

"How much will he win by?" I asked.

"I didn't say he would win. I said he'd be the next president."

Enormous state power exists in Russia whether the head of this state is elected or elects himself. And with such power goes tremendous governmental inertia. This either meant that no matter who got elected, nothing would change, or it meant that all the changes would keep happening, no matter who got elected. The Russians didn't know, and, busy as they were trying to make a living, they weren't that eager to find out. If Zyuganov and his ilk got in, the corrupt bureaucratic Soviet holdovers, the so-called dingycrats, would continue to run things. And if Yeltsin was returned to power, the dingycrats' partners in corruption, the crime-and-business parvenus called New Russians, would continue getting rich.

The New Russians are an amazing bunch. The men wear three-piece suits with stripes the width and color used to indicate no passing on two-lane highways. Shoulder pads are as high and far apart as tractor fenders, and lapel points stick out even farther, waving in the air like baseball pennants. The neckties are as wide as the wives. These wives have, I think, covered their bodies in Elmer's and run through the boutiques of Palm Springs, buying whatever stuck. Their dresses certainly appear to be glued on—flesh-tight, no matter how vast the expanse of flesh involved. Hair is in the cumulonimbus style. Personal ornaments are astonishing in both frequency and amplitude. There was a David Bowie concert in Moscow in June 1996, and according to the *Moscow Times,* the loudest sound from the expensive seats was the rattle of jewelry.

Most of the New Russians, like the dingycrats, had government connections in the old Soviet Union. They were at the heart of the socialist beast, and when it collapsed, they found themselves in perfect position to feast on the carcass.

Drinking with Dmitry Volkov one night, I said, "Maybe you should have cleaned house in Russia. Maybe after the attempted coup in 1991, you should have hanged the Communists."

"No," said Dmitry. "What would it have mattered if Goebbels had hanged Himmler?"

Like many other places in the world, Russia is a land of contrasts between old and new. But these are not the cute contrasts between old and new that telecommunications companies love to use in TV commercials—Zen masters faxing each other blank pages. In Russia, the contrasts are all scary. I visited a radio station on election night, a radio station still using vacuum tubes in its broadcast equipment. There was a Toshiba laptop in the studio. And this ordinary piece of journalistic equipment was alarming. The laptop, with its crisp design and neat finish, made the whole building look like it had been built by apes. Apes on the take. The place was no more than fifteen years old, and the plaster was flaking, the floor tiles were buckling, the walls were crooked, the windows didn't fit. The carpet was unraveling into long, smelly coils. You could break down the doors with a blunt remark. And there, on a wobbly table with a veneer top wrinkled like a relief map of the Urals, sat the little Toshiba, doing the one thing that nothing made in the Soviet Union ever seemed to do: It worked.

I was blaming this wild incompetence on marxism until I walked in St. Basil's Cathedral, that mountain of Persian domes and painted dazzle that is the very symbol of Russia, not to mention the symbol of U.S. TV anchormen broadcasting from Russia and telling us what's what. One thing they don't tell is that the inside of St. Basil's is a dusty jumble of catacombs and closets, badly made and primitively decorated—that the whole thing is really just a pile of bricks and timber, and more like something molded out of mud by kids than a real piece of architecture.

St. Basil's was commissioned by Ivan the Terrible in 1552, 350 years after the cathedral at Chartres. According to legend, Ivan had the architects blinded to keep them from building another. Perhaps he went too far, but he certainly should have had them beaten over the head with a book of lessons about how to make vaults and arches.

Barbaric touches persist in Russia. Packs of wild dogs roam the streets of Moscow. One pack lived by Red Square, lurking on Vetoshny Street in the back doorways of the GUM shopping mall. Another pack lived behind the best hotel in town, mine, in an alley directly below my window. They barked all night and slept all day, tempting me to open my casements in the middle of the afternoon and shout, "Sit! Fetch! Roll over!" for a couple of hours.

Russia possesses more recent vulgarities, too. Lenin remains on display by the Kremlin walls, laid out like a bad ideological salad under a big glass sneeze guard. Not many people come to see the dead maniac anymore, but the military sentinels are still there, as serious as ever, and still empowered, as all government authorities in Russia always have been, to make your life a misery if you laugh or moon the sarcophagus.

A few days after the election, I took the night train to St. Petersburg. It was still dusk when I left at midnight. I dozed for a while in my compartment, but by 4:30 the sun was up. I sat on my bunk watching the dormant countryside, sipping terrible sparkling apricot wine that I'd bought by mistake at a party-hearty kiosk. The meadows, marshes, and birch forests were spread with a low-hanging mist and dusted with Queen Anne's lace. In the little clusters of farmsteads, only the corrugated roofing and the occasional single thread of electric wire indicated modern times. The houses were built of logs with gables, eaves, and small, deep-set windows decorated with hand carvings.

There is an open-air museum, the Skansen, in Stockholm, where dwellings like these have been preserved. The home that I saw in the Skansen that most resembled the homes I was looking at now dated from the sixteenth century. In Russia, people are still living in them. Potato plants grew up to the front doors. Open wells and outhouses stood in the yards. I counted one truck and a motorcycle. This is the part of Russia that's closest to Western Europe. This is the route between the nation's two historic capitals. And for one complete hour, looking out that train window, I did not see a paved road.

In the morning in St. Petersburg, I went to the Winter Palace. From across the Russian-size expanse of Palace Square, it was an impressive building, becoming less so as I walked toward it, following the path that charging Bolsheviks didn't actually take when they didn't really storm the Winter Palace, which wasn't in fact defended by the czar and his minions but by members of a moderate provisional government. But it made a great visual in the Sergei Eisenstein film *October,* and that is more than the Winter Palace does in person. It is painted call-the-lawn-service green picked out in lardy white and cheap gilding. Ugly statues and clumsy urns line the cornice tops. Whole families of servants used to live up there, performing such tasks as keeping the royal plumbing from freezing by dropping hot cannonballs into the cisterns. They built huts between the chimneys and fed goats on the grass that grew on the roof.

The building was designed in 1754 by Bartolomeo Rastrelli. He spent most of his life in Russia, and it shows. The look is Go for Baroque. In unimaginative decoration, coarseness of detail, and infelicity of proportion, the Winter Palace has everything Stalin would want 200 years later.

The Hermitage museum, housed inside, is not much better. There is spectacular art—El Greco's *The Apostles Peter and Paul,* Filippo Lippi's

Adoration of the Infant Christ, Leonardo da Vinci's *Benois Madonna,* Rembrandt's *Descent from the Cross.* But there is so much art that, just as a statistical matter, some of it would have to be spectacular. And most of it's junk. There are Titian rent-payers, Peter Paul Rubens factory seconds, Watteaus painted by the yard, rooms full of Dutch genre paintings that explain the phrase "in Dutch," and a batch of Fragonards that should have gone to the guillotine with Marie Antoinette. All of this is slapped on the walls at random, hanging in full sunlight in galleries with the windows standing open.

The place looks like Art Club for Czars. Which it was. Catherine the Great bought European art collections wholesale and shipped them to her private quarters. "Only the mice and I admire all this," she gloated.

Russia is a country that didn't even become medieval until Ivan the Terrible introduced feudalism in the late 1500s, a country where the small landowner was known as a *smerd,* a "stinker." Russia never had a Renaissance, never had a Reformation. There was no Enlightenment here, no Romantic period, no *Rights of Man,* no parliamentary reform. What little Industrial Revolution Russia had was nipped and twisted by the Communists. Russia never had a Roaring '20s, a Booming '50s, a Swinging '60s, or a Me Generation. There was just one Them Generation after another. Standing in the Hermitage, you realize just how far out in the suburbs of Western civilization Russia is.

Of course, America is pretty far out in sophistication's subdivisions, too. An American instinctively understands big, silly, sprawling, clumsy St. Petersburg. It's an artificial capital like our own, willed into existence from nothingness, built in a swamp as worthless as the District of Columbia's, and designed and laid out the way Washington was by arty-farty foreigners who loved grand vistas and hated places to park.

St. Petersburg was founded in 1703 by Czar Peter the Great as a base for Russia's navy. Russia didn't really have a navy. Russia didn't even own the land. This corner of the Baltic coast was occupied Swedish territory and didn't officially become part of Russia until the Peace of Nystad, in 1721. The climate was terrible. There was nothing to eat. No building supplies existed. The Neva River regularly flooded. And

Russia already had a principal city and seat of government that no one was interested in leaving.

Peter the Great was no more daunted by these things than a good American would be, though he used some Russian methods to overcome the difficulties. He press-ganged 40,000 workers. They died of cold, starvation, and disease. The next year, he press-ganged 40,000 more. And so on. For nearly six decades, every carriage, wagon, boat, barge, or sled entering St. Petersburg had to pay a toll of building stones—very inconvenient things to carry in the troika's change tray. In 1712, Peter simply ordered a thousand families to the new capital and told them they were "required to build houses of beams, with lath and plaster, in the old English style," the first recorded instance of a "themed" development.

That stuff rapidly succumbed to fire and rot, but St. Petersburg retains the fake-o-la look of an eighteenth-century Epcot Center. The mansions are supposed to be like Italian villas, but they're crammed wall on wall, as though they were town house condominiums. The czars had pads all over the map—Summer Palace, Winter Palace, Small Hermitage, New Hermitage—each looking like it came from Palaces for Less. And St. Petersburg has canals. The city is sometimes called the Venice of the North. But not very often. This is Venice as interpreted by a U.S. real-estate mogul: "Give me a bigger ditch. And lose the canoes."

St. Petersburg is a city of largeness. You could hold the Reno air races in Palace Square. St. Isaac's Cathedral is big enough for God to come down from heaven and feel like He was rattling around in there. The hall corridor on each story of the Grand Hotel Europa makes a loop sufficient in size for a high-energy-particle accelerator. (No doubt some interesting quarks could be produced by collisions between protons and room-service waiters.)

And Russians are a people of largeness, too—large bodies, large gestures, large voices. In fact, Russians are enormous. Being an average-size American in St. Petersburg is like being a girl gymnast at a Teamsters convention. And these are Russians who were raised on potatoes and suet and bread that you could use for a boat anchor. Envision them after a generation of good nutrition. Twenty years from now, Americans may ask themselves if winning the cold war was worth losing the Super Bowl.

To an American used to cute, fussy little Western Europe, Russia is . . . not a breath of fresh air, certainly, since the place is kind of *smerdish,* but it's like mail from home. News that your dog died, maybe, but mail from home nonetheless. There's something very American about Russia, despite a history as deprived and unlucky as ours has been hopeful and rich. The historian Ronald Hingley says the saga of Russia has been marked by "a peculiarly Russian tendency for tragedy to mingle with high farce." But Hingley is British, and what would he know? That doesn't sound peculiarly Russian to Americans. It sounds like the Clinton administration.

Speaking of pumpkin rollers in the corridors of power, I went to see the house where Rasputin was assassinated. The overblown and butt-ugly Yussupov Palace belonged to a family who owned, basically, everything in Russia. Rasputin, a Siberian peasant, was a televangelist. TV had not been invented, however, so he had to swindle people one at a time. The one he picked was Alexandra, wife of the last Russian czar. It's a shame that Alexandra didn't live long enough to talk to Nancy Reagan about horoscopes.

Some of the czar's advisors decided Rasputin had to go. Young Prince Felix Yussupov volunteered to do the honors. Felix liked to cross-dress. He took a chef, a chauffeur, a valet, a housekeeper, and a groom with him when he went to college. He didn't sound too tightly wrapped. I kept waiting for the tour guide to tell me that Felix killed Rasputin to impress Jodie Foster.

The prince lured Rasputin to the Yussupov Palace and fed him on cyanide-enhanced cakes and wine. These had no effect. So Felix shot Rasputin in the heart. The charlatan seemed to expire, but an hour later, when Felix returned to get the body, Rasputin reached up and grabbed him by the throat. Yussupov managed to free himself, and Rasputin ran into the garden, where one of the coconspirators shot him three more times. The prostrate Rasputin was put in a car trunk and dropped through the ice into a tributary of the Neva. Even then he didn't die. His body was found downriver, clutching the pilings of a bridge. Rasputin was the Richard Nixon of Russian politics. Don't tell me our countries haven't got a lot in common.

† † †

In comparing free-market and collectivist systems, the temptation is to prove too much. Socialism is not the simple cause of Russian bungling any more than laissez-faire is the simple cause of Albanian larceny. Economics is too complicated for that.

Economics is probably too complicated, period, for somebody who was beginning to think of Russians as a Yankee lost tribe. Maybe I hadn't been getting enough sleep. It was the summer solstice—the White Nights—and daylight lasted until 3 A.M. Even then, night came only to street level. Above, the sky was still glowing.

During the White Nights, everybody walks around the city from supper until breakfast in a genial haze. There are concerts and dances, and busloads of army cadets bring their dates to Palace Square and whistle and yell to see the sun up at midnight. All the people in the streets are solicitous and cheerful. Which is quite a change, because another thing that's American about this country are the manners. Russians have American-style manners and then some. Russians have American professional-athletics-style manners.

Russians don't, won't, can't line up for anything. At every turnstile, ticket booth, or cash register, they shove in from all sides like piglets on a sow. They have no sense of personal space. They'll walk across an empty Red Square to stand on the toes of your shoes.

Every question or request, at even the most "Western" hotels and restaurants, is met with a stare of dull surprise and a grudging, laconic response.

"Do you have soup today?"

Waiter pauses, frowns, grimly considers. "Yes."

"What kind of soup?"

"Different kinds."

"Could you tell me some of the different kinds?"

"Soup of the day."

Small boys, when they see a passing train, give it the finger. An Intourist travel agent, queried on whether it would be worthwhile to visit Khabarovsk, rolled her eyes and said, "*Pfft*. I don't know. *I've* never been there."

I asked a long-distance operator, "Will you put this call through to the United States?"

"Maybe," he replied.

Suggested slogan for post-Soviet tourism promotion campaign: Russia—Barge Right In.

People who weren't in Russia before 1991 sometimes think Russian rudeness is a product of freedom. "I guess the Russians are finally free to be rude," they'll say. They're wrong. Manners were worse yet in the USSR and were accompanied by a public atmosphere of defeated fatigue and indefatigable suspicion. Plus, half the people were drunk— a thrashing, helpless, hello-coma kind of inebriation I saw almost nowhere on this trip except occasionally in the mirror.

So socialism causes rudeness. And capitalism causes rudeness. But if you go to Sweden, where they've got both, everybody's polite. You figure it out.

I gave up and took a boat trip to a palace complex built by Peter the Great—Peterhof, named after Peter, as everything that Peter named was. Here were four or five residences too big to live in, plus one too big to walk through without taking a break for lunch.

Fountains, cascades, and other waterworks clutter Peterhof's grounds. The ordinary garden hose has taken much of the thrill out of fountains, I think. Right in our backyards we have something that sprays water beautifully into the air, and you can squirt your wife with it. Also, we have electricity. Spumes, spritzes, and artificial drizzle received more *oohs* and *aahs* when viewers knew that hundreds of serfs were scrambling uphill with buckets to make them happen.

Peterhof's fountains have been under restoration since World War II. Some spitting gargoyles had a plaque that read, THE DRAGONS WERE RAVAGED BY THE NAZIS. Which must have been a sight to see. Not satisfied with sexually molesting the garden ornaments, Hitler's troops ruined all of Peterhof during their unsuccessful siege of what was then Leningrad.

I went to the appalling Throne Room and looked at the gilded rococo moldings slobbered all over the walls and ceilings. A dozen immense purple glass chandeliers from a whore's idea of paradise ruined the space overhead. Underfoot, an ugly jigsaw puzzle of parquet flooring spread for acres in all directions, so much of it that there were once servants whose job was to skate through the palace in big socks, keeping everything buffed. The throne itself was preposterous, and above it was a portrait of fat Catherine the Great, the picture bracketed by personifications of Justice, Truth, Virtue, and other things that Catherine wouldn't have known if they bit her.

An afternoon at Peterhof is enough to explain the whole Bolshevik revolution, especially in 1917 to starving sailors on the Kronshtadt fleet, freezing soldiers at World War I's Eastern Front, and semichattel peasants hauling water buckets for the Peterhof fountains. I was ready to join the revolution myself if I'd get a chance to heave that throne through a window, make a penny-arcade shooting gallery out of the chandeliers, and play ducks and drakes with a hand grenade on those parquet floors.

The problem is, the Bolsheviks didn't do those things. And when the Germans did, the Bolsheviks spent the next four and a half decades carefully restoring the place. This is because marxists are insane.

Marxism has had such an impact on this century and remains, even after the fall of the Soviet bloc, such a potent intellectual force that we tend to forget how loony are its fundamental tenets.

Karl Marx believed that man is created by economics, not the other way around. No soul is involved. Nebuchadnezzar, Jesus, Attila the Hun, Leonardo da Vinci, George Washington, Albert Schweitzer, and Alanis Morissette are all just different versions of investment maven Warren Buffett. And mankind, like Warren Buffett's Berkshire Hathaway company, moves ever forward economically. History, to Marx, was nothing but the inevitable evolution of economic systems. First there was snatch and grab, followed by hunt and gather, then feudalism, capitalism, and, finally, there will be snatch and grab again, as much as you like, in the communist utopia.

Marx insisted that these economic systems determine everything. He lived in the capitalist age, so all of what he saw around him was a construct of capitalism: marriage, family, religion, government, nation. When communism came, these would disappear. *Poof!* No more wife and kids, and you don't have to go to church on Sunday, you can play golf. Unless golf is a capitalist construct, too, in which case you'll be standing in the grass with a *niblick* in your hand and no idea what to do.

Faith in the primacy of economic determinates is, in brief, putting a price on your mother. As I pointed out in the last chapter, a good economist can do this, if pressed. But Marx was not a good economist. He espoused the Labor Theory of Value, the idea that the value of a product is determined by the work required for its production. Thus, a hole in the ground is worth more than a poem. (Although this actually happened to be the case with much of the poetry written in the Soviet Union.)

Marx also believed that once private property was eliminated and communism had arrived, all of humankind would be gathered into one huge, cohesive, all-pervading socioeconomic cooperative. How this would happen, however, Marx hadn't a clue. He hinted it would be accomplished in a big, gooey, spontaneous, Woodstock way. In Russia, it was done with guns.

There's a problem with such an immense, omnipotent, and ubiquitous organization (a problem, that is, besides the millions of people killed to create it). What is this thing supposed to *do?* Karl Kautsky, another leading crackpot left-wing theoretician of the nineteenth century, said, "In the socialist society, which is after all just a single, giant industrial enterprise, production and planning must be . . . organized as they are organized in a modern, large, industrial enterprise." But a modern, large, industrial enterprise producing what? Game Boys? Inner peace? Blow jobs? Candy and gum? Without rational prices, how do you know what to produce? Without private property, how do you get these products? Without products, how can there be markets? Without markets, how can prices be set?

Between 1918 and 1921, the Lenin government actually attempted to develop a system of nonmonetary accounting. Try this in your bankbook. "Let's see, I withdrew the clean dishes from the dishwasher, and I deposited my kids at day care . . ."

Absent the automatic commonsense mechanisms of supply and demand, what really happens is that all production and consumption decisions are made by . . . Joseph Stalin. Stalin went so far as to claim that economic policy was a Kremlin matter and economists should stay out of it.

The absurdity of socialism made a dog's breakfast out of the Soviet economy, just as it continues to ruin Cuba's. But a visit to Russia is more interesting to an amateur economist than a visit to Cuba, because the truth about how socialist thinking beggared the USSR is now being told. Even some socialist thinkers are willing to tell it. Mikhail Gorbachev, in his *Memoirs,* says, "The costs of labor, fuel, and raw material per unit of production were two- to two-and-a-half times higher than in the developed countries, while in agriculture they were ten times higher. We produced more coal, oil, metals, cement, and other materials (except for synthetics) than the United States, but our end-product was less than half that of the U.S.A."

This end product was not, of course, insignificant. The Soviet Union was able to manufacture moon rockets and atomic bombs and enough AK-47s to make every shoeless jackanapes in the Third World into an NRA life member. But Soviet industrial might mostly ended up doing doughnuts on the lawn. The Russians used to say, "We build huge machines that dig coal and ore out of the ground. We burn the coal to smelt the ore to build huge machines that dig coal and ore out of the ground."

Even when Soviet factories produced something useful or necessary, central planning bunged it up. The government in Moscow would send commands called gross-output targets to all manufacturing facilities. The gross-output target told the factory manager what to make and how much of it. Anyone who has dealt with bureaucrats who are accountable only to other bureaucrats knows what happened next.

The trouble wasn't that the factory managers disobeyed orders. The trouble was that they obeyed them precisely. If a shoe factory was told to produce 1,000 shoes, it produced 1,000 baby shoes, because these were the cheapest and easiest to make. If it was told to produce 1,000 men's shoes, it made them all one size. If it was told to produce 1,000 shoes in a variety for men, women, and children, it produced 998 baby shoes, one pump, and a wing tip. If it was told to produce 3,000 pounds of shoes, it produced one enormous pair of concrete sneakers.

The factory managers weren't doing this because they were evil or stupid. They did it because their livelihoods, their futures, and sometimes their necks were at stake. They didn't have to satisfy customers. They didn't have to please stockholders. What they had to do was meet the gross-output target, no matter what.

Getting the raw material and machinery to meet the gross-output target was as hard on Soviet factory managers as wearing enormous concrete sneakers was on Soviet consumers. Soviet factories were not allowed to deal directly with each other. All requisitions had to go through the State Planning Committee (the well acronymed GOSPLAN) and the State Committee on Material-Technical Supply (the wonderfully acronymed GOSSNAB). These entities worked as well as everything else worked in the Soviet Union. Thus when a factory manager was told to produce 1,000 shoes, he ordered 1,000 tons of leather. That way, maybe he'd get at least a couple of pieces of cowhide. And if he got too much, great, he'd hide it.

A black market of strange bartering grew up among factories as managers traded unneeded things to make unwanted stuff. And a special class of bureaucrats called *tolkachi,* "pushers," arose to facilitate these deals. *Tolkachi* were, essentially, hired to be white-collar criminals. Many of today's filthy-rich New Russians were *tolkachi* and still are, since the Russian government has by no means untangled itself from the economy.

Members of the Soviet managerial class were forced to become liars and thieves, and ordinary workers took the hint. The amount of on-the-job theft in the Soviet Union was astonishing. In 1990, the USSR Academy of Sciences reported that "losses of the objects of labor total approximately 70 percent" and "losses during the use of the means of labor [i.e., tools and raw materials] total 40 percent to 50 percent."

If any of that contradicted the spirit of marxism, you'd be hard put to learn it by reading Marx, especially reading the Theory of Surplus Value. The value of a thing is, as Karl Marx decreed, determined by the labor required for its production. The amount a thing sells for, minus the amount paid to the workers who made it, equals the capitalist rip-off to which all good socialists are so strongly opposed. The Theory of

Surplus Value means that anytime you hire someone, you are exploiting him. If you pay someone to fix your automobile, he has the right, by virtue of being your mechanic, to steal your car.

The terrific corruption that now exists in Russia was not caused by the collapse of Marxism-Leninism. It was caused by Marx and Lenin.

Well, sort of. Russian authorities had been inclined to steal everything in sight at least since the reign of Ivan "Moneybag," 1328–41. Until Peter the Great, Russian officials were paid no salaries. They were expected to "feed themselves from official business." And when the Marquis de Custine traveled through Russia in 1839, he encountered a member of the czarist aristocracy who said, "They tell me that in France, at present, the highest noble can be put in prison for a debt of two-hundred francs; this is revolting: How different from our country! There is not in all Russia a tradesman who would dare to refuse us credit for an unlimited period."

The world's corruption, incompetence, and rudeness can't all be blamed on socialism. In fact, to be fair, a socialist society seems to produce solidarity among people. It does so in Sweden. And it does so in Cuba, even if that is a solidarity of suffering and anger. Socialism, however at odds with economic sense, engenders brotherhood.

Or so I was thinking as I arrived in the Siberian city of Irkutsk. The twentysomething Intourist guide who met me at the airport certainly seemed a younger-brother type. Ivor was affable, outgoing, and . . .

"You'll notice there are no niggers here," said this product of socialist childhood and schooling.

We'd been standing in the dumpy baggage hall, waiting for my suitcase and talking about the elections and Ivor's great good fortune as a translator. He'd never even been to Moscow, and he was now going to Atlanta with the Russian Olympic team.

"Jesus Christ, Ivor!" I said. "You *can't* use that word. It's a really serious insult."

"Don't black people commit a lot of crimes in America?"

"Ivor, in America, *everybody* commits a lot of crimes. You can't ever use that word. It has a meaning of bigotry, hatred."

"But isn't it true that many Americans don't like blacks?"

"No!" I said. I scanned my conscience on that. "Americans aren't prejudiced at all. And we're getting over it, too."

Ivor looked dubious. He was too Russian to believe it was really okay for some people to go around being, you know, *different* from other people. This is a country that considers Warsaw an exotic southern city whose hot-blooded natives are not quite to be trusted.

Capitalist or socialist, there's a stumbling-around-in-the-daylight quality to the Russians. Almost 7 million square miles of territory, and still they don't get out enough. My six-hour flight to Siberia took two days. We were lined up to board six or eight times before we finally got on the plane. Airline employees circulated with walkie-talkies. Not satisfied with individual screwups, they apparently wanted to coordinate them.

"Everything's unready to go in the cockpit."

"Roger that. We've got the baggage lost."

"Seat selection's a mess."

"Wait a minute. Wait a minute. Catering's not fucked yet."

Fortunately, Russia is a country where you can bring your own vodka bottle, mixer, and highball glass right into the boarding lounge— bring your own dog and pony, for that matter. And, anyway, what were they going to do—send me to Siberia?

Unfortunately, I had not packed the two-day-sized bottle. I tried to order a drink on the plane.

"Vodka."

"Huh?"

"Vodka. You invented it. Vod-ka."

"Water?"

I consulted my *Berlitz*. The Russian word for vodka is *vodka*.

She brought me a hard candy and a lime drink.

Ivor showed me around Irkutsk, a city of half a million people that is 2,600 miles east of Moscow and still only two-thirds of the way to the Pacific. The modern parts of town were a mess, but the dumpy, old, run-down neighborhoods were fine. The nineteenth-century houses are log cabins, but on *Beverly Hillbillies* scale. The trunks of straight Siberian larch were so perfectly squared that the joints are almost invisible. The copper roofs are capped by ornate brick chimneys. Elaborate fretwork embellishes the doors and windows. This is the kind of place where Abraham Lincoln would have grown up—if his mother had been Martha Stewart.

A frontiersman like Abe would recognize Siberia. Russia's far east is our Wild West—the same fur traders, gold rushes, homesteadings, and murders of the people who lived there originally—always, however, with the slightly off-center Russian spin. For one thing the settlers *still* haven't settled the place. Only the strip of land along the Trans-Siberian Railroad has a population density of more than twenty-five people per square mile. And the Russian version of *Wagon Train* has been going on since a cossack high-plains drifter named Yermak chased away the pesky Tartars in 1582.

There's also a whiff of the highbrow in Siberia. For a hick town, Irkutsk had too many opera houses, theaters, museums, and academic institutes. This is because, for hundreds of years, the smarty-pants reformers, annoying idealists, and know-it-all do-gooders were sent here for life. It's as though everyone who voted for George McGovern was packed off to Lubbock, Texas. A mixed blessing for the locals, as you can imagine.

Ivor was a local, and he considered the vast surrounding wilderness to be another mixed blessing. We drove for an hour southwest along the Angara River toward Lake Baikal, to a craggy overlook above a thousand square miles of virgin conifer forest. I was experiencing the egotistical swelling that comes upon urbanized man facing vast, uninhabited spaces. I was thinking, "There's nothing! There's nothing here! There's nothing here but ME!"

"There's nothing here but bears," said Ivor. "We call it Bear Angle."

Actually, Debris Corner would have been more like it. Trash lay all over the clearing. The largest rock on the hillcrest was covered halfway to its top with broken glass.

"Did the place look like this under communism?" I asked.

"Sure," said Ivor. So there is no correlation between socialist systems and tidiness.

Also, the surrounding bushes and trees were covered by small strips of cloth, tied to almost every branch and twig.

"What's that about?" I asked.

"Oh, this place is sacred to the Buryats; they are of Mongolian type," said Ivor, eyeing me carefully to see if "Mongolian type" was another of the terms that might set me off.

Some visitors—of Russian type—arrived at the overlook. There were a dozen of them in three cars. They were young and dressed for a ball, although it was 11 in the morning. They took dramatic and gurgling drinks of vodka and champagne, threw their bottles at the big rock, got back in, and drove away at high speed. One of the car roofs was decorated with a pair of pizza-size gold-foil rings.

"A wedding," explained Ivor. "When people here are getting married, they drive around the countryside very fast and have drinks."

Which is also what they do when they aren't getting married. We were doing it ourselves. We drove to Lake Baikal, very fast, and had drinks.

An impressive chaser is Baikal—395 miles long and 50 miles across at its widest point. Eighty percent of Russia's freshwater is here, and 20 percent of the world's—more than the Great Lakes put together. Baikal's water is famously pure and so clear that you can look all the way down to . . . nothing, because the water is almost a mile deep.

Cows were sleeping on the highway by the shore. "There's not much to do in Siberia," said Ivor.

"But it's beautiful," I said.

"Mmm," said Ivor.

A spectacular and almost empty locale like Baikal should maybe be kept as some kind of public property—a park or nature preserve. And yet, the capitalist in me agreed with Ivor. Looking out at the smooth, vacant waters of a lake bigger than Belgium and almost as dull, I kept having visions of Hobie Cats, cabin cruisers, float boats, outboards, and Jet Skis.

I went down to the stony beach and put a toe in the water. Yow! Christ! Brr! The place should be a nature preserve.

We drove up a hill to the Baikal Hotel, which has one of the world's spectacular views, and its restaurant and bar are in the basement.

At lunch I talked to some other Intourist clients, four Russians on a day trip from Irkutsk. They had a lot of questions. What was my opinion of the current intrigue in the Duma? What were my thoughts on local government reform? What did I believe was Russia's proper geopolitical posture? These were beyond me. But I guess when your nearest world capital is Ulan Bator, any wandering rubberneck is worth pumping. Besides, I was an American and was supposed to know all about the problems of liberty. "You have had over two-hundred years of democracy," said one of the Irkutsk men, sighing as though self-rule were something that had to be achieved by Darwinian selection, like an opposable thumb.

The Russians did have queries I could answer, however. "Are there really cowboys in America?" (They were delighted that it's so.) "Do you still use coins in the U.S.?" (The largest Russian coin was, at the time, worth 1/50th of a cent.) And I had something just as naive to ask them. "How is Russia *doing*?" I said. "I mean, you know . . . Are people better off? Worse off?"

Because I really couldn't tell. I'd heard disaster stories about the Russian economy, but Moscow and St. Petersburg appeared prosperous. On the other hand, these were the wealthiest places in the country and, as a tourist, I'd spent my time in the best parts of town. Judging Russia by a couple of weeks of sightseeing in its two principal cities would be like judging America by walking up Madison Avenue from Fifty-seventh Street to the Whitney Museum.

Irkutsk looked more like the old Soviet Union, shabby and drab, but tokens of economic success were scattered around. Some decent apartments were being built. There were Japanese cars on the streets. The Intourist Hotel offered actual hospitality, and its restaurants served real food. Dozens of privately owned stores had opened, including a grocery next to one of the Martha Stewart log cabins. And that grocery could have been stocked by Martha herself: ten varieties of Hong Kong tea biscuits.

As for the Russian countryside, I'm not sure it ever looks different. Genghis Khan probably saw the same things in the Russian countryside that I did, although he stopped to burn them.

I was flummoxed. Russia was richer than it was when I'd been there in 1982 and 1988. But experts and statistics said just the opposite. According to the Russian State Committee for Statistics, the gross domestic product was only 61 percent of what it had been in 1989. Russians couldn't have more stuff and less stuff at the same time, could they? The World Bank estimated that one-third of Russia's population had an income below the minimum sustenance level: One out of three people was keeling over from hunger. This wasn't happening. Indeed, three out of three Russians could use some time on a StairMaster. Tatyana Y. Yarygina, deputy chairwoman of the State Duma's Committee on Labor and Social Policy, claimed that a full quarter of Russians couldn't find employment. Thirty-eight million or so folks were sitting on their duffs— yet the day-trippers from Irkutsk were almost the only Russians I saw doing nothing.

What did they think? "Oh, things are better now." "Much better." "Better, better, better now." Of course, a whole bottle of vodka had been drunk at lunch, and things *were* better. But, in fact, the Russians told me what I wanted to know by asking another question of their own, a question that only the citizens of a few nations would bother to ask. "Tell me," said one, in the serious and important manner that comes with drinking too much in the daytime, "where is life harder? In the U.S. or in Russia?"

Measuring the current Russian economic situation against the old Soviet economy is like trying to do arithmetic by tasting the numbers. The Soviets invented statistical methods that were almost as strange as Lenin's nonmonetary accounting. Instead of using the definition of gross domestic product accepted by every Western nation—the value of the production of all labor and property located in a country—the Communists had something called gross material product. To oversimplify, gross material product ignored services and counted products every time they moved.

Not that this mattered, since all of the USSR's statistics were Cuban in their unreality. The figures used to calculate the gross material product were drawn from bureaucratic reports about fulfillment of the notorious gross-output targets and, hence, were all lies.

Besides, the USSR's output was stated in rubles, a currency with no value at all. Or, rather, the ruble had up to a dozen different values by the end of the Soviet era. There was the international ruble, the official currency with an exchange rate of about $1.75; the commercial ruble, used for trade with hard-currency countries and usually pegged at fifty-seven cents; the tourist ruble, introduced to undercut the black-market ruble; the auction ruble, with value determined by sales among foreign banks; the enterprise ruble, which could only be spent on products from a specific Soviet industry; and so on. Russians are still suspicious of the ruble. A store clerk in St. Petersburg rejected my tattered 1,000-ruble bill on the grounds, I guess, that it was a torn ruble with yet another special exchange rate.

We don't know how much of the Soviet economy shrank after the collapse of communism, because the Soviet economy was unknowable. But we do know that electrical consumption fell by only 18 percent. This argues against the amount of GDP contraction claimed by the Russian government. We also know that black-market activity grew, although by how much is also unknowable. (Amazing how little you can find out from the people running things when they're flanked by enormous thugs.) I talked to one of Communist presidential-candidate Gennady Zyuganov's economic advisors. She claimed to be an expert on the "black economy" and said she believed that 45 percent of Russia's industry and trade was now conducted off the books.

Some of the shrunken parts of the USSR's economy will not be missed. In a leftover Soviet-era guidebook, I found a passage about how "a giant wood-pulp and paper mill polluted the pristine waters of Lake Baikal." I saw no sign of that thing. And some of the downturns in economic indicators are actually signs of progress. From 1986 to 1990, the part of the USSR that's now Russia produced an average of 105 million tons of grain per year. Now it produces only 69 million tons. But at the end of the communist period, 27 million tons of grain per year were being imported, while today, Russia is a net grain exporter. This is no paradox, considering the USSR's transportation and storage facilities. As much as 60 percent of the Soviet Union's food used to be lost moving it from field to face.

Still, the Russian economy did have conniptions in the 1990s. There was the wallet-popping inflation. In 1992 the inflation rate reached 1,353 percent. When the Soviet Union went to pieces, all of its former republics were left with central banks that had the equipment to print rubles, and no one was there to stop them. In effect, Russia had fourteen estranged wives, each with a duplicate of the Kremlin Visa card.

And many of the country's largest industries collapsed. The cars, refrigerators, and TVs they made were junk. The only way they'd been able to sell them before was through a Soviet retail system so screwed up that no one could buy any cars, refrigerators, or TVs, and so there were no complaints. Tens of thousands of jobs disappeared, or, worse, the jobs stayed but the paychecks vanished.

By all rights, Russia should have been in the kind of great depression mess that led to Hitler in Germany and whiny, nasal Woody Guthrie songs in the United States. But Russia, mysteriously, was not singing "This Land Is Your Land." And Russia was pretty stable, considering all the asses-and-elbows political events of the past decade.

With the reelection of Yeltsin, the Russians had voted for a sort-of democratic, kind-of free-market government. And that government's finances weren't even a total mess. Inflation was down to between 1.5 or 3 percent a month, nothing to amaze an American old enough to remember Richard Nixon's wage-price controls. National debt as a percentage of GDP was lower in Russia than in any country in Europe except Luxembourg. Probably this was because only a crazy person or the International Monetary Fund would loan Russia money. But, even so, the 34 percent of GDP Russian debt was a big improvement on America's 70 percent and Sweden's 100 percent. And Russia's budget deficit was only 4 percent of gross domestic product, about the same as the average for European Union countries. Russia's economic situation defied standard analysis.

Russia's economic situation defied standard analysis because its numbers didn't add up in any standard way. Russian industrial output had declined by half since 1990, but its export trade flourished. The nation had a $19.9 billion trade surplus.

Russia reportedly exported $88.3 billion in goods in 1996—mostly timber, cellulose, ferrous metals, coal, oil, and gas. Russian extraction industries weren't the flop that the Russian manufacturing sector was, but there was more to it than that. When the Soviet Union collapsed, Russian industries were found to be hoarding enormous amounts of raw materials, perhaps as much as $700 billion worth—in a country with chronic shortages of everything. This senseless inventory glut resulted from a combination of realpolitik cynicism and cynicism of the regular kind. The leaders of the old Soviet Union thought a nuclear war could be won. They meant to survive and rebuild the (now socialist, of course) world. It was to be, I gather, a world made of timber, cellulose, ferrous metals, coal, oil, and gas. The managers of Russia's industries were happy to go along with the daft stockpiling because they could use these heaps and piles of superfluous stuff for black-market bartering through the *tolkachi* system. Now many Russian industries were keeping themselves in business by fencing the assets of paranoid Kremlin megalomania.

Then there was the matter of Russia's continuing inflation. The inflation was dinky compared with what it had been, but nonetheless it verged on 30 percent a year. Why did a country with low national debt, a moderate budget deficit, a supposedly shrinking GDP, and a trade surplus have any inflation at all?

And if there was a trade surplus, why was the ruble losing value? Russia had issued new currency and solved the problem of rogue central banks in places like Trashcanistan. But the ruble exchange rate fell anyway.

The answer was that none of Russia's official economic figures properly took into account the "black economy," the informal market. The trade surplus was an example. According to the government import-export accounts, Russia spent only $59.8 billion of its annual export earnings on foreign goods. That left an amount equal to more than a month's salary for every person in the country. Where was this money going? It wasn't being spent on deficit financing. The IMF was loaning Russia $10 billion over three years for that purpose. And the money wasn't being used for the capitalistic purposes that Russia's Soviet forefathers so loathed. Investment in fixed capital had fallen by 36 percent since 1993. The Russians were spending it on the sly.

The Russians were spending money on uncounted and unrecorded foreign goods brought into the country by small traders. In 1996 you were allowed $2,000 in duty-free imports when you entered Russia, and no real Russian came back to the country with a penny's worth less. Clothing, toys, and small appliances were packed into enormous burlap sacks so that the baggage-claim area of any Russian airport with international flights seemed to be populated by hundreds of Santa Clauses in their off-duty clothes. Myriad Russians were doing this for a living. They were known as *chelnoki,* or shuttle boats. They went back and forth to Turkey, Poland, Italy, South Korea, Egypt, Thailand, Dubai—anywhere with cheap products for sale—flying bargain charters to obscure provincial airports. Ankon Airport, in eastern Italy, was visited by 38,677 Russians in 1995. The *chelnoki* bought with cash, and they sold unencumbered by taxes, licenses, permits, or any of society's other parasitical attachments on trade.

There were two ways to shop in Russia. You could walk down the main streets, and here were the same stores that America had, full of the best-known brands of everything. Or you could go around the corner, down the alley, and into one of the broad paved courtyards in the middle of Russia's gargantuan city blocks.

I didn't know these places existed until I was walking down a side street in St. Petersburg and caught sight of a huge bustle at the end of a dank, narrow passage. I walked through and emerged upon a Gotham of cardboard boxes. In other poor countries, people would be living in them; here they were minding shop. All the world's handiwork was for sale, at least all the world's handiwork that's cheap—from Chinese canned hams to Malaysian underpants. It was illegal, of course. But the only signs of that were two enormous thugs demanding a buck to let me in.

This was where ordinary Russians cruised the mall. They shopped for old-fashioned necessities. They shopped for newfound pleasures. And I hope they shopped a little bit just to make the people at the Russian State Committee for Statistics look like saps.

The day after I got back from Lake Baikal, I boarded the Trans-Siberian Railroad for Vladivostok. I'd gone to Intourist to look into traveling across

Russia. "What about a train ride?" I'd asked the clerk. "Is the Trans-Siberian Railroad any fun?"

She stared at me. "It will be long remembered," she said.

It will—four days and three nights with no scheduled stops longer than eighteen minutes in accommodations that were Spartan. Trojan is more what I mean—like the inside of the horse of that name after a whole platoon of sweaty Greek hoplites had been squished in there for, oh, four days and three nights.

Public transport in Russia is not for the faint of nose. I don't mean to hurt any feelings, but I'm a professional journalist with certain duties, and conscience compels me to provide the information that Russians smell. They smell with a big, mildewy, musky, left-the-gym-clothes-in-the-car-trunk-all-summer stink. And they didn't start smelling any better between Irkutsk and the Pacific, because Russian trains don't have baths in the bathrooms, or showers or hot water or soap or towels or toilet paper. The toilet itself empties directly onto the roadbed, with its waste pipe aimed out to the side in a way that must provide surprises to the occasional bystander.

There's one bathroom to a car. It's the size of a high-school locker, and everything in there, including the toilet seat, is made out of sheet metal. There's no drain in the floor, and what with spills and leaks of one kind and another, the cubicle quickly fills with a variety of liquids to a height above your shoe tops. Bring Handi Wipes.

The passenger compartments are slightly larger than the bathroom, almost large enough to contain the four bunks with which each is equipped, plus maybe one and a half of the four adults who are supposed to be accommodated therein. You can stretch out on these bunks in comfort if you answered the casting call for Tattoo on *Fantasy Island*. The compartment window does not open, and there's no fan or other form of ventilation, and no window shade. In the summer in southern Siberia, the sun shines eighteen hours a day. If your compartment is on the south side of the train, as mine was, you can use it to bake pies. A few of the windows in the corridor do open, and some relief can be had by sticking your head out and letting your jaw hang open in the breeze. I saw most of Siberia the way your dog sees I-95.

Each train car carries two middle-aged ladies whose job, as far as I could tell, is to walk up and down the corridor making sure no one smokes. You can drink on the train, you can puke on the train, you can yell and quarrel and party all night, you can cook tripe on alcohol stoves and make fetid picnics of smoked fish and goat cheese, but you can't smoke. In order to smoke, you have to stand between the cars and risk getting shoved under the wheels by all the people from the adjoining compartments who are standing between the cars, too, because everyone smokes in Russia.

And this is the first-class section of the train. In second class, the corridor runs through the middle of doorless compartments with four bunks on one side and a fifth above the window across the aisle. Below this bunk are two seats with a hinged flap between them. Raise the flap and you get yet another bunk. There haven't been so many people on top of each other at bedtime since the U.S.A. in the 1960s.

Russian trains are reeking, grubby, airless, and clamorously loud. The cars sway in sudden and violent motions. Rail sections are laid haphazardly, with large gaps between rail ends. Instead of clickety-clack, Russian trains go KA-WANK! KA-WANK! KA-WANK!

I ended up angry, but not about the discomfort or lack of services. What was maddening was more abstract—how the train had been designed with no consideration for anyone on it. In fact, there seemed to have been active malice. Mere negligence wouldn't explain that bathroom. In the old Soviet Union, nobody had to like this train—or anything else. Nobody had a choice. People couldn't go on a competing railroad. People couldn't go on a Greyhound bus. People couldn't even—considering what a trip to Siberia usually meant—not go. So the trains weren't built to satisfy the needs of the passengers. They were built to satisfy the whims of people in the Kremlin, and to satisfy the personal agendas of the managers and technocrats putting that whimsy into practice.

This is central planning. And anybody who advocates central planning—from Gennady Zyuganov to Sidney Blumenthal—should be made to get down on his hands and knees and lick the Irkutsk-to-Vladivostok train.

† † †

The trip had its compensations, however, even without a pair of prominent political figures lapping the couplings. I'd bought a whole compartment so I could loll around in my boxer shorts while keeping myself
hydrated with Stolichnaya. Though this didn't taste exactly like the
Stolichnaya we get stateside. Stolichnaya may have a paint-thinner subsidiary.

There was a shabby dining car about half a mile up the train, and,
though the galley was dirty enough to start a worm farm, the food was
good. I don't know what the food was, but it was good. It was a bird, I
think, and had a great flavor, and I only got a little sick afterward.

I'd brought my own food along, too, purchased in Irkutsk's Martha
Stewart grocery. And when the train made its brief stops, I could go to
the market stalls that lined the station platforms and buy fresh bread,
homemade pickles, smoked fish, and—even in Ust'-Urluk, on the fron-
tier of Outer Mongolia—Pepsi. I also bought carbonated Russian min-
eral water. This tastes like Spic-and-Span, but I could shake the bottles
and use my thumb to direct squirts of household-cleaner-type liquid at
the cockroaches eating Hong Kong tea biscuits under my bunk.

Whether everyone's better off in Russia these days, I still don't
know. But the people in the market stalls certainly were. In 1990, Cato
Institute, the libertarian think tank, reported on this same rail trip, saying: "At isolated rural stops, peasants burst onto trains to buy oranges,
apples, and milk from a train staff eager to pocket additional rubles."
Now the bursting was in the opposite direction.

The stops came every few hours at little cities which appeared
without preamble in the wilderness: Ulan-Ude, Mogocha, Birobidzhan.
They are ugly little cities, with immense factories where suburbs usually are, and everybody lives where you'd expect the stores and offices
to be. So devoted to standardization were the Soviets that high-rise concrete worker housing was built even in Siberia, with nothing but land
in every direction. The cities of the Russian east are the only places on
earth that need urban sprawl.

And what a place to sprawl in. There is confounding beauty here
in bewildering amounts. Half a day was required just to skirt the southern shore of Lake Baikal. The scale of Siberia is baffling. And so is every-

thing else about it. Lake Baikal has seals—1,500 miles from an ocean. Using a pair of flippers to drag tail all the way from the Bering Strait must make a Trans-Siberian train ride seem comfortable.

We went east from the lake, through sandy plains and pine barrens, then into meadows and birch groves, riding through them all night. If the Iroquois had had these—and a capitalist free market—they might have founded a General Motors of canoes.

In the morning we were out on the rolling grasslands. You could imagine the Mongol hordes riding their horses across the horizon if you wanted. I preferred to imagine the Mongol hordes playing golf. Business—even the professional-sports business—is an improvement on war. The Mongols would have been better received if they'd invaded on a PGA Tour. (And they would have won, too, what with practicing on 100,000-yard fairways. Par 900.)

We traveled into the Yablonovyy Mountains and the wilds north of Manchuria, following the Amazar River and threading between heights on a roadbed chipped from the riverbank cliffs. The Amazar looked to have white-water-rafting potential. But Russia has not yet reached the stage of development where its yuppies feel the need to risk their lives on weekends. In an economy as Mafia-infested as Russia's, they get enough danger 9 to 5.

Beyond the mountains was the *taiga,* the boreal forest that covers an area of Russia larger than Western Europe. Anton Chekhov said, "You don't pay attention to it on the first day of travel; in the second and third you are surprised; the fourth and fifth day give you a feeling you'll never get out of that monster of the Earth."

Of course, Chekhov was a fussy little Western European type at heart. To an American the *taiga* just looks like God got carried away with the recipe for northern Maine. The only thing monstrous about the Russian woods is that they bring back memories of summer camp.

There were, however, no signs of sing-along or capture the flag or any other social activity outside the train windows. Siberia is mostly a giant resource being unused. And it's not being unused in a sweet, preservationist way. All along the Trans-Siberian Railroad's tracks were huge pieces of discarded industrial equipment; big, twisted nests of twelve-foot I beams and enormous shattered chunks of rebar and cement. It was as if the gargantuan Soviet industrial complex had been trying to use Siberia and kept getting it wrong and would then—Godzilla-like—crumple up its mistakes and throw them away.

There were also lone graves along the tracks, neatly fenced and marked with handsome headstones. Maybe these are hero workers who died while getting it wrong. Or maybe these are Trans-Siberian bathroom tragedies—people who stood too close to the track when someone in a passing train was on the can.

I would have asked my fellow passengers about the graves, but nobody spoke English. People were friendly, and they shrugged and smiled at me, but for four days I couldn't actually say anything to anybody, and for a yammering mick like myself, this was as bad as AA.

Our route took us along the Amur River plain, and the country opened into an empty paradise. It was land that seemed to have been made for a human habitation and enterprise that never came—ungrazed prairies, unfarmed bottom land, unfished trout streams, unhunted bird covers. In the marshes, acres of wild irises bloomed, fated never to join a bouquet. Plenty of wilderness has been spoiled by man. This had been spoiled by lack of him.

However, beyond the Amur River and for the last 400 miles south to Vladivostok, the countryside has been domesticated. That is, I saw a person every fifteen or twenty minutes. Usually the person was a babushka, one of those Russian grandmothers who look like Boris Yeltsin in a dress. There were babushkas hanging laundry, babushkas chopping wood, babushkas in bikinis weeding their gardens, babushkas riding in motorcycle sidecars. It was Granny Nation. The men I saw were mostly piloting those motorcycles—motorcycles seemed to be the only form of transport. I didn't even see tractors. Hay was still being cut by hand. There was one ancient bearded fellow, leaning on his scythe and watching the train, who looked too much like Father Time. Russia needs modernizing. I'd rather deal with Father Daylight Saving Time, who wears shorts and shades, and carries a weed whacker.

The land was good. But like so many good things in Russia, nothing good had ever been done with it. And I didn't see any young people around to bring in Toros and Lawn Boys to replace the grim reaper. I suppose the young people are off in the cities seeking their fortunes.

† † †

Well, fortune may be found in Russia, and fame and beauty and truth, and all that. And not just for the young or the mobbed-up or the connected. It could be the best country in the world—richer, roomier, grander than our own. Russia has fine prospects, big possibilities, wonderful potential—everything you could wish for in a future. Also, everything you could dread in a past. The Russians now have the freedom to escape that past and the means to use the freedom. Will they blow it?

Probably. The Russians are, as their history has proven too well, human. Humans can blow anything if they put their minds to it. And there, at the end of my journey, was Vladivostok as an example of things blown.

The great metropolis of Russian Asia occupies a tiara of hills overlooking the Sea of Japan. The headlands embrace one of the finest deepwater ports in the Far East. It is a magnificent site for a city—too bad there's not one there. Vladivostok is St. Petersburg without the monuments, palaces, and art. It is Moscow without the money, crowds, and fun. Vladivostok looks like, in the words of Russian writer Gleb Uspensky, "what could have happened to San Francisco if the Bolsheviks ever got there." Fortunately, they were stopped in Berkeley.

Vladivostok should be among the Pacific Rim's foremost marketplaces for food, fuel, and raw materials, but Soviet military paranoia kept the docks closed to foreign trade until 1990. Now the town is notable only for Chinese border smuggling, Mafia activity, trash on the beach (Vladi*dump*stok), and a Japanese restaurant with the second-worst-imaginable name: Nagasaki. About half the Russian navy sits in the harbor, out of money to go anywhere. The people who do have money, the New Russians, are building themselves lumpy condominium towers. The only architectural grace notes are balcony railings made from rows of vodka bottles set in mortar.

I had been in Russia for a month, and my ideas about reform had been refined and simplified. By this time, I wanted to enact just one basic and fundamental reform—the one my dissident acquaintances, Donna and Carlos, had attempted in Cuba. I wanted to leave. And here is a change that has taken place in Russia that is unequivocally good. I was free to go.

8

HOW TO MAKE NOTHING
FROM EVERYTHING

❖

TANZANIA

The problem in Russia is how to reform an economic system. The problem in many places is how to get one. The World Bank claims that some two billion of the world's citizens live on $1 a day or less. These people have livelihoods governed by the plain rules of subsistence. They don't buy, sell, or trade much because they don't have much to buy, sell, or trade. They're poor.

And nowhere have people been poor longer or more thoroughly than in Africa. According to World Bank statistics, the ten poorest countries on earth are all African. Not one of the fifty-three members of the Organization of African Unity—not even diamond-infested South Africa or oil-soaked Libya—has a decent general standard of living. And this is the continent where man evolved, where the first great civilization arose. This is the human hometown.

I went to Tanzania in February 1997. Probably every child whose parents weren't rich enough has been told, "We're rich in other ways." Tanzania is fabulously rich in other ways.

The Tarangire reserve is a thousand square miles of branching river valleys sheltering some of the last great elephant herds in the world.

To the northwest, the wildlife-covered Serengeti Plain stretches away forever more, oceanic in its flatness. The only landmarks are the kopjes, wind- and rain-polished bubbles of granite ranging from back porch to state capitol building in size. At night lightning bolts can be seen eighty miles away on the shores of Lake Victoria.

The nearby Ngorongoro Crater is a collapsed twin of Kilimanjaro, a mountaintop chasm 1,500 feet deep and ten miles across, containing a miniature perfect universe of grassland and rain forest.

One dawn I rode a dizzy-pitched, rut-ulcerated switchback road into the crater. Maasai boys were leading a hundred cattle down to a salt lick. The young herdsmen were dressed in pairs of plaid blankets, with one worn as kilt and the other as toga. Beadwork swung at their necks and dangled from the piercings at the tops and bottoms of their ears. Each carried a long stick with the war-lance aplomb young boys give to long sticks. The air was clean and sharp. The clear sky was just beginning to light up. The cowbells plinked like a half-audible cheery tune. There are probably worse things to be than a Maasai boy taking cattle into the Ngorongoro Crater at dawn. Although the usual Maasai diet of curdled milk and cow's blood wouldn't provide enough roughage for an American my age.

There is an all-day, all-night rush hour of animals in Tanzania: Cape buffalo jam, zebra lock, and wildebeest backup. Thomson's gazelles bound about with a suspicious black swipe on their sides—enough like the Nike trademark to raise questions about sponsorship. Warthogs scuttle with their tails up straight in the air, endlessly acknowledging some foul in the game of hogball. Hyenas are all over the place, nonchalant but shifty, in little groups meandering not quite aimlessly—greasers at the mall. Hippos lie in the water holes in piles, snoring, stinking, sleeping all day. The correct translation for the Greek word "hippopotamus" is not "river horse" but "river first husband." And lions doze where they like, waking up every day or two to do that famous ecological favor of culling the weak, old, and sick. (Do lions ever debate the merits of weak versus old versus sick? "Call me oversophisticated, but I think the sick wildebeest have a certain piquancy, like a ripe cheese.")

† † †

The nation of Tanzania might seem to be a Beulah Land—if you stick to
the parks and the game preserves, and get back in your hotel by sunset.
It can be done. I have a fatuous article from the March 2, 1997, Sunday
New York Times travel section in which some publishing-industry pooh-
bah tells how he and his wife flew in chartered planes to the Ngorongoro
and the Serengeti, "and returned dazed by the wealth of wildlife and
the vastness of the terrain."

But, putting the tourist daze aside, Tanzania is a truly poor country. I arrived at Kilimanjaro Airport, near that mountain but not much
else. It was evening, time for the overseas flights to land, and mine had,
and that was it. The airport is one of those grand, 1970s reinforced-
concrete foreign-aid projects now going grim from mildew and falling
to pieces. Surely it is one of the few international airports without a visible clock. There are no hustling taximen or begging children outside
the door. It costs fifty cents to enter the airport grounds, and they can't
afford it.

A safari guide named John collected me in the minivan in which
we'd spend the next two weeks. It was a beaten, slew-wheeled, butt-
sprung vehicle. John managed to keep it working (except for flat tires
and getting stuck, and a rear hatch that sprang open in a remote corner
of the Maasai Steppe with a lion on one side of the road and an irritated
mother elephant on the other).

We drove for an hour and a half through the smoky African night.
Smoky is not an adjective chosen for artistic, evocative reasons. According to Tanzanian government figures, 90 percent of the country's energy generation is just plain lighting fires. Virtually all the cooking,
heating, lighting, and manufacturing in Tanzania is accomplished by
the same method you use with burgers on weekends.

We arrived on the outskirts of Arusha, the principal city in northern Tanzania. Here was another stained and flaking assistance-to-
developing-nations structure—the best hotel. No air-conditioning, no
screens, and not much happening in the bar.

In the morning we drove to Arusha proper, a low sprawl of ne-
glected stucco buildings, with here and there a large government office
made of that inevitable aid-donor cement. Half the businesses down-

town had something to do with doing something with tourists, and the rest sold used refrigerators. The thin and sluggardly traffic was made up of colonial-era Land Rovers and large, woebegone trucks with obscure South Asian brand names. A few trucks were full of farm produce. A few were full of people. All the others were broken down by the side of the road, with men lying under them, occasionally working on the truck mechanicals, but usually sleeping. In the center of town, in a traffic circle where one bus seemed to be permanently circling, was a monument to the fact that Arusha is, geographically speaking, halfway between Cairo and Cape Town. This is something that Arusha has never been accused of being, metaphorically speaking.

Outside the small business district, the roads were lined with scrapwood and palm-thatch stalls, some with signs that overreached the mark—HOLLYWOOD BAR—others selling modest goods, such as scrap wood and palm thatch. Vendors who couldn't afford sheds sold goods more modest yet: pieces of bicycle tire and strips of rubber cut from old inner tubes. There were a few industrial buildings at the city's edge, but nothing industrious seemed to be happening in them. An open-air market was busy but looked more full of people than goods. John laughed to point out a Christian revival tent next to a brewery.

The Tanzanian men wore shirts and slacks that had a clothing-drive look, but, if so, they were picked from the Goodwill bin with more taste than most Seattle bands show and more use of detergent, too. The Tanzanian women had on T-shirts or Western blouses, but also *kangas*—yard-wide, twelve-foot lengths of brightly printed cotton cut in two to make a skirt and shawl. The *kangas* were spotless, even when the women were working in the fields (something Tanzanian women have an equal opportunity to do; in fact, there seems to be an affirmative-action program in force). It's not a dirty country—if you don't count dust.

It's not a squalid country. There are no droves of the crippled and diseased, no beseeching for alms, no pestering of strangers, no evident public violence. Tanzania is not a nation suffering social collapse, but I'm not absolutely sure I mean that as a compliment. There's the sad possibility that they just don't have the cash for booze, drugs, and handguns.

Seeing the people in Arusha going about their business—or lack thereof—should have been more depressing than it was. Describing the

English poor of 150 years ago, George Eliot noted "the leaden, blank-eyed gaze of unexpectant want." But with Tanzanians, there was a twinkle in that gaze. The women walked down the roads bearing all the burden of Tanzanian material possessions. These are few enough, but still a lot to carry on your head. And more often than not, the women were smiling. Their *kangas* swayed and billowed. The printed cloths are embellished with slogans or catch phrases, such as PENYE KUKU WENGI HAKUMWAGWIMTAMA: "Don't dry the millet where the chickens are." Children rushed home from school as gleefully as if they were headed for rec rooms full of Sega games and *Anastasia* videos. (Tanzanian kids all wear school uniforms, in case you think that regulation is the answer to all ills.) Just the names of things in the country are cheerful: the No Competition grocery, the New Toyota Shoe Shine, the Buy-n-Bye minimart, and a long-distance motor coach christened So What. Merchants are nice to the point of chagrin over any commercial aspect of a visit to their stores. One shop had an apologetic sign posted in the window:

You are my friend
Yes
You are my relative
Yes thank you
But my business does not know you

A few weeks after I left the country, Hillary and Chelsea Clinton came to Arusha on a fly-through tour of Africa. The silly young daughter of the President of the United States told an audience at Kilimanjaro Airport that in America "we have a big problem with people not thinking they have a future. Young women and young men . . . there's a lot of hopelessness." The Tanzanians were too nice to pelt her with things.

Beyond the town, people were even poorer. Arusha is green, irrigated by the waters of Kilimanjaro's smaller companion, Mount Meru, which hulks 15,000 feet over the city. The farmland is lush, but the farms are hodgepodges: a banana tree here, a cassava plant there, here a maize stalk, there a bean sprout, everywhere a chicken (and several children chasing it). Hollow logs hang lengthwise in the branches of the taller trees. Fetishes of some kind, I assumed, but I had the sense to ask John.

They're beehives. One whole chapter in the *Tanzanian National Budget* is devoted to beekeeping. People can't afford sugar. Sugar sells for twenty-eight cents a pound.

The average Tanzanian smallholding is less than one and a quarter acres. The homesteads are just shacks topped with sheets of tin or one-room bunkers built from very irregular concrete blocks made, one by one, in wooden molds.

Farther west, the land gets worse, rocky and dry and barren as a stairwell. Goats seem to be the only crop. Here, people don't have the luxury of shacks. The tiny houses are thatch roofed, with walls made from stick-work lattices, the spaces between the sticks filled with little rocks, and the whole plastered over with mud if—water being scarce— the family can afford mud.

Women sat by the side of the road, hitting rocks with stumpy hammers, making gravel by hand—to give some idea of the value of labor hereabouts. Little boys stood resolutely in the middle of nowhere next to gunnysacks of charcoal that the passing trucks can't burn and the walkers and bicyclers can't carry. If you wonder where all the old, fat-tired, one-speed, backpedal-to-brake American bicycles went, the Huffys and the Schwinns, they're in Tanzania, complete with reflectors, mud flaps, rocket-shaped battery lamps, and handlebar baskets with little brothers stuffed in them.

The road to the Rift Valley is paved and reasonably smooth from lack of traffic, but it's only as wide as an alleyway. At Makuyuni ("Place of the Fig Tree"—and there's not one) is the turnoff to Tanzania's most important tourist attractions: the Ngorongoro Crater, the Olduvai Gorge, the Serengeti. And at Makuyuni, the pavement illogically ends. We headed west across the Rift Valley on a road that was just a pile of rocks—like driving lengthwise on a New England stone wall. We were slammed so badly inside the van that John steered out into the arid, rutty bush, where we were engulfed in dust, dropped into holes, and launched aloft by boulders. John went back to the road until we could take it no more, then back to the bush. And so we traveled to Ngorongoro, veering from the Scylla of African topography to the Charybdis of the Tanzania Highway Department, a journey of thirty-odd miles that took three hours.

In the Rift, the Maasai still live with their livestock inside corrals of piled thorn bush, in flat-topped, windowless hovels made from straw smeared with cow dung and entered through a crawl hole.

The Greek Cynic philosopher Diogenes is said to have slept in a barrel. And supposedly it was a happy revelation to him that he could drink out of his cupped palms and thus throw away one more possession: his mug. But Diogenes had a barrel, a fairly complex piece of technology. Compared with the way some Tanzanians exist, Diogenes was a Sharper Image customer.

Statistically, there are poorer countries than Tanzania; that is, countries so chaotic that all their statisticians have been chased up trees—Liberia, Somalia, Congo—and countries which are so reclusive—North Korea— that it's impossible to tell what's going on. But Tanzania is right at the bottom of the aforementioned barrel, which would probably have to be imported from an industrially advanced nation. According to the *World Bank's 1996 World Development Report,* Tanzania is poorer than Uganda, poorer than Chad, poorer than godforsaken Burundi. Haiti is 80 percent wealthier than Tanzania. Papua New Guinea is almost ten times more prosperous, never mind that some of its citizens have just discovered the wheel.

Tanzania is so poor that its poverty is hard to calculate. Eighty-five percent of the workforce is employed in agriculture, if *employed* is the word. They grow things. They eat them. This does not generate W-2 forms or register on the stock exchange that Tanzania doesn't have. ("Money and capital markets" are to come "in the near future," says the Ministry of Finance.)

There's a sad little econometric debate about Tanzania's per-capita gross domestic product. Tanzanian government figures (given foggy population projections and a Tanzanian shilling with an exchange rate that varies between worth-little and worthless) work out to approximately $128 a person a year. The World Bank believes it's about $117. The CIA, in its *1997 World Factbook,* estimates Tanzanian per-capita GDP at $650. But this is from the organization that—as late as 1989—thought the Soviet Union's per-capita GDP was nearly as high as Britain's. The

CIA uses something called the purchasing-power-parity (PPP) method to measure gross domestic product. PPP is supposed to compensate for the lower living costs found in poorer countries. It's like having your boss tell you, "Instead of a raise, why don't you move to a worse neighborhood—your rent will be lower and so will your car payments, as soon as someone steals your Acura."

Let's take the Tanzanians' own figures—it's their country after all: $128 per-capita GDP. And here we see the fallacy on the bottom line of utopian economic ideas. If theoretic social justice were enacted—if all the income in this nation were divided with complete fairness and perfect equity—everybody would get thirty-five cents a day. This (using the PPP method, by the way) is half a pack of Sportsman cigarettes and nine ounces of dried beans.

I mentioned the thirty-five-cents figure to an American friend, who said, "Christ! You can find that much lying in the road." Not in Tanzania you can't. There's nothing on or near the roads. The things we throw away—broken scraps of plastic, bits of tin sheeting, snips of copper wire—are collected by the Maasai and made into the centerpieces of beadwork necklaces and bracelets. These are sold by old women at the tourist spots for about a dollar apiece. Sell one and that's three days of per-capita gross domestic product.

There are probably better ways to measure extreme poverty than GDP. Tanzania has a population slightly less than California's and is slightly more than twice California's size, and Tanzania has 1,403 miles of paved roads. The District of Columbia has 1,104 miles (although, to be fair, our capital has worse potholes than their capital does). Telephone lines for Tanzania's approximately 29 million people number 85,756. Cell-phone service, I was told, was coming "next month," which is when you usually get a dial tone. Outside the cities, there are no phones, just three shortwave-radio call stations.

I sat in a hotel bar one night, listening to the howling, shrieking distortions of a ham-radio set on which a frantic husband in the Serengeti was explaining that the tour guide's jeep had gone into a hyena den, and he thought his wife's spine was fractured. Garbled plans were being made to fly the wife hundreds of miles to Nairobi, Kenya, for medical treatment. At last count, there was one doctor for every 28,271 people in Tanzania, and, I suppose, 28,270 patients were in line ahead of the poor woman with the fractured spine.

Only 260,171 Tanzanian households or businesses have electricity, and that electricity arrives with the frequency and predictability of Publishers Clearing House sweepstakes wins. Speaking of such, the average Tanzanian receives 2.14 pieces of mail per annum. In 1990, the most recent year in which the Tanzanian government has managed to count these things, 3,314 cars, 2,385 four-wheel-drive vehicles, and 6,445 trucks were imported. Number produced domestically: zero.

Five percent of Tanzania's teenagers are enrolled in high school (though this is better than the percentage of American high-school students actually paying attention). The average Tanzanian family devotes 70 percent of its expenditures to food. In Cuba, where they claimed the American embargo was starving them, that figure was 50 percent. And a U.S. family allots about 14.5 percent of its spending to food—$6,592, which is 1,739 Big Mac meals and a large order of fries, and may explain why Americans are so fat. Tanzanians are not. According to the World Bank, 29 percent of Tanzanian children age five or less are underweight.

Why is Tanzania so poor? The nation is by no means overpopulated. The countryside is mostly dry plains and mild badlands, a sort of tropical South Dakota with seacoast, but it's not infertile. Tanzania is a net exporter of edibles. Agricultural products make up 75 percent of foreign-trade earnings. Forty percent of the country is meadow or pastureland, enough to supply all the burgers missing from local lunch breaks. And Tanzania has resources: tin, phosphates, iron ore, coal, diamonds, gemstones, gold, natural gas, and nickel, says the CIA World Factbook, and salt, gypsum, and cobalt, adds the U.S. State Department's 1997 Country Commercial Guide. Plus, there's said to be hydroelectric potential. (I did notice a lot of water running downhill—as it tends to do.)

Tanzania has not suffered the wars, civil and otherwise, that have riven sub-Saharan Africa. It did fight one brief conflict against Uganda, in the good cause of ousting Idi Amin. But peace has been the general rule since independence. Domestic peace, as well. Tanzania isn't wracked by tribal conflicts. Julius K. Nyerere, the high-minded and high-handed schoolteacher who ruled the country for its first twenty-four years, opposed tribalism and was helped in his opposition to tribes by the fact that Tanzania has more than 120 of the things. None is large enough to predominate. Besides the well-known Maasai, there are the Ha, the Hehe, the Gogo, etc., etc. It's silly enough to murder somebody because he's a Serb or a Croat, but to kill a person for being a Gogo is much too absurd for the sensible and even-tempered Tanzanians.

Tanganyika, as it used to be called, did not have a very bad colonial history, as those things go. The Germans arrived late, in 1885, and left early, in 1918, after muffing World War I. Local people fought the Germans persistently—in the Hehe Rebellion of 1891, the Maji Maji War of 1905, and a variety of other spirited (and oddly named) uprisings. The British took over Tanganyika as a League of Nations protectorate rather than as a colony, so the Tanganyikans were spared the influx of wastrel coffee planters, lunatic white hunters, and Isak Dinesen that plagued Kenya. Resistance to British rule was nonviolent and well-organized, and the Brits left in 1961 with a minimum of puling and fuss.

Tanzania does have various of the other evils on which Third World poverty is blamed—corruption, for instance. Tanzania has that. But so do Newt Gingrich and Al Gore. The wild, venal jobbery of politicians doesn't, by itself, make a country poor. Nor does colonial exploitation. Virginia and Massachusetts were colonies, too, and more effectively exploited than Tanzania was.

Then there's socioeconomic lag, the late introduction of the ideas that propel the developed world. Yet Tanzania, or at least its coast and its islands such as Zanzibar, were exposed to science, math, and, technology by Muslims, beginning in the eighth century. That's 800 years before anybody who could read or recite multiplication tables arrived in North America. True, Arab traders came for the purposes of stealing slaves and pillaging ivory. But the harbingers of civilization rarely go anywhere in order to deliver Girl Scout cookies. The poverty of Tanzania is a puzzle.

Lack of education is, of course, a problem. But Tanzania's literacy rate is estimated to be almost 68 percent. Even if that estimate is overhopeful, the proportion of Tanzanians who can read and write now is higher than the proportion of Europeans who could do so at the beginning of the Industrial Age. Also, illiterate is not ignorant. The most backwoodsy of Tanzanians speaks a tribal tongue or two, plus Kiswahili and, often, English. At my tourist hotel on the rim of the Ngorongoro, I asked the bartender why Tanzania was so poor. He said "lack of education" and then held forth with a fifteen-minute dissertation on the mathematics of the exchange rate that left me heavily shortchanged and in some doubt about his theory.

One answer is that Tanzania's *not* poor—by the standards of human experience. Admittedly, these are grim standards, but until creatures from other planets really do invade, we have no others. The World Bank claims that 48 percent of rural Tanzanians and 11 percent of the country's city dwellers are living in "absolute poverty," which the World Bank defines as an "income level below which adequate standards of nutrition, shelter, and personal amenities cannot be assured." But when and where on earth were the poor ever guaranteed three hots and a flop, let alone "personal amenities"? According to the Organization for Economic Cooperation and Development, Tanzania's current per-capita gross domestic product is something like Japan's or Brazil's at the beginning of the nineteenth century, and about the same as that of India or China in 1950.

Tanzanians live the way people usually have since we quit being apes. No, they live better. Tanzanian life expectancy is approximately 52 years. Life expectancy in the United States was 52.6 years in 1911. The infant-mortality rate in Tanzania is 84 deaths per 1,000 live births. The American infant-mortality rate was 85.8 as recently as 1920.

After we had crossed the Rift Valley, John and I drove to the Olduvai Gorge, where Louis and Mary Leakey did their archeological work, showing just how ancient mankind is. More than a million years ago *homo erectus*—who resembled modern man at least as much as Neil Young does—was wandering around here on open savannas very similar to those of modern Tanzania.

The hominid tools on display in the museum at the Olduvai Visitor Center are not reassuring as to the lifestyle of our early relations. You'd have to be an expert to tell they're tools at all and not just stones that broke funny. Of course, there's always the possibility that the Leakeys were pulling our leg and Ralph Reed is right, and man was created by divine miracle last Wednesday at noon. But I was watching CNN, and something would have been mentioned. Anyway, the stuff that Grandfather Erectus was working with in his Paleolithic basement shop gives you a second thought about what poverty really means. I wouldn't care to be turned loose in the African underbrush with nothing but a couple of sharp rocks—not even for an hour and knowing that John was parked back by the road with our box lunches.

Man was born into a state of nature, and nature, I'm sad to report, is woefully underdeveloped in an economic sense. The wildlife herds were sad reminders that there are only two ways to obtain a thing; either agree upon a price for it or take it by butting heads. Wildebeest must depend upon the latter method. Due to a lack of pockets, wildebeest cannot carry cash or credit cards. Among animals, only marsupials have pockets, and then just to keep their young inside. And there are various difficulties, practical and theoretical, with an economic system based on inch-long blind and hairless kangaroos.

No medium of trade is one reason that wildebeest aren't very productive. No brains is another. About the only thing wildebeest can do to increase productivity—of crap and other wildebeest—is eat more. This they accomplish to the best of their ability, standing around all day with their choppers in the groceries. Leaves and grass aren't much more nutritious for them than they are for us. Consider how much lettuce and oat bran you would need to gain weight. Consider how much a 500-pound wildebeest would.

Wildebeest also sleep, but not peacefully. A significant minority of creatures on the African veldt aren't grazers or browsers, or members of PETA. They're hungry, too. And buff. Running down a 500-pound herbivore is an excellent exercise program. Plus, John said that cheetahs and leopards will kill—as will many a lesser hunter in a duck blind—for fun. So wildebeest wake up a lot in the night, and when they wake up, they eat. They mate, of course. Once a year. Fun-o. They migrate to find other things to eat. They go to water holes, but these are haunted by crocodiles, lions, jackals, wild dogs, hyenas, and minibuses full of tourists waiting to see the violence and strong-language portions of safari. That's about it for the wildebeest lifestyle. The young ones frisk, but they get over it.

Nature is poor, and the Tanzanians haven't gotten nearly far enough away from nature. Coming back from the Serengeti, John and I drove by a small airport. There were vultures on the landing strip—never a good sign. We descended into the Rift to the marshy village of Mto-wa-Mbu, which means "Mosquito River," a name of stunning obviousness, like calling Kansas "Flat State."

We went to the market, a jolly, if unhygienic, huddle of teetering sheds and precarious vegetable heaps. I was taking notes on food costs. This nosiness might have raised suspicions or hackles elsewhere, but Tanzanians have experienced more than three decades of foreign-aid mavens, development experts, and academic investigators of Third Worldery. They got with the program at once. Three or four helpful loafers showed me into every corner of the bazaar, and merchants gave price quotations with the speed and facility of NYSE specialist brokers.

The market smelled. The whole of Tanzania smells. It's an odor of smoked, spoiled milk with undertones of compost and beef jerky. Amazingly, it's not a bad smell. But it's not the smell of success.

Along the main street, Mto-wa-Mbu resembles a ghost town in the American West—if cowboys had had a marvelous sense of color, and also if they'd stuck around. Mosquito River is fully populated. Its leaning, sagging, dilapidated buildings are made of cinder block. This isn't usually a "rickety" building material but, with lack of mortar and abstention from use of the level or plumb bob, a tumbledown effect can be achieved.

All the small towns in Tanzania look like hell. The crudity of ordinary things is astonishing: fences, gates, window frames, doors, and let's not mention toilets. Every place is makeshift, improvised, jury-rigged, askew (and in the case of toilets, amok). Americans are so querulous about mass production that we forget the precision afforded by machinery.

Handmade often means made with ten thumbs. Examine the shelves you put up in your garage. Now take a log and a machete and build them.

Lots of things are started in Tanzania. Not much is finished. Scattered everywhere are roofless masonry walls—literally a few bricks shy of a load. Paint appears on the fronts of buildings but never on the sides or backs. The country seems as if it was built by hippies. And in a sense, it was.

Julius Nyerere was born two years after Timothy Leary. Nyerere, called *Mwalimu,* "the teacher," was elected president of Tanganyika in 1962, just when Professor Leary began advocating LSD use at Harvard. Nobody has ever accused Nyerere of being a "head." He's lived an abstemious life (although he does have twenty-four grandchildren). But some of the same generational fluff filled the skulls of both Julius and Tim.

Nyerere embraced the collectivist ideology that has run riot in our century, and from this embrace was born a particularly spacey and feckless socialism call *ujamaa,* or "familyhood." Excerpts from Nyerere's writing sound like a 1969 three-bong-hit rap from somebody going off to found an organic tofu-growing commune: "Our agricultural organization would be predominately that of cooperative living and working for the good of all. . . . Some degree of specialization would be possible, with one member being, for example, a carpenter." Dig it. "If every individual is self-reliant . . . then the whole nation is self-reliant." Heavy.

The 1967 Arusha Declaration, a government manifesto cataloging the right-on goals and groovy ideals of *ujamaa,* states that agriculture and animal husbandry are where the Tanzanian economy is at. Industrialization would mean a bummer money trip. In the words of the tuned-in *Mwalimu,* "We make a mistake in choosing money—something we do not have—to be the big instrument of our development." Development being something else they don't have.

Issa G. Shivji, a law professor at the University of Dar es Salaam, has written an article summing up *ujamaa.* He says, "There were two central premises of this ideology: equality of human beings and developmentalism." Equality is the thirty-five cents a day mentioned earlier. Developmentalism sounds like some even worse offshoot of Scientology. "The problem," Shivji continues, "was that the ideology of *ujamaa* was not supported by any explicit social theory," and that the Tanzanian government "pursued this policy logically and consistently."

In other words, *ujamaa* made about as much sense as most things in the 1960s. Slogans were coined, such as the Hitlerish *"Uhuru na Kazi,"* which sounds even more Hitlerish when translated: "Freedom and Work." Price controls were instituted, lasting until 1986. In 1981 farmers were being forced to sell corn to the government for 20 percent of market value, and that market value is nothing to write to Iowa about. In Mto-wa-Mbu, price-uncontrolled corn now sells for twenty-three cents a pound. Local industries were nationalized, foreign companies were expropriated, and compensation for these takings was, in the words of the U.S. State Department, "extremely slow and ponderous." Much of commerce met the same ponderous, if not so slow, fate. East Indian and Arab minorities were the targets. The history textbook used in Tanzanian public high schools blandly states, "The monopolistic position of Indian wholesale traders was abolished."

A program of "villagization" was begun, which sounds benign enough: "Hey, get a picket fence." The idea was to persuade rural Tanzanians to move to 8,000 "familyhood villages," *ujamaa vijijini,* where the government could provide them with water and education, and, by the way, keep an eye on everybody. The planned communities did not come up to plan: The water didn't arrive; neither did the education, nor the people who were supposed to move there. When persuasion wouldn't work, force was used. By the end of the '70s, more than 65 percent of the population in the Tanzanian countryside had been deported to the *ujamaa vijijini* gulag. But, this being Tanzania, the population just wandered away again and built houses of their own in the bush.

Other vaporous ideas were being tried. According to *Ideology and Development in Africa,* a terribly fair-minded book published by the Yale University Press in the early '80s, "There was a sharp reorientation of medical outlays away from high-cost, Western-model, curative medicine and toward rural, paramedical, and preventive health care. By 1974 the fraction of the health budget allocated to hospitals had dropped from 80 percent in the late 1960s to 50 percent," with results such as the hyena hole/fractured spine crisis I overheard on the shortwave radio.

Meanwhile, the Tanzanian economy went concave. Tanzanian National Accounts figures indicate that the per-capita GDP has yet to return to its 1976 level. And the purchasing power of the legal minimum wage fell 80 percent between 1969 and 1987. So another answer to the question, "Why is Tanzania so poor?" is *ujamaa*—they planned it.

They planned it, and we paid for it. Rich countries underwrote Tanzanian economic idiocy. There's a certain kind of gullible and self-serious person who's put in charge of foreign aid. (e.g., ex-head of the World Bank Robert McNamara. I rest my case.) This type was entranced by modest, articulate Julius Nyerere and the wonderful things he was going to do. American political-science professor Ali Mazrui dubbed it "Tanzaphilia." In the midst of the villagization ugliness, Tanzania was receiving Official Direct Assistance (or ODA, as it's called by the sucker/succor professionals) of $300 million a year in big, fat 1975 dollars. That was twenty dollars a head, and it wouldn't surprise me if twenty dollars was about what it cost to build a *vijijini* hovel, catch a Tanzanian, and stick him inside.

Countries such as Sweden were particularly smitten, seeing in *ujamaa* a version of their own sanctimonious social order, but with better weather and fewer of those little meatballs on toothpicks. By the beginning of the 1990s, Sweden, Norway, and Denmark were sending Tanzania more than $320 million a year—nine times the amount of American aid.

Then there is the aforementioned World Bank, financed by the United States, Japan, and other wealthy nations. Its purpose is to loan money to underdeveloped areas, and I can't understand why it won't loan money to me, as I am in many areas as underdeveloped as it gets. The World Bank charges interest rates like your dad does when you borrow a twenty. Thirty-three percent of the projects funded by the World Bank are considered failures by the bank itself. The World Bank thus operates on the same business principles as a Reagan-era savings and loan. And apparently on the same moral principles—because villagization was just fine with the World Bank; in fact, it had already proposed something on that order in the reams of busybody economic advice with which international organizations pester the globe. How would we like it if the Organization of African Unity told us to get out of our suburbs and move downtown?

The World Bank loaned Tanzania oodles of money. Further oodles were loaned by other kindly aid agencies. Tanzanians now have a total foreign debt equal to almost two years' worth of everything produced in the country. Tanzania is $7.4 billion in hock. The money will be repaid . . . when Rush Limbaugh becomes secretary general of the UN.

But don't worry, the International Monetary Fund is on the case. If a country gets in trouble by borrowing too much from places like the World Bank, then it qualifies for an IMF loan. As long as Tanzania promises to abide, more or less, by free-market guidelines and doesn't print more worthless paper money than it absolutely has too, the IMF will "help."

Tanzania has been smothered in help. It's received loans, grants, programs, projects, an entire railroad from the Chinese government (running 1,200 miles to nowhere in particular), and just plain cash. In 1994, by World Bank tally, foreign aid made up 29.1 percent of the Tanzanian GDP, more than the budget of the Tanzanian government. Whatever that government does, we better-off citizens of the world foot the bill. And we've been doing it for thirty-seven years.

Tanzania is said by Africa scholar Sanford Ungar to be "the most-aided country in all of Africa." In the period immediately after independence, Tanzania was getting half a billion dollars a year in aid. Between 1970 and 1989, the CIA estimates, another $10.8 billion arrived. According to the World Bank, $5.4 billion more was given between 1990 and 1994. This is more than $20 billion, without even trying to pump the figure by adjusting for inflation.

John told me that good farmland in Tanzania sells for a million shillings an acre, about $1,650. Since there are 29 million Tanzanians, $20 billion would have bought each family a larger-than-average farm plot, and everybody could have gone back to doing what they were doing before *ujamaa* was thought of. One more reason that Tanzania is poor is that we've paid them to be.

† † †

John and I took the hammering ride back across the Rift. When I got green from being jiggled, John said, "*Safari* means 'hard journey.'" Dust devils the size of major-league ballparks roamed across the Maasai home-steads. The Maasai didn't bother to glance at these swirling circles of debris, which hit us with high-speed curtains of dirt and filled our van like a window planter. The Rift Valley is the work of continental drift. Africa is being pulled apart. Some day, Tanzania will float away from Rwanda, Burundi, Congo, and Uganda. And Tanzanians deserve the move. Tanzanians deserve a lot of things.

Tanzanians certainly don't deserve what they've had since 1961. The scum tide of *ujamaa* has receded, but it's left behind such things as the awful road to Makuyuni we were on. *Ujamaa* woozy thinking has also left the Tanzanian public mind strewn with intellectual jettison. The na-tional budget, in its "Agriculture" section, asserts that the government is encouraging "private sector participation in production," and, in its "Land" section, claims that the government seeks "to ensure equitable distribu-tion and equal access to land by all citizens." So you're encouraged to farm your private plot, and everyone else is encouraged to farm it, too. The high-school history book gives a disapproving economic analysis that's a combination of marxism and Ross Perotology: "General Tyre Corpora-tion built one tyre factory for the whole of East Africa in Arusha. But soon after this decision, another corporation, Firestone, built a similar factory in Nairobi. This meant the competition of imperialist capital." And even John, who was completely sensible, said, "We have lots of bananas, but we don't do anything with them—just use them for food."

I said, "Huh?" John did tell me, however, that nobody even thought about trying to put the Maasai into *ujamaa* villages. Say what you will against the blood sports, people who spear lions for fun are well-prepared for political rough and tumble.

And Julius Nyerere apologized, which is more than most '60s icons have bothered to do. When he relinquished the presidency in 1985, he said, in his farewell speech, "I failed. Let's admit it."

We drove on from Makuyuni to the Tarangire River basin on the far edge of the Maasai Steppe. The Maasai are fit and towering, despite what is—by the standards of Tanzania itself—a life of extreme hardship. They customarily knock out a couple of their children's teeth so that the kids can be force-fed when they get lockjaw. Administering a liquid diet is easy enough, because Maasai cuisine is nothing but, basically, gravy. It would be food suicide for any other people and may cause even the Maasai a certain amount of indigestion. They call Europeans *iloredaa enjekat,* "those who confine their farts with clothing." The Maasai try to avoid pants and other items of Western apparel. They stick to their tartan wraps. From toddler to granny, they possess a martial bearing. No Maasai man goes outdoors without a lance or quarterstaff. As a result of this public dignity, seeing a Maasai engaged in any ordinary activity— riding a bicycle, walking down the road with an upside-down dishpan on the head, drinking a soda pop—is like seeing a member of the Joint Chefs of Staff skateboarding. But the Maasai do know how to wear plaid-on-plaid. So Ralph Lauren is history if the Maasai ever get start-up capital and a marketing plan.

This brings us to a question much sadder than, "Why are the Tanzanians so poor?" which is, "Why do we care?" An economist would answer that a Maasai line of Lion Kill sportswear would drive down the price of Ralph Lauren Polo clothing and that we, as consumers, would profit. But the idea that the increased productivity of others benefits ourselves is not something most noneconomists understand or believe. It would be nice to think that we worry about Tanzanian poverty out of some *ujamaa*-like altruism—or maybe not, considering the results of *ujamaa.* Anyway, altruism toward strangers is mostly a sentimental and fleeting thing, a small check dashed off to Save the Children. Twenty billion dollars' worth of it is rare. In the cold war days, of course, we were giving money to Tanzania on the theory of: "Pay them to be socialist so they won't be communist and figure out what the difference is later." But now, I'm afraid, the ugly truth is that we care about Tanzanians because they have cool animals.

And they do. John and I spent most of our days together driving around and looking at them. The minivan had a kind of sunroof on legs that, instead of sliding out of the way, popped up to form a metal awning. Thus, while John drove, I would stand in the back and, holding the awning's supports, be bounced and jiggled around like some idiot of the raj in a mechanical howdah. Then, John would shout things such as, "Elephant!"

And I would shout, "No kidding!" because the elephant was twenty feet from us, walking across the road without so much as a sideways glance for traffic. It was an enormous solitary bull. His back was powdered with the dust that elephants fling over themselves to ward off bugs, a pink dust in this case, collecting in the deep gray wrinkles and making his hide look like an old actress betrayed by her pancake base. The bull's tusks were as long as playground slides and thick beyond consideration of billiard rooms or piano keyboards. This fellow could have delivered ivory bowling balls if such a thing were thinkable nowadays. He was the most impressive living creature I've seen—for about a minute. Then he got more impressive, growing an immense erection for no reason. (I hoped it was for no reason. A mad infatuation with our minivan would have been unwelcome.) "Fifth leg," said John. Africa is not the place to soothe insecurities.

The elephant walked off into a forest to strip the bark from the legal-pad-colored fever trees and snap the branches off for snacks. Elephants leave a real mess in the woods. They leave a mess wherever they go. You can see how in a country supported by humble agricultural endeavors, the big browsing animals get killed. And not just by poachers. We love elephants in North America, where they never get into our tomato plants or herbaceous borders, much less destroy the equivalent of our fax machines and desktop computers.

On the other side of the forest and keeping their distance from the tourist track were three more big browsers: black rhinos. There used to be thousands of rhinoceros in Tanzania. Now there are not. The poachers did get the rhinos, as they've gotten most of the rhinos in Africa, all because middle-aged men in Asia believe the powdered horn gives rise— as it were—to potency. Like the world needs middle-aged men with extra hard-ons.

The Cape buffalo are still around in droves, however. Their horns don't seem to do anything for Asians. And it's harder to kill them. The Cape buffalo is just a cow, but a gigantic and furious one—the bovine as superhero, the thing that fantasizing Herefords wish would burst upon the scene between feedlot and Wendy's.

Most of the animals were not shy. They've discovered that the round-footed noisy things on the roads do not claw or bite, and are not—on their outsides, anyway—tasty. We were able to drive to within tollbooth-change-tossing distance of some young lions lying on a sand-bank at a water hole.

"These are stupid young males," said John in a tone that (he being as fiftyish as I) implied the unlikelihood of any other young male type. "They are hunting badly. A female would be behind the sand, not on top of it." The lions didn't seem to care. They didn't seem to care about us, either. And they didn't care about the half dozen other jeeps and vans full of tourists that, seeing us seeing something, eventually gathered around.

A trip to the game lands of Tanzania isn't a lonely, meditative journey. Everything I saw was also being ogled by dozens of other folks from out of town, and they were reeling off enough videotape to start a Blockbuster chain devoted solely to out-of-focus fauna. But the tourists pay money, and money is what it takes to keep the parks and preserves more or less unspoiled, and to buy the bullets to shoot poachers. If the animals of Africa aren't worth more alive to rubberneckers than they're worth dead to farmers, pastoralists, and rhino-horn erection peddlers, then that's that for the *Call of the Wild*. (Besides, romantic as the idea may sound, how solitary do you want to be in the presence of stupid young lions?)

One of the lions got up, walked a couple of steps away, took a leak, and—with no thought for the grace and style that Western-educated people so admire in African wildlife—lay down again in the piss.

At the next water hole, we saw a pair of lions dozing in the midday heat. A herd of wildebeest surrounded them, evidently thirsty yet mindful of trespassing's consequences. "But every now and then," said John, "one of them forgets."

The male lion was crashed out on his back, immobile. The female was lying prone and panting hard. "They have just mated," said John. "Lions mate every six minutes and then gradually decreasing until it's every half hour, every hour, every few hours, and so on for seven days." So the primitive economics of nature may have its compensations.

John had a variety of information about the sex lives of animals. "Do you know why there are so few giraffes?" he asked at a moment when we had quite a few in sight. "They have no natural enemies," John continued. "Their hooves are too sharp. Their legs are too strong, not like wildebeest or zebras. But there are wildebeest and zebras everywhere." He paused. "The guidebooks will not tell you this, but giraffes are homosexual." John had no more said this than the two giraffes closest to us—one definitely female and the other very emphatically male—began to (and never has this slang term been used with more scrupulous precision) neck.

"You're wrong about *these* giraffes," I said. "They're going to mate."

"Not yet," said John. "She has to kick him first."

Besides kinky sex, the economics of nature does seem to generate leisure time, at least for some species. On a riverbank meadow in the Tarangire, John and I came across a huge troop of baboons, more than a hundred of them. They were just, well, monkeying around; lollygagging, dillydallying, scratching their heads and other body parts, putzing, noodling, airing their heels, and engaging in constant chatter. About what I can't say, but John told me baboons are a favorite food of the big cats. Baboons aren't much different than we were in *Australopithecus* days. I wondered if this troop was us four million years ago. If so, the baboons are probably plotting revenge upon the predators. "Soon as we evolve, we take the natural habitat and *pave its ass*."

But not just yet, I hope. Tanzania has creatures of such breath-catching magnificence that they turn the most hardened indoorsman into a mush on the glories of the natural world. It happened to me when I saw a mother cheetah stretched under a gum arabic tree with four cubs a couple of weeks old. The mother cheetah bore a startling resemblance to my high-school sweetheart from St. Ursula's, Connie Nowakowski—the same tawny coloring, the same high cheekbones, the same little uptilt of the nose, and the exact, the identical eyes. Connie died in her thirties, years ago, and it would be just like her to come back as a cheetah. She'd love the drama, and the coat looks great. But how any male cheetah got four cubs—or even a hand-job—from Connie Nowakowski is one of the mysteries of nature.

A full quarter of Tanzania's geography is some kind of conservation area. For so poor a country, this is a remarkable bit of ecoconscious forbearance. It's not like the big game couldn't be put to use. "Are wildebeest edible?" I asked John.

"Yes."

"How about Cape buffalo?"

"Yes, yes."

"I'll bet a gazelle steak is nice."

"Oh, yes."

"Are warthogs any good to eat?"

"Yes," said John, "delicious."

I wasn't even going to ask about elephants. Lions, anyway, are horrible. I had a lion steak once, at a German restaurant in, of all places, Springfield, Massachusetts. The flavor was of militant liver.

Keeping the conservation areas conserved is not just a matter of Tanzania sucking up to the International Wildlife Fund. Vast sections of Tanzania are infected with sleeping sickness borne by the tsetse fly. The fly's devastating effects are similar to those of other known sleeping-sickness carriers, such as the tsetse professor, tsetse boss, and tsetse *New York Times* op-ed page writer. Sleeping sickness does not bother wild animals, but it does kill people and—something that's more economically important in Tanzania than people are—domestic cattle. The Sierra Club's travel guide to East Africa says, "A good number of African parks undoubtedly owe their existence not to an animal that humans wanted to preserve, but to one we couldn't get rid of." The tsetse is the size of a housefly but manages a bite like an enraged fox terrier. Dozens of them would get in the minivan and hang out behind the dome light and under the sun visors, waiting for their chance. Tobacco fumes seemed to be the only effective repellent. Cigarette packs should come with a printed message: "Smoking may prolong life in areas of tsetse fly infestation."

If we want to save Tanzania's wildlife, we'd better do something about its poverty. Otherwise the Tanzanians may give up on safari tourism, spray the Ngorongoro, the Serengeti, and the Tarangire with DDT, and start playing the *Bonanza* theme song. Who wouldn't rather be a cowboy than a busboy?

In fact, no matter what our motives are for being appalled by Tanzanian poverty, we'd better do something about it. There's suffering humanity to be considered. And that suffering humanity will be us if we're not careful. Only a few million of the world's people are relatively wealthy, but two billion live like the Tanzanians. One of these days those billion are going to figure out that they can buy guns in Florida without much of a background check.

On my last night on safari, I gathered an armload of Serengeti beer and went to sit on the small terrace of my ground-floor hotel room. There was a stretch of flowering shrubs on the other side of a knee-high wall and, beyond that, miles of pitch-dark Africa. I heard a *crunch-crunch* in the decorative landscaping. Then a *crunch-crunch, crunch-crunch.* I turned off my room lights. It was a moonless night, but I thought I could see something moving. I got out my travel flashlight, its beam is about as wide as a finger. I shone it this way and that, and then down along the ground, and there was a pair of eyes. They were big, round, red eyes, and they seemed to be very far apart. I shone the flashlight around some more, and there was another pair of eyes. And a third. *Crunch-crunch, crunch-crunch.* The eyes were coming in my direction. I ran into the room and pulled the screen door shut. As if that was going to help. The glass slider wouldn't budge. I chugged a Serengeti and thought . . . I don't know what I thought. I went back out on the terrace and said, "Ahem," and, "See here, you animals . . ." I aimed the flashlight directly into the scarlet orbs and wiggled it vigorously. The eyes kept coming. The crunching got louder.

The eyes came up to within three feet of my wall. Then they seemed to turn away, and in my flashlight beam I saw the enormous head of a Cape buffalo, scarfing the bougainvillea. I switched the room lights back on. Here was the animal "considered by hunters to be the most dangerous of the big game" (said my tourist guide). In fact, here were three of them. And they were acting like well-mannered parochial-school football players in the lunchroom cafeteria line—at the expense of the hotel's gardening staff. The Cape buffalo were unperturbed, not interested in me, and eating everything in sight. They munched their way next door. I had another beer. It goes to show how even the most wrathful of earth's residents can be rendered dull and domestic—if the chow's good enough.

How is Tanzania supposed to get rich? Well, there's "improvements in agricultural yield," always a favorite with development-aid types. The British Labour government tried this after World War II in what became known as "the groundnut scheme." The Labourites decided that Tanganyika was going to become the world's foremost producer of groundnuts— that is to say, peanuts. They selected three huge sites and cleared the land by running a chain between two tractors, pulling the chain through the bush, and destroying thousands of acres of wilderness. Thirty-six and a half million British pounds were invested, an amount nearly equal to the whole Tanganyikan government budget from 1946 to 1950. It was then discovered that peanuts wouldn't grow in Tanganyika.

The Tanzanian government budget contains more pages on agriculture than would ever be read by anyone, except a journalist in a hotel room with dysentery and nothing but a copy of *The Mill on the Floss*. But the only mentions of land *ownership* in the budget are an admission that buying land entails "lengthy and bureaucratic procedures," and this weasel sentence: "A new land law being formulated proposes to introduce different structural arrangements." Julius Nyerere (apologizing again) has said it was a mistake to collectivize the individual small farms, the *shambas*. But it's a mistake that hasn't been corrected. John said, using the same word the Russians use, that farms must be bought "informally." (Another note from the budget: "FISHERIES—the sector still faces problems from dynamite fishing.")

I did see one swell coffee plantation, Gibb's Farm, at the foot of the Ngorongoro Crater. This is run by English people and has thousands of neatly clipped coffee bushes lined in parade file. A smoothly raked dirt road winds up through the property with woven-stick barriers stuck in the drain gullies to hinder erosion. A profusion of blossoms surrounds the main house. The very picture of a Cotswold cottage yard has been somehow created from weird, thorny African plants which need to be irrigated every minute. The English will garden the ash heaps of Hades if hell lets them.

I suppose the farms of Tanzania could all look like Gibb's Farm, but it turns out that Gibb's Farm doesn't make any money as a farm but prospers because upscale tourist lodgings have been installed. So there's tourism.

According to the U.S. State Department's *Country Commercial Guide,* "Tourism is currently the second-largest foreign-currency earner for Tanzania, after coffee." (Actually, the largest foreign-currency earner for Tanzania is foreign aid. But never mind; with Republicans in Congress and 13 percent unemployment in Sweden, foreign aid is not a growth industry.) All the tourists I talked to were voluble in their praise of Tanzania—as soon as they'd recovered enough from their road trips to form words. And Tanzania's tourist hotels produced $205 million in revenue in 1995. But that's only 6.7 percent of the country's GDP. This compared to the 6 percent of GDP produced by Tanzania's "transport and communication sector." Tanzania doesn't have any communication. As for transport, according to the same State Department guide that talks up tourism, "It takes approximately three days to travel by road from the capital, Dar es Salaam, to the second-largest city, Mwanza," a distance of about 500 miles.

I talked to the manager of a luxury hotel near Mto-wa-Mbu, a Kenyan whom I'll call Shabbir, and his friend, a Tanzanian named, let's say, Mwambande, who ran the plush tented camp down the road. Shabbir said it was difficult to get these resorts to work. What was going on in his kitchen right now "was hell." And at another hotel in Tanzania, I did watch a waiter just arrived from rural climes being utterly confounded by a soda-can pop-top. I asked Shabbir and Mwambande if tourism could make a country like Tanzania rich. Shabbir didn't think so. He was leaving for better opportunities in Vietnam. Mwambande didn't think so, either, but more optimistically. "Tourism acts as a showcase," he said. "It helps people come see a place for them to invest."

They explained that tourism itself isn't very profitable for Tanzania because so much of what's spent is "yo-yo money." The foreigners arrive via foreign-owned airlines in planes built by foreigners. They stay at hotels constructed with foreign building materials, ride around in foreign-made cars, and eat food imported from foreign places. The money rolls in, pauses for a moment, and rolls back out.

Some of the foreigners are, indeed, rich people. "Is the Tanzanian government giving them any incentive to invest?" I asked.

"Oh, yes," said Mwambande, "if you build a plant here you get a five-year tax holiday."

"But," I said, "it normally takes a new enterprise five years to make a profit." Mwambande and Shabbir laughed. "And what about after the tax holiday?" I said. "What are taxes like then?" Mwambande and Shabbir laughed and laughed.

In a February 10, 1997, story about a Tanzanian crackdown on illegal tour operators, *The East-African* newspaper mentioned these taxes just in passing: "a hotel levy (20%), sales tax on food (15%), sales tax on fresh juices and cakes (30%), stamp duty (1% of turnover), with-holding tax on goods and services (2%), training levy (10% on expatri-ate employees' taxable income), payroll levy (4% on gross taxable income of all employees), vocational education training agency tax (2% on gross taxable income of all employees)."

Forget about tourism. How about trade? Trade benefits everyone. Anytime I've got something you want more than I want it, or vice versa, and we swap instead of steal, the economy is improved. But trade in Tanzania has—surprise—its problems, too. Starting right at the dock. Says Foggy Bottom's *Commercial Guide:* "The Customs Department is the greatest hindrance to importers throughout Tanzania. Clearance delays and extra-legal levies [note diplomatic wording] are commonplace." And until a couple of years ago, Tanzanians, like Cubans, weren't allowed to have real money. They had to make do with Tanzanian shillings, which no one wanted.

The current Tanzanian government (which is to say, the same old government after some cheaty elections to stay current looking) claims to have a "trade liberalization policy." But that government shows no understanding of what trade is. It talks about local industries "facing stiff and often unfair competition from imports." That's the point. Back in the States, we'd be driving DeSotos and browsing the Web with room-size Univacs if it weren't for the Japanese. The Tanzanian government also claims that "the domestic market is now more or less saturated with imports." Sure. Until the early 1980s there were only nine computer installations in the country, and a ban on importing computers wasn't completely lifted until 1994.

Nor does "trade liberalization" seem to be aimed at people doing the actual trading. A story in the Dar es Salaam *Guardian* began, "Petty traders along Ali Hassan Mwinyi Road . . . yesterday received a city commission notice to quit the area in five days—and a demolishing grader erased their kiosks a few hours later." Or if bulldozers won't do it, a value-added tax is being instituted this year. An exaction of between 14.2 and 17.5 percent will be charged on the sale of most goods and services. In Tanzania, no one ever says, "You can't stand in the way of progress."

Still, trade does happen. I went to the largest and most prosperous-looking store in Arusha. I'll give it the moniker Safari Barn. It sold souvenirs to tourists. A Maasai warrior in full fig stood sentry by the door, looking as quietly mortified as a Coldstream Guard placed at attention in front of a Victoria's Secret outlet.

The souvenirs were beautiful: black wood carvings of hippos, rhinos, Cape buffalo, giraffes. (Could America's unemployed carve squirrels and mice as well?) And Safari Barn also sold the best *kangas* I'd seen. I picked out one with orange hearts and black wiggle lines like a Keith Haring print. SEMENI MNAYOJUA MSIKAE MKAZUA, said the slogan along the material's edge. I asked the saleswoman to translate. She blushed, the blood rising in her dark complexion and turning her cheeks maroon. John began giggling. "It means," he said, "'Don't sit down and spread your legs and tell everything you know.'" Besides the *kangas* and wood carvings, there were comely Maasai beads, sparkling "Tanzanite" gemstones, and a terrific selection of masks. Literally terrific, most of them, with gobbly teeth and vexed expressions, and fulsome trimmings of what I hoped wasn't human hair. "What are these masks used for?" I asked another saleswoman. You can't come back from Africa without a mask. But I might be shy about having certain ceremonies represented around the house.

"Mostly they're for dancing," said the saleswoman.

"What kind of dancing is done in this one?" I said, pointing to a handsome white striped false face with a box for a mouth and nose.

She hesitated: "Dancing . . . at night."

I got an antelope mask.

I talked to the man who owned Safari Barn, whom I'll call Nisar. By his faintly Middle Eastern speech and pallor (and wow of a wristwatch), I judged him to be a foreigner. But, though Europeans are rare, Tanzanians cover all skin-color bases. There is a sizable population with roots in India, Persia, and Oman, plus people of mixed African-Arab and whatever-whichever ancestry. Nisar's family had been in Tanzania for six generations.

Nisar said Julius Nyerere's "economics were no good." The British tradition of understatement survives in Tanzania. Although only sometimes. "I have queued for a loaf of bread for two weeks," said Nisar. "Under Nyerere, even if I had enough money for a dozen Rolls-Royces, if I drove a Mercedes, I'd go to jail for seven years—languish in jail." So he hated Nyerere's guts. No. "Nyerere destroyed tribalism in Tanzania," Nisar said and claimed he encountered no prejudice for being non-African. He praised Nyerere's insistence that everyone speak Kiswahili: "It unified the nation."

Safari Barn was successful, said Nisar, because "I poured money into Tanzania when others were afraid to spend a shilling." It was hard getting Safari Barn built. Nisar's description of working with Tanzanian contractors was the same as Shabbir's description of work in the hotel kitchen. Nisar had received no tax holidays, no subsidies. To get them, he would have had to go to Dar es Salaam and hang around. "'The Minister is here.' 'The Minister is there.' 'The Minister is gone for a week.' It could take a month to see the right guy. I'm a one-man show here." Then, Nisar said (without a *but* or a *however* or an *even so*), "Tanzania is the best country in Africa. And I have traveled all over. If there is a food shortage in Tanzania, people won't riot. There has never been that tradition here. They will get through it. They will share, help each other. They will organize to complain. They will have meetings. They are very political. But not violent. This is not a violent country." He paused and thought that over for a second. "These people," said Nisar, "are so damn lazy."

† † †

Well, not lazy—not when half the teenage girls in the country are walking around with five-gallon buckets on their heads. Five gallons of
water weigh forty pounds. But Tanzanians are *country*. Rural labor is
hard and long, not busy-busy. Cassava plants don't crash on deadlines.
Chickens don't form quality teams. The sun does not take work home
at night. And Tanzanians are political but, again, not in a way an American always understands. During the 1995 elections, John had run for
the legislature, the Union Assembly, on the opposition NCCR ticket.
But he couldn't remember what the party's initials stand for. (National
Convention for Construction and Reform, incidentally, and I defy you
to remember it until the bottom of the page.) Tanzania has been ruled
by Nyerere's CCM Party (*Chama Cha Mapinduzi*, Party of the Revolution) since independence. Tanzania is a one-party state but has dozens
of political parties, anyway. According to Louisa Taylor, Africa correspondent for the Canadian *Ottawa Citizen*, "Every party stands for clean
government and well-equipped hospitals, good roads, and higher crop
yields, and all are equally vague on how they would make it so."

Even when making it so is a simple matter. I was talking to an expat
Brit who'd come to East Africa as a colonial administrator after World
War II. I said, "That washboard from Mto-wa-Mbu to Makuyuni—all
they'd have to do is send a road grader over it." (The one from Ali Hassan
Mwinyi Road seems to be available on short notice.)

"Oh, less than that," said the Brit. "They used to just drag a big log
behind a tractor—up and back. The fellow'd get to one end and turn
around and go back to the other. Took all the corrugation out. You'd
watch for the dust cloud having gone your way and then take off. I'd
run my little MG right up to the Ngorongoro rim."

The dysfunction of Tanzania is comic, depending on the cruelty of your
sense of humor. Here is an exhibit label from a Tanzanian Museum:

The Soda Bottle (ancient)
The soda bottle which in use up to 1959. This bottle contain a marble
and rubbering which jointly (wished) as stopper for the gas.

Then you take a swig of the locally produced purified water and
notice brown, gelatinous things floating in your own bottle (modern).

John and I visited a high functionary of the Tanzania Chamber of
Commerce, Industry and Agriculture, Arusha branch.

"What does the chamber of commerce do?" I asked.

"Our main activity is getting new members," said the functionary.

"Is the chamber doing anything to attract business to Arusha?" I
asked.

"We haven't reached that level yet," said the functionary. "I think
Arusha has everything to attract business."

"Except telephones," I mentioned.

"Telephones will be privatized next year," he said. "Arusha has two
million people in the whole town." He thought about that. "Arusha has
300,000 people. It is second to Dar es Salaam in importance. If all goes
well, it might become first important."

"Do you have any brochures?"

"We used to have the newsletter, but of recently, we have not done
any printing."

"But *what* does the chamber of commerce actually *do*?"

"We are a pressure group," said the functionary with emphasis.

"Have you been a successful one?"

"We have! To some good extent. The chamber of commerce played
a big role in formulating the budget. We were invited to Dar es Salaam
to give our opinion. We complained about the postal-service box rent
going from 3,000 shillings to 50,000 shillings."

"Did they change the rate back?"

"No."

The chamber of commerce office was located in a long, tin-roofed
shed adjacent to the former headquarters of the East African Community or EAC. The latter building is of a truly stupendous international-
donor type, featuring not only discolored concrete but also oxidized
aluminum, rust-stained stainless steel, and a row of empty flagpoles all
bent at different angles. The EAC was an attempt by Tanzania, Kenya,
and Uganda to form a common market, and it fell apart when Kenya's
president, Daniel arap Moi, started getting huffy and Uganda's dictator,
Idi Amin, started eating people. But nothing in Africa that receives for-

eign assistance ever really goes away, and the EAC continues to exist in the guise of East African Cooperation. In the parking space reserved for the EAC's deputy secretary was a BMW. In the executive secretary's parking space was a new Mercedes sedan. These plenipotentiaries are members of what Kiswahili-speaking Africans call *waBenz,* "People of the Fancy German Cars." So the comedy of errors has a happy ending—for some folks.

And not for others. When John isn't guiding, he and his wife live in northwestern Tanzania, on an informally purchased farm near the Burundi border. They have two grown sons and did have two young daughters, but the five-year-old girl had died a couple months before John and I met. She had malaria. John took her to the local dispensary, where she was injected with a massive dose of something, and she went into a coma. When the girl had been unconscious for five days, medics at the dispensary said she needed a tracheotomy. The nearest surgeon was a hundred kilometers away. John told the medics to radio ahead and hired a car. The drive took all day. By the time John and his daughter arrived, the surgeon—the only surgeon; in fact, the only doctor—at the hospital had left. "Oh, the doctor goes home around 5," said the hospital staff. "Go get him!" said John. And they said, "We don't know where his house is." John hired another car and searched for hours. Meanwhile, his daughter died.

I flew to the capital of Tanzania, wherever that may be. "In 1973 it was decided to move the capital city from Dar es Salaam on the coast to Dodoma in the center. . . a dry and desolate area," says the *East Africa Handbook.* The move to Dodoma is "anticipated around the turn of the century," says the *Globetrotter Travel Guide to Tanzania.* "Dodoma is now the official capital of Tanzania, displacing Dar es Salaam," says the *Brant Guide to Tanzania.* "Some government offices have been transferred to Dodoma," says the CIA's *1997 World Factbook.* And an article in the February 20, 1997, Dar es Salaam *Guardian* begins, "Dodoma branch members of the Tanzania Chamber of Commerce, Industry and Agriculture have asked the government to clarify a minister's statement that Dodoma is not the country's legally recognized capital."

Anyway, I flew to Dar es Salaam. A jolly soldier rummaged through my carry-on baggage, airily dismissing my pocketknife as a possible weapon and telling me that the woman operating the metal detector was his sister and would love to go along. I was ushered into the "boarding lounge" for the requisite two- or three-hour wait before anything airplane-like happens in Tanzania. Warm soft drinks were for sale by a young lady with no change.

As I walked to the tired prop plane, John was on the roof of the airport, shouting goodbye. He'd been waiting the whole time outside in the heat to see me off.

The plane flew over Mount Kilimanjaro. Hemingway begins "The Snows of Ditto" by noting that there's a frozen leopard carcass at the top. "No one has explained what the leopard was seeking at that altitude," writes Hemingway. A clean bathroom is my guess.

In Dar, as knowing travelers call it, I was met by a driver named Nzezele (pronounced "Nzezele"). Dar es Salaam is a seaport without the bustle and sin that implies. Probably due to lack of ships and sailors. A few rusty tubs are moored in the harbor. Much of the commerce with nearby Zanzibar is still conducted in sailing dhows. Goats graze in the main rail yard.

Dar sports some stucco buildings in the art-deco style but with Arabian embellishments: horseshoe arches and crenellated roof lines, all in a poor state of repair, as if a sheikh had come to Miami Beach with the District of Columbia's public school system maintenance staff. The dusty moderne, however, is being supplanted by dusty glass boxes. Here and there are signs of history, or history's ugly half-sister, politics: a squatty palace built by the sultan of Zanzibar when he ran the place and a small, tile-roofed, half-timbered Lutheran church, like a misplaced molecule of Bavaria. The predominant tint of the city is beige, a color with a bad name for being middle class and bland, but Africa can use some bourgeois dullness. There's a golf course right downtown.

Traffic dribbles around unimpeded by many stoplights, none of those being at the busier intersections. Buses and taxis bear pictures of Bob Marley. Pedestrians wear T-shirts emblazoned with Rastafarian slogans. BACK TO AFRICA is—confoundingly—a popular slogan in Tanzania.

There are some nice houses up on Oyster Bay, but not ridiculously nice. There are some slums out in Kariakoo, but not horribly slummy. The neighborhoods where Nzezele told me to lock the car door wouldn't make a New Yorker button his wallet pocket. A Swedish expat told me that he'd been robbed once. The big wad of Tanzanian shillings that it takes to amount to twenty dollars had been picked from his jeans. A crowd chased the thief, who dropped the money. Bystanders picked it up and brought it back to the Swede, asking him to count it, to make sure it was all there. The crowd chasing the thief caught him and beat him to death.

There's no garbage on the streets in Dar, no rats, no stray dogs. There are some beggars, but they're halfhearted. Dar es Salaam has a clunky charm. The International Cashew and Coconut Conference was being hosted February 19–21. You'd be nuts not to sign up. And you have to love a city with a thoroughfare name Bibi Titi Mohamed Street.

Of course, Dar es Salaam has its troubles. The city is out of water. Hundreds of women stand in line at the few open taps, their plastic buckets making brightly colored dots in the pathos. The problem is not drought or depletion of ground supplies. Dar's water system has a 40 percent leakage rate.

The February 19, 1997, *Guardian* carried a story about corruption—in all senses of the word—at a city-hospital morgue: "Certain persons had raised objections that hospital staff were preventing relatives from picking up bodies of identified persons until they paid either fees or consideration to the staff." The hospital had been forced by "congestion of dead bodies" to put some corpses "outside the cold room. . . . Nurses, doctors, patients, and passersby were exposed to a choking smell, which invited swarms of flies from all directions." A photo accompanying the story showed the garbage truck in which the bodies were hauled away.

Does poverty lead to this kind of thing, or does this kind of thing lead to poverty? It is a question that economists have never managed to answer. Maybe there's some inherent cultural failure that is keeping Tanzania poor. But even if that's so, there are legal and political failures helping poverty abide. We don't know if we can change culture. At least we don't know if we can change it for the better. But we do know we can change other things. More freedom and responsibility can be given to individuals. I went to the government of Tanzania to see if it was doing any of that.

And here was an odd glimmer of hope. Poor and shabby countries ought to have poor and shabby governments. They usually don't.

There is some misappropriated opulence in Tanzania. The compound where the president lives has a house and grounds that make Bill Clinton's residence look like Roger's. But the actual government of Tanzania is run out of the same colonial administration offices constructed by Germany ninety years ago, and they haven't been mopped since Kaiser Bill.

The buildings are on the harbor in a line along the Strand (renamed Wilhelms Ufer by the Germans, renamed Azania Front by the English, renamed Kivukoni Front by the Tanzanians). They are substantial train-shed-like wood and stucco structures with a few architectural flourishes—arabesque lintels and tile-roofed porches—indicating a Germanic attempt to go native.

I went to the Bureau of Statistics, President's Office, Planning Commission at 3:30. Just too late. Everyone had gone home, although there was one man left in a large, dusty room stacked with copies of government publications and pamphlets, many of them yellowing and dating back to the '60s. These were for sale, but for some reason, the man couldn't sell them to me. But he showed me several that he said would be excellent for me to buy, including the *Tanzanian Statistical Abstract* (most recent available: 1994), the *Tanzanian Budget* (most recent available: 1994), and the *National Accounts of Tanzania From 1976 to the Present* (the present, in Tanzania, being 1994). He then gave me a heartfelt speech about current politico-economic conditions in Tanzania, of which I didn't understand much. As the American accent tends to flatten most vowels into an *uh,* the Tanzanian accent tends to flatten most consonants into a sound somewhere between an *l, n, t, d,* and *r.* He did wind up, however, by saying, "Until that, you can pour aid in, and all you'll get is . . . ," and he pantomimed a fat man.

There was exactly such a fellow at the bar in the Sheraton that night, in the very largest size of Armani clothes, with a great deal of jewelry. It's rare to see a stout Tanzanian, but, now that jail time for driving a Mercedes is no longer the practice, it happens. And when Africans use the phrase "big man," it's not a metaphor. The big man had his cell phone, his Filofax, his double Johnny Walker Black, and a pile of U.S. dollars on the bar in front of him and coolly left them lying there as he made frequent trips to the pay telephone, because Tanzania didn't have cell phones yet.

I went back to the Bureau of Statistics at 9:30 the next morning. Just too early. No one had arrived yet. I wandered unchallenged through the offices, a dark bafflement of low warrens and vaulted passageways with broken tile underfoot and crazed and damp-stained plaster on the walls. It gave a sinister impression until I noticed that the place was furnished with beat-up Ikea-modern furniture and bulletin boards covered with photos of kids, cutout newspaper cartoons, and postcards from vacationing pals. The government offices of Tanzania look like what would happen if Franz Kafka designed the national PTA headquarters.

I found the correct person to sell me the *Statistical Abstract* and national accounts summary, but he explained that what I really wanted was the *Rolling Plan and Forward Budget for Tanzania for the Period 1996/97–1998/99 Volume I.* "Stacks and stacks of them have just been printed," he said. He didn't have any, however. He sent me, with Dungeons and Dragons directions, through the building to an office with its number Magic Markered on the door. Here, another bureaucrat did have the budget. His desk was covered with copies. "Stacks and stacks of them," he pointed out, but he wasn't authorized to sell me one. "You should go to the planning commission," he said. Although that's where I thought I was.

I got in the car and told Nzezele that we needed to go to the planning commission. He drove me the thirty feet there. At the planning commission a puzzled security guard, a puzzled secretary, and someone else who was puzzled considered my request, and after a closed-door consultation with a boss, they pointed me down a long hall containing several motorbikes and a lot of automobile tires. I emerged into a courtyard with extraordinarily grimy paint. Something good was cooking nearby. I climbed a couple of flights of creaking, swaying stairs, crossed a shaky breezeway, and found myself in the office of the head of environmental planning. A rattling air conditioner was creating a dank environment. He told me he had "only a very few" budget copies. I told him—just between ourselves—about the fellow in the next building who had stacks and stacks of them on his desk. He made a note. I may have set off an enormous turf war within the Tanzanian bureaucracy.

Anyway, the head of environmental planning said that he couldn't give me a budget. I looked disappointed, and he immediately offered to loan me his personal copy on the condition that I bring it back the next morning. So I spent a festive night at the Sheraton copying Tanzanian budget information into a spiral notebook.

Not that I was missing much. The nightlife in Dar es Salaam consists of a few tourists being robbed of their running shoes on the downtown beach. Besides, contained in the *Rolling Plan and Forward Budget* were further glimmers of hope. Right on page two the document states, "The government is being reoriented to play the role of facilitation of development other than continue being seen as 'provider' of development." The English may have gotten out from under them, but this is still a clear explanation of what government should do. Compare it to the Republican "Contract with America." And for brevity and bluntness, it tops anything that's come out of the Oval Office since Nixon yelled "Fuck" on the Watergate tapes.

There are lots of honest admissions in the Tanzanian budget: about civil-service reform "launched in 1992–93 against a background of grossly overstaffed, underpaid and barely performing workforce," and about poverty—"The living conditions of the majority of the people, particularly in rural areas, are quite alarming." And no easy, *It Takes a Vijijini* solutions are proposed. The budget says "poverty-borne problems" must be "tackled," but "this needs to be achieved under conditions of macroeconomic stability." Which may be translated as, "Curing poverty equals allowing people to get rich." This very simple equation has eluded some of the deepest thinkers of the world's advanced nations.

Naturally there is also claptrap in the Tanzanian budget—the mealy-mouthing about property rights that I mentioned before and scary sentences such as "expenditure management control system will be enhanced by setting up five additional sub-treasuries, bringing the total to 10." But taken as a whole, as an example of a government going on public record, the *Rolling Plan and Forward Budget* might almost be called refreshing.

The Tanzanian government has an idea, a slight inkling of what to do—or, rather, what not to do. Often, the most important government action is to leave people alone. That brings us to what we prosperous Westerners should do for Tanzanians. We should leave them alone, too.

Not the cheap, easy kind of leaving them alone. There are plenty of charities and causes in Tanzania that could be supported—and lavishly, if we're the kind, decent folks we like to think we are. Individuals can be helped. But can you "help a nation"?

Official Development Assistance has funded disasters and fostered attitudes of gross dependence. Yoweri Museveni, the president of Uganda, says his country "needs just two things. We need infrastructure and we need foreign investment. That is what we need. The rest we shall do by ourselves." This is the "if we had ham, we could have ham and eggs, if we had eggs" philosophy. Or as Nzezele put it as I was leaving Dar after having given him a large and not very well-deserved tip, "When you get back to America, if you find that you have any extra money, could you send me a wristwatch?"

Delivering our cash to a dictorial and silly government was bad, but even worse was delivering our big ideas about centralization, economic planning, and social justice to a country that had 120 university graduates at the time of independence. Not that the Tanzanians didn't understand our big ideas; they understood them too well. They just had no experience with how bad most big ideas are. They hadn't been through Freudianism, Keynesianism, liberalism, *www.heavensgate.com,* and "Back to Africa." They don't have 10,000 unemployable liberal-arts majors sitting around Starbucks with nose rings.

There's even some evidence that getting ahead in the world comes from a lack of big ideas. Call this the Bell-Dip Theory. The United States is arguably the most-successful nation in history, but not—by any argument—the smartest. Japan, even in a recession, is an economic powerhouse, but we're talking about a people in love with Speed Racer, whose most sophisticated art form is the haiku, an itty-bitty poem on the order of:

> *An old pond.*
> *A frog leaping in.*
> *Sit on a pickle.*

Tanzania is one of those places called "developing countries," as if the Family of Nations had teens, as if various whole geographical regions were callow, inarticulate, clumsy, but endearing, of course—you know, going through an awkward phase.

And that's about right. Every twenty-four hours of Tanzania is like a crib sheet on adolescence. There's the dewy-aired, hopeful dawn. All is beautiful. All is fresh. Then, as the day goes on, the dust rises. The noise builds. Everything is seen in a too-vivid light. The glaring inadequacies of life are revealed. Enormous confusion develops. There's a huge stink. And just when you've really had it—when you're ready to call for the International Monetary Fund's equivalent of "grounding," when you're about to take the keys to the goat or something—the whole place goes to sleep for eighteen hours.

9

HOW TO
MAKE EVERYTHING
FROM NOTHING

❖

HONG KONG

How a peaceful, uncrowded place with ample wherewithal stays poor is hard to explain. How a conflict-ridden, grossly overpopulated place with no resources whatsoever gets rich is simple. The British colonial government turned Hong Kong into an economic miracle by doing nothing.

Hong Kong is the best contemporary example of laissez-faire. The economic theory of "allow to do" holds that all sorts of doings ought, indeed, to be allowed, and that government should interfere only to keep the peace, ensure legal rights, and protect property.

The people of Hong Kong have been free to do what they wanted, and what they wanted was, apparently, to create a stewing pandemonium: crowded, striving, ugly, and the most fabulous city on earth. It is a metropolis of amazing mess, an apparent stranger to zoning, a tumbling fuddle of streets too narrow and vendor choked to walk along, slashed through with avenues too busy and broad to cross. It is a vertical city, rising 1,800 feet from Central District to Victoria Peak in less than a mile; so vertical that escalators run in place of sidewalks, and neighborhoods are named by altitude: Mid-Levels. Hong Kong is vertical in its building, too, and not just with glossy skyscrapers. Every tenement house and stack of commercial lofts sends an erection into the sky. Picture Wall Street on a Kilimanjaro slope, or, when it rains, picture a downhill Venice.

And rain it does for months. Hong Kong in monsoon season has a climate like boiled Ireland. Violent air-conditioning wars with humid heat in every home and place of business, producing a world with two temperatures: sauna and meat locker. The rainwater overwhelms the outgrown sewer system, which fumes and gurgles beneath streets ranged with limitless shopping. All the opulent goods of mankind are on display in an air of shit and Chanel.

It is a filled-in city, turgid with buildings. The Sham Shui Po district of Kowloon claims a population density of more than 425,000 people per square mile—eighteen times as crowded as New York. Landing at Kai Tak Airport, down one thin skid of Kowloon Bay landfill, you fly in below clothesline level, so close to apartment windows that you can watch women at bathroom mirrors putting on their makeup. You can tell them that their lipstick's crooked.

There is no space in Hong Kong for love or money, at least not for ordinary kinds of either. A three-bedroom apartment in Central rents for $1,000 a month, but there isn't room in any of those bedrooms to even have sex with yourself. The whole home will be 700 square feet, less than ten yards long by eight yards wide, with windows papered over because, outside those windows, a hand grab away, are the windows of the apartment next door. And anything you're going to fix in the kitchen had better be something that can be stood on end—like a banana. This is how middle-class people live. Poor people in public housing will have three generations in a fifteen-by-twenty-foot room.

But when they come out of that room, they'll be wearing Versace and Dior—some of it even real. Hong Kong is a styling city, up on the trends. Truly up, in the case of platform sneakers. You can spend an entertaining afternoon on Hollywood Road watching teens fall off their shoes. Over the grinding hills, in the blood-clot traffic, men nonetheless drive their Turbo 911s. The S-class Mercedes is the Honda Civic of Hong Kong, and for the soccer-mom set, a Rolls and a driver is a minivan.

Jesus, it's a rich city. Except where it's Christ-almighty poor. Hong Kong is full of that "poverty midst plenty" stuff beloved of foreign correspondents such as myself who, when doing a Hong Kong piece, rush from interviews with day-laboring "cage men" in barred flophouse partitions to dinners in the blandly exclusive confines of Happy Valley's Jockey Club, where I could sample the one true Hong Kong luxury—distance between tables.

But those poor are going to *get* rich. Just ask them. You can call the old lady selling dried fish on the street on her cell phone.

The *bippity-beep* of cell phones all but drowns the air-conditioner racket. And each time a cell phone rings, everyone within earshot goes into a self-administered frisk, patting himself down to find the wee gadget. You can go weeks without talking to an answering machine, because you're not really dialing a telephone, you're dialing an armpit, purse, shirt pocket, or bikini top.

The cell phone has to be there, or somebody might miss a deal. Everything's a deal. In a store you ask, "What's your best price?" then "What's your Chinese price?" and on from there. I was trying to buy a bottle of cognac in a little restaurant. The owner produced a brand I'd never heard of for $100 and a brand nobody's ever heard of for $80. I got my friend Annie, who let fly in Cantonese, and we had a bottle of Remy for one dead U.S. Grant. "I didn't know you were going to bring my sister in here," said the owner. "*Hwa-aaah!*"

It's a Cantonese exclamation halfway between *oi vey* and *fuhgedaboutit*. Which is Hong Kong in a nutshell—a completely foreign city that's utterly comprehensible. It's a modern place, deaf to charm, dumb in the language of aesthetics, caught up in a wild, romantic passion for the plain utilitarian. The only traditional touches are the catawampus walls and whichaway entrances dictated by *feng shui*, the art of placing things so as to ensure luck and not disturb spirits. One building in Repulse Bay has an enormous square hole in its middle so that a certain invisible dragon can get from the mountain to the sea. Knowing Hong Kong, it was probably a scam with a paid-off fortune-teller helping architects and construction companies boost their fees. Some of Hong Kong may believe in geomancy, but it was my local bookstore in New Hampshire that had thirteen *feng shui* titles.

Everything else quaint within reach in Hong Kong has been torn down. Just a few poky colonial government buildings are left. Landfill has pushed the waterfront a thousand feet into Victoria Harbor. Ferry terminals block the water views, and tides are cramped into a raging flume between Central and Kowloon.

The statue in Statue Square is of a business manager, the nineteenth-century chief executive of the Hong Kong and Shanghai Bank. Behind the square, the Hong Kong and Shanghai Bank Building itself rises. Here the local taste for functionalism has been carried to an extreme that arrives at rococo: a massy, looming, steel Tinkertoy of a thing with its whole construction hanging, suspension-bridge fashion, from eight enormous towers. Very functional, indeed, whatever that function is. Maybe to be expensive. It cost a billion dollars to build.

To the west is Jardine House, an aluminum-skinned monolith covered with circular porthole windows—Thousand Assholes, as it's known. To the east is the I. M. Pei–designed Bank of China Tower—all big diagonals and tricky, skinny angles. Its purpose was to be the tallest building in Asia, which it was for about five minutes before being overtopped by Central Plaza a few miles away, and then by twin towers—the tallest enclosed structures in the world—being built in Kuala Lumpur.

A competitive place, Southeast Asia. And it attracts some types that can compete with anything I've seen. I sat at dinner one night between a tough-as-lug-nuts young woman from the mainland who lives in New York and deals in used motor oil—sparkling table talk—and a large and equally adamantine chick from the wrong side of somewhere's tracks in America. I turned to the suicide blond.

"I'm uh arht cunsultunt," she said.

"Come again?"

"Uh *arht* cunsultant."

"That's interesting. Who do you art-consult for?"

She named a large Saudi prince.

"What kind of art does the prince like?" I asked.

"Nineteen-cenchury reuhlist—you know, Uhmerican."

"Any particular artist?"

"Andrew Wyeth."

I'd been under the impression that Andrew Wyeth was still alive—rare in a nineteenth-century artist. And you'd think Hong Kong would be a strange place to look for one of his paintings. But who knows? They shop hard in Hong Kong. Buy hard. Sell hard.

They drink hard, too. On Friday nights, police are posted in the Lan Kwai Fong bar district because people have actually been crushed to death there during happy hour. Nobody takes it easy in Hong Kong. The only idleness visible is on Sundays, when thousands of the city's overworked Filipino maids come to Central, spread cloths and plastic sheets up and down the sidewalks, and picnic in the least attractive and most heat-baked part of town.

The Filipino maids are Hong Kongese, too. They're in Central because it's practical to get there on the subways, trams, and buses. Hong Kong is a practical place, down to earth, or, rather, down to concrete. The complimentary city guide in my hotel room gave advice on pricing whores and noted, "Some of the conservative hotels don't allow a man to toddle in with a rent-a-bird in the middle of the night. But as you can imagine there are plenty of 'cheap guest houses.'"

In the window of an antique shop, I saw an ivory carving of the familiar row of monkeys: SEE NO EVIL, HEAR NO EVIL, SPEAK NO EVIL; but this one had a fourth monkey with his hands over his balls: FUCK NO EVIL.

City of hardheads. City of rough tongues. You're a *gweilo* right to your face, meaning a white goblin or foreign ghost or old devil or any number of other things, according to how it's said (none of the meanings being complimentary). You can give back as good as you get, however (or try to, since *gweilos* are famously dim). For instance, the Cantonese really can't distinguish *l*s from *r*s. "Ah, you ordered flied lice," said Annie's *gweilo* husband, Hugh. "That's *fried rice,* you plick," said Annie.

I met two women who seemed barely into their twenties but were the publisher and the sales manager of a prominent Hong Kong business magazine.

Publisher: "You're really well-dressed."

Sales manager: "For a journalist. We understand you're a popular writer."

Publisher: "In Japan."

City of straight faces. I was looking at some animal figurines representing Chinese astrological signs. The ancient woman behind the shop counter asked, "What year you born?"

"1947."

"*Hwa-aaah*. Year of pig! Good luck!"

"Oh, 'Good luck! Good luck!'" I said. "That's what Chinese always say to shopping *gweilos*. Stolen Ming dynasty grave offerings: 'Good luck!' Can of tuna fish: 'Good luck!' Lacoste shirt: Good luck!'"

"Not so!" she said. "Some years bad luck."

"Such as?"

"Year of buffalo."

"Which year is that?"

"This one."

"This one" being 1997. I had come to Hong Kong to watch the best contemporary example of laissez-faire be surrendered to the biggest remaining example of socialist totalitarianism.

Hong Kong was (and to be fair to its new commie rulers, remains, for the moment) socialism's perfect opposite. Hong Kong doesn't have import or export duties, or restrictions on investments coming in, or limits on profits going out. There's no capital-gains tax, no interest tax, no sales tax, and no tax breaks for muddle-butt companies that can't make it on their own.

The corporate tax in Hong Kong is 16.5 percent of profits. The individual tax rate is 15 percent of gross income. Hong Kong's government runs a permanent budget surplus and consumes only 6.9 percent of gross domestic product (compared with the 20.8 percent of GDP spent just by the federal government in the U.S.). The people of Hong Kong have not been paylings of the state. They've owned their own. They've been able to blow it, Dow Jones it, start a sweater factory, hire, fire, sell, retire, or buy the farm. (And there actually are some little-bitty farms in the New Territories.)

Hong Kong has never had democracy, but its wallet-size liberties, its Rights-of-Man-in- a-purse, have been so important to individualism and self-governance that in 1995 an international group of libertarian think tanks was moved to perhaps overstate the case and claim, "Hong Kong is the freest nation in the world."

Free because there's been freedom to screw up, too. Hong Kong has no minimum wage, no unemployment benefits, no union-boosting legislation, no Social Security, no national health program, and hardly enough welfare to keep one U.S. trailer park in satellite dishes and Marlboro Lights. Just 1.2 percent of GDP goes in transfers to the helplessly poor or subsidies to the hopelessly profitless.

Living without a safety net, people in Hong Kong have kept a grip on the trapeze. The unemployment rate is below 3 percent. In America, a shooting war is usually needed to get unemployment that low. The "natural rate" of unemployment is considered to be about 5 percent in the U.S., which rate would cause natural death from starvation in Hong Kong. But they aren't dying. Although smoking is the city's principal indoor athletic activity, life expectancy in Hong Kong is about seventy-nine years, compared with seventy-six in the States. And the infant-mortality rate is comparable to our own. This from people who consider crushed pearls, dried sea horses, and horns from the dead rhinos of Tanzania to be efficacious medicine. Even the babies are too busy to die.

Economic growth in Hong Kong has averaged 7.5 percent per year for the past twenty years, causing gross domestic product to quadruple since 1975. With barely one-tenth of 1 percent of the world's population, Hong Kong is the world's eighth-largest international trader and tenth-largest exporter of services.

I'm not exactly sure what "exporter of services" means, unless it's fly-by dim sum, but, anyway, it's a fine statistic and helped make dinky, terrifying Kai Tak Airport the third-busiest passenger terminal in the world and the second-busiest air-cargo center. And Kai Tak's solitary runway sticks out into a container port that's the world's most busy of all.

Hong Kong's per-capita GDP is $26,000. Average individual wealth is greater than in Japan or Germany. It's $5,600 greater than what Hong Kong's ex-colonial masters back in Britain have, and is creeping up on the U.S. per-capita GDP of $28,600. Besides Americans, only the people of Luxembourg and Switzerland are richer than those of Hong Kong. And these are two other places where capital is allowed to move and earn freely.

True, there has been an "Asian crisis" since the above statistics were compiled. The Hong Kong stock market has flopped. Indonesia, Thailand, Malaysia, South Korea, and maybe Japan are experiencing depressions. The entire business world of Asia is supposed to be in ruins. But a mere continent-wide financial collapse is unlikely to faze the people of Hong Kong.

Hong Kong's economy was destroyed by the Japanese occupation of World War II, destroyed again by the UN embargo on trade with the Communists in 1951, and almost destroyed a third time by worry about the 1997 handover to China. The territory has been squeegeed by typhoons, squished by mudslides, toasted by enormous squatter-camp fires, and mashed by repeated refugee influxes. Hong Kong has no forests, mines, or oil wells, no large-scale agriculture, and definitely no places to park. Hong Kong even has to import water. So in Hong Kong they drink cognac instead, more per person than anywhere else in the world. They own more Rolls-Royces per person, too. So what if there's no space at the curb? They'll hire somebody fresh from the mainland to drive around the block all night.

Why did the British allow this marvel of free enterprise? Why did Britain do so little to interfere with Hong Kong's economic liberty? This is especially hard to answer because, back in London, an ultrainterfering socialist Parliament had taken charge after World War II. This government would bring the U.K.'s own economy to a halt like a hippo dropped on a handcart.

Actually, the British did piss in the colonial soup when they could. The crown government held title to almost all the land in Hong Kong and the New Territories, and dealt it out slowly to keep sales revenues high. Thus the crowding in a place which, in fact, comprises some 402 square miles of dry ground—enough, in theory, to give everybody a bean-sprout garden. Instead, half the population is stuck in claustrophobic government housing. Then in the '70s, one of Hong Kong's thicker governors, Sir Murray Maclehose, set aside 40 percent of the colony as parkland—cramped comfort to the fellow living in 300 square feet with his wife, mother, kids, and their Tamagotchi pets.

But the British never tried to install a European-style Pampers-to-June Allyson welfare system in Hong Kong. Maybe the Labour M.P.s were unwilling to invest vast quantities of groundnut scheme–type pinko planning genius in a place that could be gobbled up at any time by the pinko planning geniuses across the border. Maybe the colonial administrators were overwhelmed by the number of refugees from pinko planning jamming into town. Maybe the mother country was too broke from ruining its own economy in the British Isles. Or maybe the Brits just didn't care about pushing social justice down the throats of people who were, after all, only Chinese.

On the other hand, the British were not irresponsible. The "doing nothing" mentioned at the beginning of this chapter is a relative term. Laissez-faire isn't Tanzanian administrative sloth or Albanian popular anarchy. Quite a bit of government effort is required to create a system in which government leaves people alone. Hong Kong's colonial administration provided courts, contract enforcement, laws that applied to everyone, some measure of national defense (although the Red Chinese People's Liberation Army probably could have lazed its way across the border anytime it wanted), an effective police force (Hong Kong's crime rate is lower than Tokyo's), and a bureaucracy that was efficient and uncorrupt but not so hideously uncorrupt that it wouldn't turn a blind eye on an occasional palm-greasing illegal refugee or unlicensed street vendor.

The Brits built schools and roads. And the kids went to school because they knew if they didn't, they'd have to hit that road. And the U.K. gave Hong Kong a stable currency, which it did totally by cheating—first pegging the Hong Kong currency to the British pound and then, when everyone got done laughing at that, pegging it to the U.S. dollar at a rate of 7.8:1. Now when there's any money-supply dirty work to be done, Hong Kong can blame everything on Alan Greenspan.

Hong Kong was also fortunate in having a colonial government which included some real British heroes, men who helped the place stay as good as it was for as long as it did. The most heroic of these was John Cowperthwaite, a young colonial officer sent to Hong Kong in 1945 to oversee the colony's economic recovery. "Upon arrival, however," said a *Far Eastern Economic Review* article about Cowperthwaite, "he found it recovering quite nicely without him."

Cowperthwaite took the lesson to heart, and while he was in charge, he strictly limited bureaucratic interference in the economy. He wouldn't even let bureaucrats keep figures on the rate of economic growth or the size of GDP. The Cubans won't let anyone get those figures, either. But Cowperthwaite forbade it for an opposite reason. He felt that these numbers were nobody's business and would only be misused by policy fools.

Cowperthwaite has said of his role in Hong Kong's astounding growth: "I did very little. All I did was to try to prevent some of the things that might undo it." He served as the colony's financial secretary from 1961 to 1971. In the debate over the 1961 budget, he spoke words that should be engraved over the portals of every legislature worldwide; no, tattooed on the legislators' faces:

> . . . in the long run the aggregate of decisions of individual busi-
> nessmen, exercising individual judgment in a free economy,
> even if often mistaken, is less likely to do harm than the cen-
> tralized decisions of a government; and certainly the harm is
> likely to be counteracted faster.

Even *Newsweek* has been forced into admiration: "While Britain continued to build a welfare state, Cowperthwaite was saying 'no': no export subsidies, no tariffs, no personal taxes higher than 15 percent, red tape so thin a one-page form can launch a company."

During Cowperthwaite's "nothing doing" tenure, Hong Kong's exports grew by an average of 13.8 percent a year, industrial wages doubled, and the number of households in extreme poverty shrank from more than half to 16 percent.

"It would be hard to overestimate the debt Hong Kong owes to Cowperthwaite," said economist Milton Friedman. And it would be hard to overestimate the debt Hong Kong owes to the Chinese people who sanctioned and supported what Cowperthwaite was doing or, rather, doing not. Because Hong Kong didn't get rich simply as a result of free-dom and law. Economics is easier than economists claim, but it's not as easy as that. Chinese culture was a factor in Hong Kong's success. And yet, almost by definition, Chinese culture must have been a factor in mainland China's failure. Culture is complex. Complexities are fun to talk about, but, when it comes to action, simplicities are often more effective. John Cowperthwaite was a master of simplicities.

Yeung Wai Hong, publisher of Hong Kong's most popular Chinese language magazine, *Next,* has suggested erecting an heroic-scale statue of John Cowperthwaite. (To be paid for by *private* subscription, thank you.)

In less than one lifetime, Hong Kong created the environment of comfort and hope that every place on earth has been trying to achieve since the days of *homo erectus* in the Olduvai Gorge. And Hong Kong's reward? It has been made a "Special Administrative Region" of the People's Republic of China.

At midnight on June 30, 1997, the British sold six million five hundred thousand souls. No, gave them away. Nearly a Londonful of individuals, supposed citizens of the realm that invented rights, equity, and the rule of law, got Christmas-goosed in July. Hong Kong was on the cuffo, a gimme, an Annie Oakley for the mainland Communists.

At the stroke of 12, I was watching TV in my Hong Kong hotel room. The handover ceremony was being broadcast from the hideous new convention center three-quarters of a mile away. A British military band wearing hats made from Yogi and Smokey and Poo played "God Save the Queen." The Union Jack went south. Prince Charles had just given a little speech. "We shall not forget you, and we shall watch with closest interest as you embark on this new era of your remarkable history." In other words, "Goodbye and bolt the door, bugger you."

Outside, on my hotel-room balcony, the floodlit convention center was all too visible on the harbor front, looking like somebody sat on the Sydney Opera House. Directly below the balcony, a couple thousand not very noisy protesters stood in the rain in Statue Square, looking like somebody was about to sit on them. They were listening to democracy advocate Martin Lee. Mr. Lee was a member of the first freely elected legislature in the history of Hong Kong. And the last. It was unelected at midnight. Mr. Lee was speaking without a police permit. And speaking. And speaking. Every now and then a disconsolate chant of agreement rose from the crowd. Mr. Lee kept speaking. No one bothered to stop him.

Back inside, on the TV, president of China Jiang Zemin was speaking, too—introducing himself to his instant, involuntary fellow countrymen with a poker-faced hollering of banalities in Mandarin. "We owe all our achievements most fundamentally!!! To the road of building socialism!!! With Chinese characteristics!!! Which we have taken!!!" he said, interrupting his speech with episodes of self-applause, done in the official politburo manner by holding the hands sideways and moving the fingers and palms as if to make quacky-ducky shadow puppets.

The big men on the convention-center podium—Jiang, Prime Minister Li Peng, and Foreign Minister Qian Qichen—seemed to have made their own suit jackets at home.

Tung Chee-hwa, the Beijing-appointed chief executive of the new Hong Kong Special Administration Region, came to the microphone next, making pronouncements that combined a political-reeducation-camp lecture ("Our thoughts and remembrance go, with great reverence, to the late Deng Xiaoping") with a Dick Gephardt speech ("We respect minority views but also shoulder collective responsibility. . . . We value plurality but discourage open confrontation. We strive for liberty but not at the expense of blah, blah, blah.").

This also was said in Mandarin, which is not the native tongue in Hong Kong. In fact, no one uses it there, and having the HK chief executive lipping away in an alien lingo was like hearing an American politician speak meaningless, bizarre . . . it was like hearing an American politician speak.

Outside on the balcony again (covering the Hong Kong handover required a journalist to give his utmost—what with AC-chilled binocs fogging in the tropical heat and a minibar running low on ice) I watched the HMS *Britannia* pull away from the convention-center dock. A nondescript, freighter-shaped vessel painted white, *Britannia* looked to be more an unfortunate cruise-ship choice than a royal yacht. It steamed through Victoria Harbor, hauling butt from now foreign waters. On board were the last British governor of Hong Kong, the aristocrat currently known as Prince of Wales, any number of other dignitaries, and, I hope, a large cargo of guilt.

Would the limeys have skipped town if Hong Kong was full of 6.5 million big, pink, freckled, hay-haired, kipper-tucking, pint-sloshing, work-shy, layabout, Labour-voting . . . Well, in that case . . .

Maybe Hong Kong just wasn't one of those vital, strategic places worth fighting for—like the Falklands. Maybe the Poms only intervene militarily where there's enough sheep to keep the troops entertained.

Why didn't the British give some *other* island to China. Britain, for instance. This would get the U.K. back on a capitalist course—Beijing being more interested in moneymaking than Tony Blair. Plus, the Chinese have extensive experience settling royal-family problems.

Or why didn't Britain sell England to Hong Kong? Hong Kong can afford it, and that way anyone who was worried about the fate of democracy in the Special Administrative Region could go live in Sloane Square, and the rest of England could be turned into a theme park. There's quaint scenery, lots of amusements for the kiddies ("Changing of the Wives" at Buckingham Palace is good), and plenty of souvenirs, such as, if you donate enough money to the right political party, a knighthood.

But this didn't happen. And the people of Hong Kong (unless they were very rich) were stuck in Hong Kong. Sure, they had British passports. But these were "starter passports"—good for travel to . . . Macao. Of course, they could have gotten passport upgrades. For a million Hong Kong dollars, they could have gone to Toronto. Very fun.

Oh, let's give the limeys a break. It's not as if we Americans gave a damn, either. We could have threatened to stealth-bomber the Red Chinese or, for that matter, Margaret Thatcher when she started gift-wrapping Hong Kong for Deng Xiaoping. We could have told China to go kiss Boris Yeltsin's ass if it wanted to be a most-favored nation. And we could have handed out 6.5 million green cards.

Imagine 6.5 million savvy, hardworking citizens-to-be with a great cuisine. What a blessing for America. And how we would hate them. Pat Buchanan would hate their race. The AFL-CIO would hate their wage rate. The NAACP would hate their failure to fail as a minority. And Al Gore would hate 6.5 million campaign contributors who didn't have to sneak pro-free-trade money to the Democratic National Committee anymore but could go right into polling booths and vote Republican.

† † †

The surrender of Hong Kong was a shameful moment. But if you missed Martin Lee's soggy peroration in Statue Square, you might never have known it. The stock market was still on a swell, up 30 percent from a year before, with bulging, steroidal gains in the so-called red chips, the mainland holding companies promoted by the ChiComs. Trade and foreign investment were at unexampled heights. No one was running from the real-estate market. Tiny condominiums in unglamorous districts were going for $500,000.

A five-day weekend was declared, though no one closed shop. Retail sales were 30 percent to 40 percent above the usual. Important people had flown in from all over the globe. I saw the back of Margaret Thatcher's head in my hotel lobby.

On July 1 ("Dependence Day," I guess) people who should have known better sent messages of cheer, fulsomely printed in the *South China Morning Post*:

> China has made important commitments to maintain Hong Kong's freedom and autonomy.
>
> —Bill Clinton

> Hong Kong can be an even better place in which to live and work.
>
> —Madeleine Albright

> I feel pretty relaxed about it.
>
> —George Bush

Skyrockets splattered in the evening skies. The British Farewell Ceremony for 10,000 invited guests had featured not only bands from the Scots Guards, Black Watch, and various other men without pants, but also the Hong Kong Philharmonic Orchestra and (I saw this) a dance troupe with performers dressed as giant deutsche marks, enormous circuit boards, and huge powdered wigs. At the other end of the lifestyle continuum, there was a One Nation Under a Groove 11 P.M. to 9 A.M. rave.

In between were thousands of parties, from impromptu expat booze-ups in the Wan Chai lap-dancing district to dinners with courses incalculable by abacus at Hong Kong mogul David Tang's China Club. Here the whole food chain was ravaged, from depth of sea slug to bird's-nest height.

The China Club is decorated colonial style in big-wallah mahogany, except the walls are covered with Mao-era socialist-realism art, and the waiters and waitresses are dressed as Red Guards. Meaning? I have no idea.

I also have no idea why my hotel kept giving me handover gifts: a bottle of champagne, a coffee-table book about Hong Kong titled *Return to the Heart of the Dragon* (less ominous-sounding in Chinese, I gather), and a silver mug bearing crossed British and Chinese flags, and inscribed:

Resumption of Sovereignty
to
China
1 July 1997
Hong Kong

To which I intend to have added:

Bowling Tournament
2nd Place

Whimsical handover T-shirts, many making hangover puns, were for sale around the city, as were such humorous novelties as "Canned Colonial Air—Sealed Before June 30th." I suppose the same sort of things were being marketed in Vienna in 1938: "Last Yarmulke Before *Anschluss*," and so on. Maybe in occupied France, too: "Vichy Water," ha-ha.

There were grumbles in Hong Kong, of course, such as dissidentish shows by artists objecting to censorship, in case there was going to be any. Martin Lee and his fellow Democratic Party members gave a glum press conference, at which they promised to keep representing their electoral districts, even if they didn't anymore. And a certain amount of fretting in the press was seen, but mostly of the affectless editorial page kind that mixes AFTER GENOCIDE—WITHER RWANDA? with AFTER GRETZKY—WITHER HOCKEY? Hong Kong, on the whole, was awfully darn cheerful.

Why weren't 6.5 million people more upset about being palmed off to an ideology-impaired dictatorship that has the H-bomb? Even one of Taiwan's top representatives in Hong Kong was quoted saying, "As a Chinese person, I think it is a good thing that Hong Kong is coming back to China." Chiang Kai-shek, please.

There is the colonialism issue. How did the Chinese of Hong Kong really feel about being ruled by England? It's a complex question. Or, as a number of Chinese people said to me, "No, it isn't." Being an American, and an Irish-American to boot, I was, maybe, told certain things that the English didn't hear. "We hate the English," for instance.

When a Chinese friend said that, I said, "Wait a minute, I was in Vietnam not long ago, and nobody seemed to hate Americans. If the Vietnamese can forgive Americans for napalm, carpet bombing, Agent Orange, and what-all, surely you can forgive the English for the odd opium war and some 'Land of Hope and Glory' karaoke."

"It's a different thing," said my friend. "You just killed the Vietnamese; you never *snubbed* them."

Hong Kong's people are also realists. Calling in to complain on the *Larry King Show* wasn't going to do much. Thus the tepid response to the handover's endless television and newspaper "streeters," the interviews with random locals: "Excuse me, I understand you're about to get secret police in your neighborhood. Would you care to tell the world how much you hate Jiang Zemin?"

There are real reasons for Hong Kong's realism. In 1945 the population of the territory was only 1.2 million. Today, the whole city is filled with refugees and children of refugees. Until 1980, Hong Kong had a "touch base" asylum policy where, basically, anyone from the mainland who made it to downtown could stay. The Chinese who fled the civil war, the communist takeover on the mainland, and the lunatic deprivations and slaughters that followed know that there's only one real safe haven: money.

And they're serious about making it. The hours posted on the door of the fashion-forward department store Joyce are, MONDAY–SATURDAY 10 A.M.–7 P.M., SUNDAY AND PUBLIC HOLIDAYS 11 A.M.–6 P.M. Take two hours off for Christmas. And the in-case-of typhoon notice in my hotel room read:

> **Signal Number 9 and 10:**
> **When these signals are hoisted, extreme**
> **weather conditions will prevail, meaning**
> **that the typhoon is centered over Hong**
> **Kong. May we suggest that while you**
> **are confined indoors, you enjoy the**
> **facilities of our restaurants and bars.**

Finally, the residents of Hong Kong were putting a good face on things because . . . what the hell else were they going to do? There's a joke they tell in Shanghai about the Hong Kong handover. Mao asks Zhou Enlai and Deng Xiaoping, "How do you get a cat to bite a hot pepper?"

Zhou says, "You hold him down, pry his jaws open, and shove the pepper into his mouth."

Mao says, "No, that's force. We want the cat to bite the pepper of his own free will."

Deng says, "You take the pepper, wrap it in a delicious piece of fish, and, before he knows it, the cat has bitten the pepper."

Mao says, "No, that's trickery. We want the cat to know he's biting the pepper."

Zhou and Deng say, "We give up. How do you make a cat bite a hot pepper?"

"It's easy," Mao says. "Stick the pepper up the cat's ass. He'll be *glad* to bite it."

10

HOW TO HAVE THE WORST
OF BOTH WORLDS

❖

SHANGHAI

There may be an even better way of getting a cat to eat a hot pepper. Make the cat a senior vice president for sales at a global hot-pepper conglomerate and promise to open mainland China to hot-pepper imports.

I went to Shanghai to see what was taking over Hong Kong, and to Hong Kong to see what was being taken. And in the month I spent visiting these two parts of China, every employee of an international corporation I met said that the "reunification" would be good for business.

The corporations are seduced by the idea of 1.2 billion mainland customers. It has become a mantra for marketing departments around the world. "Om, one point two billion." Management is mesmerized. Right now the board of directors at Boeing is sitting around going, "One point two billion . . . boy, if just one half of one percent of those people bought a 777 . . ."

Not that the corporate executives aren't worried about communist abuse of human rights. They've been deeply concerned about this for years. Here is the chairman of Morgan Stanley Asia Ltd., quoted in

The Washington Post business section, agonizing about the events of Tiananmen Square: "The border was closed. JCPenney stock went down because their entire fall supply of shoes had to come across the border."

But on July 1, 1997, the day after the Hong Kong handover, Lehman Brothers, Samsung Electronics, Chase Bank, Singapore Airlines, Canadian Airlines, AT&T, Credit Lyonnais, Maxell Tapes, Louis Vuitton, and that White House favorite, the Lippo Group, had congratulatory ads in the former colony's English language papers. And Toshiba had decorated the top floors of its Hong Kong headquarters so that its logo was visible in almost every outdoor TV shot or still photo of the handover ceremonies.

No offense to businesspeople, of course, especially if they happen to own publishing companies or chains of bookstores. I'm just wondering if multinational executives have thought this through. There are some strange players in the Chinese communist economy. For instance, the People's Liberation Army is a major investor. Consider putting PLA officers into positions of corporate responsibility. "Sir, the merger strategy is a minefield, sir. Literally, sir." And now I've offended the People's Liberation Army. There go my 1.2 billion hardcover sales.

I don't want to disparage private enterprise. The world has political, religious, and intellectual leaders for that. But when a totalitarian government gets cozy with large financial and manufacturing concerns, it rings a twentieth-century historical bell. I'm thinking how a certain "people's car"—*ein Volkswagen*—got its start. I'm thinking, "Made the trains run on time." I'm thinking, "Greater Asian Coprosperity Sphere." There's a technical name for this political ideology.

Shanghai, on first impression, seems fine—that is, it seems to be in the dire, hideous, and enjoyable state of confusion that market freedoms always produce. I can't even tell you what Shanghai looks like, because, look again, and it looks different. Other cities have construction sites; Shanghai *is* one—a 220-square-kilometer cellar hole where the full business of urban existence is scrambled with the building trades. Tan yourself during lunch hour in the arc-welding glare. What fortieth-story

I-beam girder do I inch down to get to McDonald's? Don't call a cab; flag a crane and get hoisted back into your office window.

Everything in Shanghai seems to be going up or coming down. Maybe at the same time. Maybe, between customers, store clerks tear bricks off the shop's back wall while the saleswomen run up front to lay cinder blocks. On my first morning in town, I saw a whole platoon of the People's Liberation Army going down a manhole with plumbing tools. Which is a good place to put communist military, as far as I'm concerned. But it's beyond telling if all the activity in Shanghai makes as much sense as that did.

THIS SITE WILL DEVELOP A SUPER HIGH BUILDING, read a sign on a narrow side-street lot. Buildings were being built everywhere—on top of other buildings, smack in the middle of the street, and smack under it, too. People's Square, Shanghai's Tiananmen equivalent, the place for mass rallies and such, was torn up so that a multilevel shopping center could be installed below it. That way, if any more of those 1989-style democracy protests happen in Shanghai, the kids will be able to stand in People's Square and guess whether tanks will squash them and also run downstairs and buy a pair of Guess? jeans so they'll be dressed for the occasion.

There was so much scaffolding in Shanghai that when I saw a framework of bamboo poles holding nets over a sapling, I thought, "Christ, they're building trees." Actually not. Miles of once-shady streets have been timbered to make way for steel and glass. Although new trees were being planted. I counted a dozen. And at least two parks hadn't been completely paved. Not that Shanghai has turned its back on nature. The downtown freeway overpasses, stacked four deep, had little flowering window boxes hanging from their guardrails.

Like Hong Kong, Shanghai began as an enclave of market freedom—albeit market freedom imposed by military force (the way we've tried to impose it in Cuba several times). Both Hong Kong and Shanghai were "concession ports" granted by the Treaty of Nanjing in 1842 after the first opium war. Hong Kong belonged to Britain, but Shanghai belonged to practically everybody. A slew of foreigners threw together the Shanghai city administration, described thus in a 1911 *Encyclopedia Britannica* entry: "As there are now fourteen treaty powers represented at Shanghai, there are consequently fourteen district courts sitting side by side, each administering the law for its own nationality." Recipe, if ever there was, for a failed civic soufflé—which rose anyhow. China was experiencing one of its 4,200 consecutive years of bad government. Imagine a ruling elite so lousy that fourteen Western political systems all operating at the same time wouldn't be worse—fourteen Jesse Helmses curling your hair in the Senate, twenty-eight Bills and Hillarys bloviating at the White House, and seventy people yelling at each other on the *McLaughlin Group*.

But Hong Kong and Shanghai were havens for personal and substantial liberty on a continent where everyone's person and substance had always belonged to the emperor, the warlord, or the man with the largest hatchet. And they were havens for overseas merchants and Chinese natives alike. Even in 1885, seventeen of the top eighteen taxpayers in Hong Kong were Chinese.

Until the communist takeover in 1949, Shanghai was the more important of the two cities. It was one of the few deepwater ports on the China coast not cut off from the interior by mountains or crabby peasant rebellions. And its central location, where the Huangpu empties into the mouth of the Yangtze, made it the nineteenth-century wet version of O'Hare Airport. Shanghai is still the largest and richest city on the mainland—even though it isn't really Chinese and dates back only 156 years in a country that eats eggs that old.

Shanghai has grown from a piffling village to a metropolis with a population of 13.4 million. Or so says my 1996 guidebook—outdated while still on the press. The 1996 official estimate was 16 million. Wrong, too. The city government has since decided that 17 million people is closer to the mark. But no one keeps pace with Shanghai. I had a tourist map so current that the copyright was for the next year. I went to the spot marked Shanghai Art Museum, and the museum was gone. They'd sold the museum. A department store was going up in its place.

It took me two days to find the new art museum, though it's a whopping-big round thing with loops on the top like a granite wok—

perfect for stir-frys on Jupiter. I was usually lost in Shanghai, despite
the fact that the main part of the city is no larger than midtown Manhattan and is laid out more or less on a grid. Getting lost in right-angled
intersections with street signs in English produces a chill of embarrass-
ment and a hint of Alzheimer's-to-be, like getting lost in a Kmart.

And, indeed, familiar brand names were everywhere. The very words
for foreign goods are enough to conjure with. The most common form of
advertising is just a product's moniker in large roman letters, as if Toyota
had a billboard in Times Square reading "トヨタ自動車." Shanghai buses carry
so many logos, they look like NASCAR Chevys. Every lamppost seems to
be named after a soft drink.

The new buildings in Shanghai are like giant pages in an Ugly Man-
made Materials catalog. They are sheathed in kitchen-sink stainless steel,
storm-door aluminum, translucent-plastic disco flooring, and vast ex-
panses of chrome and smoked glass—vertical '70s coffee tables crying
out for a Mount Rushmore noseful of cocaine and a razor blade the size
of an airplane wing.

Many structures are covered in ceramic tiles like giant inside-out
shower stalls. Some have random chunks of classical decoration—pedi-
ments, friezes, Doric columns—pasted to minimalist boxes, as if the
Parthenon had been converted to ministorage units. Others aspire to
be Legoland built from Legos as big as 7-Elevens. And one spherical
corporate HQ on a cubic plinth buttressed by hulking triangles managed to be grim, silly, monumental, and cute all at once—the Tomb of
Hello Kitty.

At the top of every edifice, there's something funny going on—a
pointy or flashy or revolvy item. Favorite motifs are cocktail olive and
pickle-on-a-spike. The skewered ovoid shapes culminate in the unbe-
lievable Oriental Pearl TV Tower, 1,400 feet high, with massive geode-
sic globes at middle and bottom. It looks like a Russian Orthodox church
of the twenty-eighth century or a launch vehicle for a pair of Houston
Astrodomes or a humongous shish kebab that lost everything but two
onions in the barbecue fire.

And omnipresent amid all the frenzy of Shanghai is that famous
portrait, that modern icon. The faintly smiling, bland, yet somehow
threatening visage appears in brilliant red hues on placards and post-

ers, and is painted huge on the sides of buildings. Some call him a genius. Others blame him for the deaths of millions. There are those who
say his military reputation was inflated, yet he conquered the mainland
in short order. Yes, it's Colonel Sanders.

In some ways, Shanghai is the familiar, homogenized world city. The
restaurant at my hotel was decorated with a "Stampede '97" theme. The
waitresses were dressed in denim hot pants, checked shirts, boots, and
Stetsons—the world's only five-foot cowgirls who bow when you order
a cold one. A mechanical bull had been installed across from the salad
bar. One inebriated Japanese businessman got on it. And right off again.
Yah-hoo.

Of course, if you want to feel like you've really traveled, Shanghai
offers some experiences of the patently exotic kind. I went with some
friends to what looked like the worst pet store ever. Inside was a wall of
terrariums full of fat, angry poisonous snakes, hissing, pulling hood
boners, and making wet bongo noises when they tried to strike through
the glass. This was, in fact, a restaurant on Shanghai's Huaihai Road.
Spécialité de la maison: cobra blood.

One of the more expendable waiters opened the hinged front of
the cobra case and pinned a four-foot serpent with a forked stick. He
pried the critter out of its home, grabbed it beneath the head, and scuttled
off to the kitchen, holding the thrashing reptile aloft as though it were
a living string of furious bratwurst.

A few minutes later, the fellow emerged with a tray of brandy snif-
ters, each filled with bright, gory liquid, plus an extra glass holding the
contents of the snake's gallbladder. Bonus.

There's a ritual involved in drinking cobra blood. Of course. There's
a ritual involved in most very silly things. You have to get four males together and pledge a toast or something, and something else, which I don't
remember. Do I need to mention we were drunk? Then you slam it.

Being that a snake is a "cold-blooded" animal, I vaguely expected
a chilled beverage. But it turns out a snake is a room-temperature animal. Which allows the full flavor to come through. You know the drill
on exotic food. Cobra blood tastes like chicken . . . blood.

Drinking cobra blood makes you . . . it's very good for . . . gives you lots of . . . The explanation was in Chinese. And cobra gallbladder juices do whatever even more. We let the youngest guy drink this. He said it was okay, although he was awake all night chasing mice around his hotel room.

But a more foreign foreignness lurks in Shanghai. There's something, beyond a sip of snake squeezings, that's alien and sinister about the place. For a very full city, the town is oddly empty. First you notice there aren't any dogs. Then you notice there aren't any cats. Then you notice there are hardly any pigeons. The protein is missing.

The beggars are also missing. In days of walking around Shanghai, I encountered just two, and these of the most desperately legitimate type, one with no hands and the other a crippled dwarf. Hard to believe begging was eliminated among 17 million poor people by kind admonishment or polite request. Or that children were eliminated this way, either. Families dot the streets and parks, always in trio form. China's One Child program has succeeded (though whether at greater social costs than the success of America's One Parent program, I can't say).

The traffic jams seem normal for a moment. Modern cars look alike. But these modern cars look alike for the simple reason that they're all the same. They're all locally made Volkswagen Santanas, and all of them are painted half-gallon screw-top burgundy red.

The city streets are full to the point of stasis, but the four-lane turnpikes coming in and out of town are deserted. And in the roadside plazas where other countries would have restaurants and gas stations, there are police checkpoints instead—arrest stops.

The Chinese countryside is screwed on backward. It has vacant highways running through crowded agricultural fields. All the farmwork is being done by hand. The only tractor I saw was a rototiller thing being used in a flooded rice paddy. The operator looked like a man mowing his kid's wading pool.

Back in the city, I was walking along the Nanjing Donglu, with its store windows full of Lee jeans and Adidas shoes and Revlon eye shadow, when I peeked into an alley, and there, six feet from the makeup counter, was a man in his underwear giving himself a bath at a sink. Because that's where his sink was. If you live in the one-room warrens of Shanghai, the lavatory is in the street, shared with a half dozen other families. And a sink is luxury. Sometimes it's just a water tap, padlocked so that the folks from the next warren over don't poach. The toilet is down the block, if there is one. Wagons come through the alleys in the mornings, collecting wooden chamber pots.

The houses built when Shanghai was a treaty port were huddled into narrow streets and squeezed around dainty courtyards. They are pastiches of French style, English fenestration, German brickwork, and Chinese smiley-lip tile roofs, as odd in a small way as modern Shanghai's skyscrapers, and typically Asian in crowding. In the 1950s the little houses were divided into tiny apartments. In the 1960s the Communists inserted concrete prefab housing into every remaining open space. Hundreds of rows of two-story tin-roofed cubicles were built from tar-jointed slabs of concrete in people's areaways, in front of their doors, and along their sidewalks between the housefronts and the curb. Now the old neighborhoods of Shanghai are as intricate as Parcheesi boards and practically on the same scale.

Ground-floor rooms open directly onto the street. People live in the middle of the road, wander the snack stalls in their pajamas, tip back their kitchen chairs amid bike and motorcycle traffic, and sell cigarettes and newspapers to the passing throngs without needing to get out of bed.

And this is not poverty. Not by Chinese standards. By Chinese standards this kind of material deprivation isn't even worth noticing. It's negligible, one might say. And that's what the World Bank does say. The World Bank publication *China 2020 Series: Sharing Rising Incomes* asserts that there are "70 million absolute poor in China," and that "about 100 million additional people survive on less than $1 of income a day," and then, in the same paragraph, the World Bank states, "urban poverty is negligible."

Conditions in Shanghai are an *improvement* for the Chinese. This urban squalor is sought after. You need a government permit to move to Shanghai. People travel thousands of miles and sneak into town to live like this.

† † †

There's also another kind of living in Shanghai—living large. There are women whose every item of jewelry, apparel, and accessorization bears the mirror-image C's of Chanel—the golden ass crack. There are men in college-education-priced Hugo Boss suits (which have an unfortunate tendency to be as wide as Shanghai tycoons are high). Long black BMWs and Benzes, missing from the wino-hued daytime traffic, show up at night in front of the Hard Rock Cafe (but not, I noticed, in front of restaurants featuring cobra blood). In a real-estate-agency window was a picture of a comfy suburban house for rent: $10,000 a month. A largish three-bedroom apartment goes for $6,000 a month, a smallish one for $4,500, and golf memberships (also sold by real-estate brokers, in frank admission of snobbery's price tag) start at 83,000 yuan, which is $10,250, almost 200 times the average monthly Chinese wage.

The average monthly Chinese wage is also about what a round of drinks costs in a Shanghai bar where double-dating Chinese fifteen-year-olds were flopping and bobbling drunk on a weekday midnight while the car and driver waited outside and one of the girls cradled a cell phone like the stuffed animal she should have been home in bed with. According to *Sharing Rising Incomes,* between 1981 and 1995 the Chinese increase in income inequality "was by far the largest of all countries for which comparable data are available." The disparity of wealth is enough to turn all the people in China, me included, into Communists.

Wait a minute. They're Communists already.

In a capitalist country we can shrug off the dress-hog broads, cash brats, and limo'd pudgies. We'll put up with this kind of thing because it's the price of freedom. But China doesn't have freedom. It's illegal to strike. It's illegal to go to a church if that church isn't government approved. In January 1996, Father Guo Bo Le of Shanghai was sentenced to two years in a labor camp for, in the words of the court record, "saying Mass." Exercising rights of speech or assembly is a nonstarter. According to the U.S. State Department's 1996 human-rights review, "All public dissent against party and government was effectively silenced by intimidation, exile, or the imposition of prison terms, administrative detention, or house arrest. No dissidents were known to be active at the year's end." Sixty-five crimes are punished with the death penalty, including forging tax invoices. Torture is routine. Journalism must conform to the guidelines of the Communist Party's brazenly yclept Propaganda Department. Women are subjected to forced sterilization, and baby women are aborted so that families can get a son as their one allowable child. Most laborers belong to a *danwei,* a state work unit, that controls everything from the right to change residences to permission to have that kid. The Freedom House organization, in its annual *Freedom in the World* report, says, "China continues to have one of the worst human rights records in the world and the rule of law is nonexistent."

I had come to Shanghai for an academic conference with, of all things, a libertarian think tank. The confab was officially sanctioned and co-sponsored by a Chinese university. Why would Communists invite to their country people who are absolutely woolly on the subject of freedom? There were folks in our delegation who think Ben and Jerry's ought to be able to sell Morphine Mint, and folks who, at a certain hour of the evening—when sufficiently full of cobra blood—mutter, "I have just two things to say to Timothy McVeigh: 'IRS.' '3 A.M.'"

But it turns out that libertarians are the only policy boffins in Washington who favor free trade, no matter what. And free trade is the only freedom on the Chinese agenda at the moment. Libertarians reason that government has no business telling independent citizens whom they can do business with or why. And some libertarians have a further theory that trading fried chicken and Pepsi with the mainland Chinese is like trading smallpox-infested blankets with the Plains Indians—that the Communists will come down with a fatal case of Western values.

So the libertarians would talk about individualism and responsibility, legal self-possession, civil society, and natural law. And the Chinese would stare into the middle distance, applaud politely, and ask us if China was going to get most-favored-nation trading status without kissing the business end of Boris Yeltsin.

The other thing the Chinese wanted to know about was Social Security privatization. This, like free trade, is a policy favored by libertarians, but not for the reason the Chinese gave. A "pro-market" Party cadre told the audience that "too high Social Security benefits encourage laziness."

The academic conference was like being sent back to college unstoned and less practiced at doodling. The Chinese college students' amateur simultaneous translation didn't help. Usually the kids got just the nouns: "Problems China reforms industry strategy 1950s structure." Afternoons and evenings, there were official banquets—the Chinese version of Thanksgiving dinner twice a day. And we should be grateful that Columbus really didn't find the Orient, or our Pilgrim forefathers would have dined on chicken feet, pig's face, black "preserved" duck eggs, and many less identifiable entrées. (One thing you learn in China is: Never ask, "What's cooking?")

My reaction to academia hadn't changed in twenty-eight years. I ditched. I spent my time hiking the imbroglio of Shanghai through the First Bank of Mars architecture and the Third Supermall from the Sun shopping, pushing between construction workers in their rattan hard hats (an idea for U.S. real-estate developers who want an earth-friendly look), and weaving my way among the backstreet food vendors (don't look into a bucket of live eels right after breakfast).

Retailing in Shanghai is a matter of either megastores or coolie baskets. And industry is either corporations so large that they rate a seat on the UN Security Council, or bike shops with sales-and-service facilities on the sidewalk. There are no middle-sized businesses in Shanghai, no middle-priced goods, and being middle class seems to be actively discouraged.

Take, for example, that defining bourgeois act, buying a car. In China you have to get approval to buy it from the government's Business Administration Department, buy it, present the receipt to the revenue authorities, pay a 10 percent sales tax, and, if the car's imported, pay Customs duty of as much as 150 percent of the car's value. (China favors free trade—for *other* countries.) There's an inspection where they don't just inspect but tell you to install fire extinguishers and so forth. You need a parking permit from the traffic bureau, liability insurance at $1,000 per year, a temporary car-registration license, and a receipt for your road-maintenance fees. Then you take a photograph of your car displaying all its documentation, and present it to the Car Administration Department, which will—if it feels like it—grant you a permanent car registration after you pay to have your license number recorded.

This explains why none of those VWs in the Shanghai traffic jams is a private vehicle. They're all government-owned taxis.

The Chinese economy has grown. According to the World Bank, "China's GDP per capita has grown at a remarkable 8.2 percent a year since economic reforms started in 1978." But what, exactly, is growing? One of the professors from the Chinese university gave us a tour of Pudong, Shanghai's $36 billion commerce and industry "New Area" across the Huangpu River. We took a bus through a homemade-looking tunnel and arrived in a flat, planned sterility of immense dimensions, the office park as Nebraska. Here and there the landscape was decorated with blandly abstract corporate art. Wiggly steel shapes in red, yellow, and blue rose from the middle of a traffic circle.

"What is the meaning of the sculpture?" asked the professor, who answered himself: "I don't know." He seemed to be a reasonable guy. He didn't exactly criticize the government, but he pointed to ranks of new condominiums, unprepossessing with their Plexiglas-screened sunrooms and window air-conditioner units. He said that the condos sold for between $100,000 and $200,000. Or didn't. Almost all the units were vacant. "Why are these buildings empty?" asked the professor. "Overbuilding and overpriced."

Multinationals were visible in every direction, Shanghai booby-hatch headquarters for Hewlett-Packard, Siemens, Sharp, Coca-Cola, SmithKline Beecham, Hoffmann La Roche, Sony. There was just one thing wrong with this business district—no business. Nobody seemed to be there at all. In the middle of a Tuesday afternoon, nothing was going on. We drove up and down empty streets along concrete fences decorated with those international cross-out silhouettes indicating prohibition of this or that: No spitting. No martial arts. No cutting trees. No firecrackers. No breaking the phone.

No breaking the phone? Along the ground were miles of conduits that formed into tall pipe arches at every intersection. These were water and waste lines. Pudong had been built on a floodplain only a few feet above sea level, on ground too muddy to dig sewers in. This hadn't slowed construction. "The floor space of high-rises in Pudong," said the professor, rolling his eyes slightly, "exceeds New York City."

The real-estate glut in Shanghai is such that prices had already fallen by 30 percent in the first half of 1997. Yet the city's supply of office space was set to increase by a third in 1998.

A free market is a natural evolution of freedom. There's a missing link in Shanghai. This is not a Darwinian economy where enterprises prosper according to their ability to survive and grow. This is a creationist economy where prosperity is bestowed by a greater power.

Pudong is prosperous in just this way. An article in *The Asian Wall Street Journal* said of the government officials in charge of Pudong: "Harking back to their authoritarian instincts . . . they are deploying every tactic to fill the cavernous neighborhoods they're building." The article said that foreign banks are told they must have headquarters in Pudong if they want to do domestic-currency business, and that the International School had been moved there in hopes of luring foreign executives to the empty apartment houses. Of Shanghai in general, *The Asian Wall Street Journal* said, "The city was, quite literally, ordered to be great."

The Chinese Communists are attempting to build capitalism from the top down, as if the ancient Egyptians had constructed the Pyramid of Khufu by saying, "Thutnefer, you hold up this two-ton pointy piece while the rest of the slaves go get 2,300,000 blocks of stone."

A few months after I took my tour of Pudong, a famous economic crisis developed in Asia. And I had been staring out my bus window at the cause of it. Pudong-like senselessness had been going on all over the continent. Instead of money being invested where that money would make as much more money as possible, money was invested in strange, showy stuff. Some of these bad investments were made due to "national industrial policies," some because of corruption, some out of local pride, and some for murky political reasons. From Thailand to Japan, bad credit had been extended, bad equities had been sold, and bad ventures had been subsidized—all in the hope that success could be had by some method other than succeeding.

Of course, if I'd been able to see this disaster coming with the *fore-* rather than the *hind-* type of sight, I'd be too rich to be writing a book. But I'd have been wrong about the Asian economic crisis anyway. Since Pudong is the worst example of Pudong-style misallocation of capital, I would have expected the business failures to have started in China. But China has no floating currency rate to sink. And its securities market is not free to go into free fall. And the ordinary people of China live in desperate poverty. So when a depression comes . . . they live in desperate poverty.

On my last day in Shanghai, I went to an open-air antiques market— junk market, really—with flimsy booths containing a few old vases and bracelets, and lots and lots of Mao buttons. I found a poster from the Cultural Revolution showing sturdy figures with chins uplifted in that "who cut one?" marxist pose. The woman in the booth pointed to the date on the poster, 1966, and wrote the price on the back of her hand: 100 yuan (or *renmimbi*, "people's money," as the yuan is now called)— about $12.50. A small and bent old man walked up. He had a few teeth and thick glasses. "Would you like a translation?" he said.

The poster headline reads: REVOLUTIONARY STUDENTS MUST UNITE WITH REVOLUTIONARY FARMERS AND PARTICIPATE TOGETHER IN PLURAL CULTURAL REVO- LUTION IN THE COUNTRYSIDE. With the same results, we know now, as the sugarcane harvesting I saw in Cuba. I gave the woman in the booth 100 yuan.

"No, no," said the old man. "You should have bargained with her."

"Well," I said, "it's guilt money. When that poster was printed, I thought I was for Mao."

The old man laughed, and then he said, "Oh, yes. Because I had been sent to a Japanese school during the occupation, I was exiled to the country."

"That must have been no fun."

"How I suffered," he said. "But Mao was a great man."

"You really think so?"

"But he was dictator too long. He did many harmful things. He did . . ." The old man thought about how to put it and then summed up the entire history of government evil in the realm of economics: "He did too much."

11

EAT THE RICH

❖

We're so close to being rich. Everybody in the world could be rich as hell. The benighted masses of India could quit pedaling bicycle rickshaws and start dragging Lear jets through the streets of Calcutta. Indians in the Brazilian rain forest could be *singing* in the rain. The endangered fauna would wear thong bikinis: "Save the Girl from Ipanema." Eskimos could give up clubbing baby seals and devote their arctic vastness to building an Olympic-quality ice dancing team.

When we're all wealthy, Sally Struthers will be featured in magazine ads headlined, YOU CAN SEND THIS CHILD TO SUMMER WEIGHT-LOSS CAMP OR YOU CAN TURN THE PAGE. CARE packages will contain oyster forks and truffles. And altruistic musicians will hold benefit concerts to raise enough money to pay the Rolling Stones to retire.

Money won't solve all our problems. But money will give us options—let us choose the problems we want to have. Leisure conglomerates may open franchises in Bosnia and Herzegovina where Muslims and Serbs can blast each other in paintball wars. Self-destructive individuals will still exist, but instead of dying from drug overdoses in pay-toilet stalls, they will be able to expire in luxury at the Chateau Marmont like John Belushi. The Taliban fundamentalists might continue to keep women in seclusion, but they could do so by opening a Bergdorf Goodman's in Kabul. They'll never see those wives again.

All this is possible because the modern industrial economy works. Obviously it works better in some places than in others. But it works, even in the poorest areas. Côte d'Ivoire now produces almost as much per-capita wealth as the United States did when the Monroe Doctrine was declared, and Egypt produces more. America did not consider itself a poor country during the 1820s, and, in fact, at that time it was one of the world's most prosperous nations.

Extensive research has been done on the history of this industrial economy, much of it by the Organization for Economic Cooperation and Development. The OECD was founded by the Marshall Plan countries in the wake of World War II, and its purpose is what its name says. The OECD wants to make everyone rich as hell, although it never quite confesses to this in its literature.

In 1995 the OECD published a book by economist Angus Maddison title *Monitoring the World Economy 1820–1992*. Maddison has been studying economic growth since the 1950s, and has examined and weighed the subject's statistics and statistical estimates. On the strength of these, Maddison calculates that until the Industrial Revolution, economic growth was paltry. Measured in 1990 U.S. dollars, the world gross domestic product—the value of everything produced on earth—went from $565 per person in 1500 to $651 per person in 1820. That was an increase in wealth of about 27 cents a year.

But after the Industrial Revolution, something wonderful happened. The total world GDP grew from $695 billion in 1820 to almost $28 trillion in 1992. This planet had the same amount of arable land in 1992 as it had in 1820, and, arguably, fewer natural resources. Plus, population had grown from a little more than 1 billion to nearly 5.5 billion. But even so, world GDP per capita swelled from $651 to $5,145. Prosperity increased by $26 a year. Wealth has been growing a hundred times faster than it did before the Industrial Age.

The modern economy works, and we know how to make it work better. Free markets are extremely successful. The evidence is there for anyone who wants to look. Hong Kong, with 6.5 million people in 402 square miles, has an annual GDP of $163.6 billion. Tanzania, with 29.5 million people in 342,100 square miles, has a GDP of $18.9 billion.

Even a free market with lots of tax baggage and regulatory impediments is much better than a market that isn't free. Sweden has about the same amount of arable land as Cuba, a similar range of natural resources, a worse climate, and a couple million fewer people. But Sweden's GDP is more than eleven times the size of Cuba's.

And the free market trumps education and culture. North Korea has a 99 percent literacy rate, a disciplined, hardworking society, and a $900 per-capita GDP. Morocco has a 43.7 percent literacy rate, a society that spends all day drinking coffee and pestering tourists to buy rugs, and a $3,260 per-capita GDP.

We know what to do, and we know how to do it. So what's wrong with the world? To a certain extent, it's the same thing that's wrong with me. Because the prosaic, depressing, and somewhat shameful fact is that the secret to getting ahead is just what my parents told me it was.

The whole miracle of the modern industrial economy is based upon the things that our folks were trying to drum into our heads before we went off to college to grow sideburns and leg hair—or, as the modern case is, get pierced eyebrows and neck tattoos. It's the advice we received at the dinner table while the Jell-O dessert puddled and our friends were waiting for us at the mall. It's the clumsy set-piece speech our parents made in the heart-to-hearts they'd spring on us when we were really high. It's what we heard in capital letters when we brought home grades that looked like a collection of *Baywatch* bra cup sizes or wrecked the car.

- Hard work
- Education
- Responsibility

- Property rights
- Rule of law
- Democratic government

Actually, most parents didn't get all those items into the lecture. In fact, I've never heard of a parent saying, "Listen here, if I catch you running around without property rights again, I'll take away your cell phone." But when our parents said, "Be honest," they were assuming that property rights were real. And when our parents said, "Obey the law," they were making a logical inference that the law existed and that it merited obeying. And many of our parents had served in the military, defending democracy, and would remind us of this at length.

Of course, by "hard work" our parents didn't mean that we should be doing the hard things that constitute work for the poor people in the world. Few parents hope that their children will get jobs carrying forty-pound buckets of water on their heads. Our parents wanted us to do hard work that was intelligent, fulfilling, and promised advancement in life. (Although they also wanted us to mow the lawn.) The hard work was linked to education.

However, billions of people don't have a chance to get an education, and some of them, like religious fundamentalists and deconstructionist college professors, don't believe the education when they get one. This is one reason that dinner-table parental advice is difficult to apply to the earth's impoverished masses. There are also billions of people who don't have property rights, not to mention property. Or the property rights are arbitrary, and the property can be taken away by anybody with a gun or a government title. These billions of people have trouble being responsible because being responsible means thinking of the future. They haven't got one.

Rule of law is crucial. And it has to be good law, not Albania's Law of Lek. So if what our parents tell us is going to be globally effective, Mom and Dad will need to bring world leaders into the dining room. All the presidents, prime ministers, dictators, generals, chairman of idiot political parties, lunatic guerrilla chieftains, and fanatical heads of crazed religious sects will need to squeeze around the imitation Queen Anne mahogany veneer (with extra leaves in) and get a real talking-to.

Then there is democracy to be considered. Democracy is a bulwark against tyranny—unless the *demos* get tyrannical. People can vote themselves poor, as the Swedes seem to be trying to do.

Now all the people on the planet are coming over to the house. And when they get there, what they're going to do is . . . exactly what we did. They're not going to listen.

There is a worldwide pigheadedness about money. There is a willful and even belligerent ignorance concerning ways and means. There is a heartfelt and near-universal refusal to understand the basic economic principles behind the creation of wealth.

Not all this ignorance is irrational. Some people profit from economic privation. Economists, for instance. John Maynard Keynes couldn't have become a big shot, guiding government intervention in business and finance, if it hadn't been for the Great Depression. And Alan Greenspan is a success because we all lost our wallets when inflation scared our pants off.

We fear the power that others have over us, and wealth is power. We're afraid that Kathie Lee Gifford is going to make us sew jogging suits for thirty cents an hour. But are the rich really scarier than the poor? Take a midnight stroll through a fancy neighborhood, then take a midnight stroll a few blocks from the U.S. Capitol. Sure, we can get in trouble in Monte Carlo. We can lose at roulette. We can get suckered into a shady business deal with Princess Stephanie's ex-husband. But we're more likely to be mugged in the District of Columbia.

Not that we should begrudge the crimes of those poor people. They're just practicing politics on a small scale. If they'd listen to their own political leaders, they'd put down the gun and pick up the ballot box, and steal from everybody instead of just us.

Political systems must love poverty—they produce so much of it. Poor people make easier targets for a demagogue. No Mao or even Jiang Zemin is likely to arise on the New York Stock Exchange floor. And politicians in democracies benefit from destitution, too. The United States has had a broad range of poverty programs for thirty years. Those programs have failed. Millions of people are still poor. And those people vote for politicians who favor keeping the poverty programs in place. There's a Matt Drudge conspiracy theory in that somewhere.

Many religions claim to admire poverty. And some religions even advocate the practice of being poor. (Although all those religions seem willing to accept large cash donations.)

You'd think that businessmen, in the search for new customers, would always be opposed to impecuniousness. But Kathie Lee Gifford is not alone in depending on destitute workers to take pay-nothing jobs.

Then there is a certain kind of environmentalist who thinks that human deprivation means plant and animal wealth. Tanzania's experience of rhino-subsidizing rich tourists versus rhino-killing impoverished poachers argues against this. (And an Asia where every man could afford Viagra would be the best thing that could happen to the rhinoceros.) But many "greens" still believe that increasing human prosperity is wrong. For example, the famous population-control advocate Paul Ehrlich has said, "Giving society cheap, abundant energy . . . would be the equivalent of giving an idiot child a machine gun."

Finally, general poverty benefits specific wealth. If most people are broke, that's great for the wealthy few. They get cheap household help, low ancestral-manor real-estate prices, and no crowds on Martha's Vineyard. This explains the small, nasty plutocracies in impoverished countries. Maybe it also accounts for the rich socialists prominent on the political landscape for the last two centuries.

I began this book by asking why some parts of the world are rich and others are poor, and I naturally had prejudices about what the answers would be. I favored the free market, not because I knew anything about markets, but because I live in a free (or nearly free) country, and I'm a free man (as long as I call home frequently), and it works for me. I was skeptical about the ability of politics to deliver economic benefits because I did know something about that. I'd been writing about politics, at home and abroad, for years. I had a low opinion of the trade and its practitioners. And I considered culture, as an economic factor, to be a joke. How is ballet going to make the Tanzanians wealthy?

I was stupidly surprised to find out how important law is. Law, of course, derives from politics. And a political system is ultimately a product of a society's attitudes, ideas, and beliefs—that damned conundrum, its culture.

Which brings me back to the free market. I started out looking at the free market in terms of its effectiveness, its "efficiency," as an economist would say. I ended up looking at the free market as a moral device. My initial prejudice was right in one respect. The most-important part of the free market is the part that's free. Economic liberty cannot be untangled from liberty of other kinds. You may have freedom of religion, if the rabbi can get off night shifts on Fridays. You may have freedom of assembly, but where are you all going to go if it rains?

The U.S. Constitution is (at least I hope it is) a statement of American cultural values. The First Amendment implies a free market. Six of the remaining nine articles in the Bill of Rights defend private property specifically. And two of the others concern rights reserved to the people, some of which are certainly economic rights. We are a free-market nation, though the electors and the elected sometimes forget it.

A belief in the free market means a belief that people have an innate right to the fruits of their endeavors, and the right to dispose of the fruit the way they see fit, as long as other people don't get pasted in the face with a rotten peach or something.

There are people who don't believe this. Some of these people are just bad. They steal. Some of these people are "nationalistic" and think it's okay to take things from other people if they live more than a peach toss away or speak another language or have a different religion or look funny. And the kings, emperors, and so forth who ruled mankind during most of history were under the impression that everything belongs to kings, emperors, and so forth.

Now that the kings and emperors have been shot or reduced to pathetic ceremonial posts, the most common reason given for not believing in economic liberty is that the free market is unfair. Socialists, Social Democrats, American liberals, and all other kinds of economic levelers think that unconstrained industry, agriculture, and commerce lead to the exploitation of people who aren't very good at these things.

A little bit of immoral wealth and a great deal of unconscionable poverty is supposedly thereby created.

It was Adam Smith in *The Wealth of Nations* (published with happy coincidence in 1776) who originally argued that a free market is good for everybody. Smith seems to have been the first person to realize that all voluntary exchanges increase prosperity. Wealth is created by any swap. It may seem like an even trade, but each trader gives up something he values less in order to receive something he values more. Hence the wealth of both traders grows. When Neolithic spear makers did business with Neolithic basket weavers, the spear makers were able to carry things around in a manner more convenient than skewering them on spear points, and the basket weavers were able to kill mastodons by a method more efficient than swatting them with baskets.

The free-market outcome benefits all. It's moral. And the beautiful thing about this morality is that we don't have to be good to achieve it. In the most, perhaps only, famous passage from an economics book, Adam Smith states, "It is not from the benevolence of the butcher, the brewer, or the baker, that we expect our dinner, but from their regard to their own interest." Smith saw that a man's selfish concern with his own well-being is a desirable, indeed, a splendid thing for society. "[He] intends only his own gain," wrote Smith, "and he is in this . . . led by an invisible hand to promote an end which was no part of his intention." That end is the end this book is about: economic progress.

The general morality of the free market, however, does not answer the specific objection of unfairness. Economic liberty leads to differences in wealth. And the differences are enormous. The "wealth gap" is the subject of a critical debate about economics. The perception of unfairness is the reason that enormous numbers of the world's decent and well-meaning people, in fact the majority of them, do not rush to embrace the free market in its totality. Complete economic liberty would mean a system like Hong Kong's under John Cowperthwaite with no barriers to trade or capital flow, and no barriers to labor flow, either; no check on immigration, no minimum wage, no cost controls, and no attempt to create a fair society. This is a daunting prospect, and it's not just the Swedes and Fidel Castro who are daunted by it.

Socialists and capitalists naturally take opposing sides on the question of how economically fair life should be. But so do various political parties which claim to be pro-market. So do theologians and philosophers. And so do ordinary people when they're voting for school-bond issues or deciding how much to cheat on their taxes.

Fairness is a potent emotional issue, but how is fairness to be delivered? It's hard to build a political structure that provides economic fairness. The map is full of failed attempts, and so is this book. When a government controls both the economic power of individuals and the coercive power of the state, we get, at best, Shanghai. A businessman finds that one of his stockholders has tanks, artillery, and jet fighter planes. This violates a fundamental rule of happy living: Never let the people with all the money and the people with all the guns be the same people.

There is another difficulty with political control of the economy which keeps even the best-behaved governments from using resources well. This problem was explained by the economists Milton and Rose Friedman in their book, *Free to Choose*. The Friedmans argued that there are only four ways to spend money:

1. Spend your money on yourself.
2. Spend your money on other people.
3. Spend other people's money on yourself.
4. Spend other people's money on other people.

If you spend your money on yourself, you look for the best value at the best price—knockoff Pings on sale at Golf-*Fore*-Less. If you spend your money on other people, you still worry about price, but you may not know—or care—what the other people want. So your brother-in-law gets a Deepak Chopra book for Christmas. If you spend other people's money on yourself, it's hard to resist coming home with real Pings, a new leather bag, orange pants with little niblicks on them, and a pair of Foot-Joy spikes. And if you spend other people's money on other people, any damn thing will do and the hell with what it costs. Almost all government spending falls into category four. This is how the grateful residents of Ukraine got Chernobyl.

Also, if fairness is important, what is really fair? We may say something like, "People have a right to food, a right to housing, and a right to a good job for decent pay." But from an economist's perspective, all those rights involve making finite goods meet infinite wants. Unless the fair society generates tremendous economic growth—which societies that put fairness first have trouble doing—the goods will come from redistribution. Try rephrasing the rights statement thus: "People have a right to my food, a right to my housing, and a right to my good job for my decent pay."

Accepting the free market allows us to avoid the political abuse and financial mismanagement inherent in trying to design an economy that's fair. It also allows us to see that economies can't be designed. Economics is the measurement of how human nature affects the material world. The market is "heartless." So are clocks and yardsticks. Saying that economic problems are the result of the free market's failure is like gaining twenty pounds and calling the bathroom scale a bum.

Adam Smith recognized that markets are self-organizing. Man has a "general disposition to truck, barter, and exchange," wrote Smith. If people are protected from coercion by other people, and from coercion by that agglomeration of other people known as the state, human brains and greed create economic growth. "The strength of the mastiff is not in the least supported either by the swiftness of the greyhound, or by the sagacity of the spaniel," wrote Smith. "Among men, on the contrary, the most dissimilar geniuses are of use to one another."

I had thought that economic problems were the result of ignorance about economics. I was wrong again. I asked a friend, who's knowledgeable in the field: "Why is the concept of the 'invisible hand' so difficult to comprehend?" He said, "It's invisible." The hardest thing to understand about economics is that it doesn't need to be understood. My beatnik friends and I, when we were in college, were perfectly justified in expending our intellectual energy on love and death instead of money.

But there was one thing that we did need to learn. And still do. And it's a piece of knowledge that seems to contradict psychology, life experience, and the dictates of conscience: Economics is not zero sum. There is no fixed amount of wealth. That is, if you have too many slices of pizza, I don't have to eat the box. Your money does not cause my poverty. Refusal to believe this is at the bottom of most bad economic thinking.

True, at any given moment, there is only so much wealth to go around. But wealth is based on productivity. Without productivity, there wouldn't be any economics, or any economic thinking, good or bad, or any pizza, or anything else. We would sit around and stare at rocks, and maybe later have some for dinner.

Wealth is based on productivity, and productivity is expandable. In fact, productivity is fabulously expandable, as Angus Maddison has shown in *Monitoring the World Economy*. Yet a person who is worried about fairness can look at Maddison's figures and say that they are just averages. Per-capita GDP does not show us who actually got the cash. The worrier about fairness can recite the old saw: "The rich get richer and the poor . . ."

"Get entertained by *People* magazine stories about divorces among the rich." That is not how the worrier was going to finish his sentence. "Get lower mortgage rates because banks have more money to lend." That is not it, either. "Get better jobs because there's more capital to be invested in businesses." No, the cliché is, "The rich get richer, and the poor get poorer."

Except there is no evidence of this in recent history. Per-capita GDP is a tricky figure and doesn't tell us much about the well-being of individual people. But there are other statistics that don't present the same problems of averaging. Life-expectancy and infant-mortality rates *do* tell us how things are going for ordinary folks. No matter how rich a nation's elite, its members aren't going to live to be 250 and wildly skew the numbers. And a country can't fake a low infant-mortality rate by getting a few rich babies to live while letting all the poor babies die.

The United Nations study *World Population Prospects: 1996 Revision* contains historical statistics on life expectancy and infant mortality. Figures are given for Most Developed Regions, Less Developed

Regions, and Least Developed Regions. The last being places that are truly poor, such as Tanzania. In the early 1950s the richest countries had an average infant-mortality rate of 58 deaths per 1,000 live births. By the early 1990s the average was down to 11. During the same period the infant-mortality rate in the poorest countries dropped from an average of 194 deaths per 1,000 to 109 per 1,000. Infant-mortality rates declined in both rich and poor countries, and so did the gap between those rates. A difference of 136 deaths per 1,000 had diminished to a difference of 109 deaths forty years later. This is still too many dead babies (and it's hard to imagine a number of dead babies that wouldn't be too many, unless the fair-minded worrier is also a zealous pro-choice advocate). But infant-mortality rates give us some hopeful information about world economic growth. Yes, the rich are getting richer, but the poor aren't becoming worse off. They're becoming parents.

Life expectancy tells the same story. In the early 1950s, people in rich countries lived, on average, 66.5 years. By the early 1990s they were living 74.2 years. In the poorest countries, average lifespans increased from 35.5 years to 49.7 years (which, somewhat unnervingly, was my exact age when I wrote that sentence, and I was glad I didn't live in Tanzania and had to die that night). Anyway, the difference in life expectancy between the world's rich and poor has decreased by 6.5 years. The rich are getting richer. The poor are getting richer. And we're all getting older.

So if wealth is not a worldwide round-robin of purse snatching, and if the thing that makes you rich doesn't make me poor, why should we care about fairness at all? We shouldn't.

Fairness is a good thing in marriage and at the day-care center. It's a nice little domestic virtue. But a liking for fairness is not that noble a sentiment. Fairness doesn't rank with charity, love, duty, or self-sacrifice. And there's always a tinge of self-seeking in making sure that things are fair. Don't you go trying to get one up on me.

As a foundation for a political system, fairness may be no virtue at all. The Old Testament is clear on this point. The Bible might seem an odd place to be doing economic research, especially by someone who goes to church about once a year, and only then because that's when my wife says the Easter Bunny comes. However, I have been thinking—in socioeconomic terms—about the Tenth Commandment.

The first nine Commandments concern theological principles and social law: Thou shalt not make graven images, steal, kill, etc. Fair enough. But then there's the Tenth Commandment: "Thou shalt not covet thy neighbor's house, thou shalt not covet thy neighbor's wife, nor his manservant, nor his maidservant, nor his ox, nor his ass, nor anything that is thy neighbor's."

Here are God's basic rules about how we should live, a very brief list of sacred obligations and solemn moral precepts, and right at the end of it is, "Don't envy your buddy's cow."

What is that doing in there? Why would God, with just ten things to tell Moses, choose, as one of them, jealousy about the livestock next door? And yet, think about how important to the well-being of a community this Commandment is. If you want a donkey, if you want a pot roast, if you want a cleaning lady, don't bitch about what the people across the street have. *Go get your own.*

The Tenth Commandment sends a message to socialists, to egalitarians, to people obsessed with fairness, to American presidential candidates in the year 2000—to everyone who believes that wealth should be redistributed. And the message is clear and concise: Go to hell.

If we want the whole world to be rich, we need to start loving wealth. In the difference between poverty and plenty, the problem is the poverty, not the difference. Wealth is good.

You know this about your own wealth. If you got rich, it would be a great thing. You'd improve your life. You'd improve your family's life. You'd purchase education, travel, knowledge about the world. You'd invest in worthwhile things. You'd give money to noble causes. You'd help your friends and neighbors. Your life would be better if you got rich. The lives of the people around you would be better. Your wealth is good. So why isn't everybody else's wealth good?

Wealth is good when a lot of people have it. It's good when a few people have it. This is because money is a tool, nothing more. You can't eat or drink money, or wear it very comfortably as underwear. And wealth—an accumulation of money—is a bunch of tools.

Tools can be used to do harm. You can break into a house by driving a forklift through a window. You can hit somebody over the head with a hydroelectric turbine. Tools are still good. When a carpenter has a lot of tools, we don't say to him, "You have too many. You should give some of your hammers, saws, screws, and nails to the guy who's cooking omelettes."

Making money through hard work and wise investment is a fine thing to do. Other ways of making money aren't so bad, either, as long as everybody who's in on the deal is there voluntarily. Better sleazy productivity than none. As terrible as Albania's pyramid schemes were, Albania's riots were worse.

And the Hong Kong of John Cowperthwaite shows that even the most resolutely free-market system makes use of private means for the public weal. If the United States radically reduced the size of its government, eliminated all subsidies, price controls, and corporate welfare, and abolished its entitlement programs, we'd still pay taxes. And those tax revenues would be spent—ideally—on such reasonable things as schools, roads, and national defense, in case the British invade again and try to hand over Wall Street to the Red Chinese.

Or take the real-world example of two kids who graduate from college with honors. One is an admirable idealist. The other is on the make. The idealist joins Friends of the Earth and chains himself to a sequoia. The sharpie goes to work for an investment bank selling fishy derivatives and makes $500,000 a year. Even assuming that the selfish young banker cheats the IRS—and he will—he'll end up paying $100,000 a year in taxes: income tax, property tax, sales tax, etc.

While the admirable idealist has saved one tree (if the logging company doesn't own bolt cutters), the pirate in a necktie has contributed to society $100,000 worth of schools, roads, and U.S. Marines, not to mention Interior Department funding sufficient to save any number of trees and the young idealists chained thereto.

And if the soulless yuppie cheats the IRS so well that he ends up keeping the whole half million? That cash isn't going to sit in his cuff link box. Whether spent or saved, the money winds up invested somewhere, and maybe that investment leads to the creation of the twenty-first century's equivalent of the moldboard plow, the microchip, or the mocha latte. Society wins. Wealth brings great benefits to the world. Rich people are heroes. They don't usually mean to be, but that's their problem, not ours.

Almost everyone in the world now admits that the free market tells us the economic truth. Economic liberty makes wealth. Economic repression makes poverty.

Poverty is hard, wretched, and humiliating. Poverty is schoolgirl prostitutes trying to feed their parents in Cuba. Poverty is John driving around in the Tanzanian night looking for the doctor while his daughter dies. It's grandmothers begging on the streets of Moscow. But what poverty is not is sad. Poverty is infuriating. These things don't have to happen. These conditions don't need to exist. We can't solve all the problems of life, but we can solve the problem of gross, worldwide material deprivation. The solution doesn't work perfectly. The solution doesn't work uniformly. Nonetheless, the solution works. If we can't fix everything, let's fix the easy stuff. We know how to get rid of poverty. We know how to create wealth. But because of laziness, fear, complacency, love of power, or foolish idealism, we refuse to do it.

We think we can dabble in freedom—allow a few of its liberties and leave our favorite constraints in place. We think we can screw around with the free market—skip its costs and get all of its benefits anyway.

There is a joke that I think President Reagan used to tell to illustrate the attitude that some people have toward the blessings they get from freedom and private property. If Reagan didn't tell the joke, he should have. He won't mind the attribution. Doubtless he's forgotten all about economics now. And I'm with the president on that. I intend to start forgetting about economics as soon as I can—keeping in mind, however, a few rudimentary conceits, such as the one about the traveling salesman who is staying overnight with a farm family. When the family sits

down to eat, there's a pig in a chair at the table. The pig has three medals hanging around its neck and a wooden leg. The salesman says, "Um,
I see a pig is having dinner with you."

"Yep," says the farmer. "That's because he's a very special pig. You
see those medals around his neck? Well, the first medal is from when
our baby son fell in the pond and was drowning, and that pig dove in,
swam out, and saved his life. The second medal, that's from when our
little daughter was trapped in a burning barn, and that pig ran inside,
carried her out, and saved her life. And the third medal, that's from when
our oldest boy was cornered in the stockyard by a mean bull, and that
pig ran under the fence, bit the bull's tail, and saved the boy's life."

"Yes," says the salesman, "I can see why you let that pig sit right at
the table and have dinner with you. And I can see why you awarded
him the medals. But how did he get the wooden leg?"

"Well," says the farmer, "a pig like that—you don't eat him all at
once."